RON KALENUIK

International Family Favorites

SIMPLY DELICIOUS
COOKING SERIES™

MAGNANIMITY
HOUSE PUBLISHING

Credits

- ❧ **Project Coordinator :**

  Dianna Kalenuik

- ❧ **Editor :**

  Sharon Antoniuk

- ❧ **Cuisine Coordinator :**

  Chef Ron Kalenuik

- ❧ **Cuisine Assistants :**

  Pamela Kalenuik
  Timothy Kalenuik
  Jennifer Kalenuik
  Ruth Maier

- ❧ **Art Direction :**

  Sylvia Cook

- ❧ **Photography :**

  V.E.T. Marketing

- ❧ **Design / Graphic :**

  Sako Graphics Resource Centre Inc.

MAGNANIMITY
HOUSE PUBLISHING

© Magnanimity House Publishers
73 Greybeaver Tr.
Scarborough, On. Canada,
Telephone 416-724-7287
Fax 416-724-7857
E-Mail chefk@cycor.ca

This book is an Exclusive Edition for

250 Granton Dr.
Richmond Hill On. L4B 1H7
714-587-9207
Printed in Canada

Contents

Mr. Kalenuik affectionately known as Chef K (by those who couldn't pronounce his last name) began his culinary career in the Rocky Mountains of Alberta, Canada. Since then he has established himself as Chef de Cuisine in many of the finer restaurants in North America.

Ron has owned and operated several national award winning restaurants. He is a teacher and consultant to the hospitality industry as well as President of The North American Institute of Modern Cuisine Inc.

As an author, he expresses a unique and creative flair in all areas of cookery. Whether classic or just "down home" cookery, or in modern presentation, every style is simply given and easily prepared. This book is more than a collection of recipes, it is a collection of usable recipes that will become a favorite for family and guests.

With *International Family Favorites*, Mr. Kalenuik's writing career includes 10 other books to date. His International best sellers, *Simply Delicious Cooking, Simply Delicious Cooking 2* have sold more than 2.5 million copies. His other books include, *Fundamentals of Taste, Cuisine Extraordinaire, Pizza Pizzazz and Pastabilities, Dining In, Championship Cooking, Chef K's Cheese Best and The Right Spice.*

Many people dream of escaping their day to day lives and visiting a far off distant land. Unfortunately, for the majority of us, we must settle simply for the dream. So what does one do? The next best thing to being there is to experience the flavour of the country within the confines of your own home. The farthest one may have to journey to experience the taste of that enchanted place is the grocers, just down the street and minutes away from home.

What we are attempting to provide you with is a small journey into the land of taste. We are not giving exact national dishes, but rather the flavour of each country. The prime reason is that in the majority of national dishes many of the main ingredients are difficult to find outside the home nation. We have attempted to give recipes that do not require difficulty in finding ingredients while maintaining the integrity of taste. Most ingredients should be readily available in major grocery stores.

Come on our journey to far away lands simply through your taste buds. You will enjoy Cajun\Creole dishes just like they make in Louisiana, easily made French cuisine without strolling through the streets of Paris, wonderful Thai dishes, even delicious exciting dishes from down under. There are desserts from Germany, Austria, Australia, North America, Africa, Latin America, all to tease and tempt you and your guest.

Chocolate for the chocoholic? It's within, delicious Sacher Torte just like you would find in Austria, a very chocolaty English Tea Time Torte, or travel to the home of chocolate, Mexico, and sample Ebony & Ivory Strawberries.

Complete the experience. Decorate your dining table with authentic dishes, cutlery and flowers of the country. Why not play a little music in the background of the country! Greek music with meals from the home of the Olympics, Om-pah music from the streets of Dusseldorf with great German dining. It is the entire experience that will make the travel worth the effort.

A fork in the road takes on an entire new meaning when travelling via the taste buds. It really doesn't matter whether it be a fork, spoon, chopstick or your fingers, you know your journey will always be the one which your taste buds arrive on time. Besides travelling this way means you never lose your luggage, (unless it's the dirty dishes).

International Family Favorites is another book in The Simply Delicious Cooking Series and as you indulge in wonderful recipes, rest assured that you and each of your guests will know that is exactly what your final presentation will be - Simply Delicious. One book is to small to offer recipes from every nation in the world, so we have given you those which many persons have found to be more than acceptable during the research and writing phase of this book. If we missed your favourite, please fax the publisher a note and the recipe to the fax number on the copyright page.

Ron Kalenuik, Chef K

North America

As Italy and France have found their importance in world wide cuisine, North America has also contributed distinctive and extraordinary cuisines to the global scene. Fiery Cajun, the subtle Creole, peppery Tex-Mex, incredibly delightful Californian all speak volumes to the creative genius and the adaptability of the people and the land in which they found themselves living within.

Whether by choice or through circumstance, all quickly learned what America had to offer and would enhance the family's meal with unique new flavours never before experienced in their former home land. Flavours like corn, tomatoes, sweet potatoes, wild turkey or wild rice all would serve the founding fathers well.

Today, the same holds true. New and exciting flavours await all who journey forth. Whether it be flavours that excite the taste buds like a fresh Californian Fresh Fruit Salsa, Alligator Kebobs or taste that bites back like a New Orleans Blackened Chicken in Ancho Chile Garlic Sauce. Flavours from the Pacific northwest like Redwood Salmon or Vancouver Cioppino or from the Atlantic east coast with P.E.I. Mussels or a Maine Lobster and Salmon Mousse.

Travel with us into the heartland of America and enjoy a little bit of Main Street with a sampling of Montana Swirled Cheesecake Supreme or an Alberta Wild Mushroom Buffalo Steak Stroganoff. Don't care for buffalo, then try the best beef in the world, that of central America, whether corn fed or grain fed, it can't be beat when served as Chicago's Best Steak. Be sure to finish your journey with a trip to the dessert bar and enjoy a Nebraska Moose or a Classic Creme Caramel with Pecan Chocolate Dipped Strawberries.

All point to the fact that travelling around America is only a fork away and new family delights are to be cherished for a long time to come.

Kansas City Ribs

Ingredients:

4 ½ lbs	2 kg	pork side or back ribs
2 tsp	10 ml	salt
1 ½ cups	375 ml	beef stock (see page 42)
¼ cup	60 ml	catsup
2 tbsp	30 ml	brown sugar
3 tbsp	45 ml	red wine
¼ tsp	1 ml	oregano leaves
¼ tsp	1 ml	thyme leaves
¼ tsp	1 ml	basil
¼ tsp	1 ml	white pepper
¼ tsp	1 ml	red chili pepper flakes
1 tsp	5 ml	salt
2 tbsp	30 ml	Worcestershire sauce
pinch	pinch	cayenne pepper
1 tsp	5 ml	grated lemon peel
1 tbsp	15 ml	cornstarch
2 tbsp	30 ml	cold water

Preparation:

Trim the ribs of any excess fat. Place them on a shallow baking sheet. Sprinkle with 2 tsp (10 ml) of salt. Bake in a preheated 300°F (150°C) oven for 2 hours.

In a sauce pan combine the remaining ingredients except the cornstarch and water. Heat to boiling. Blend the cornstarch with the water and add to sauce. Simmer until sauce thickens.

Transfer the ribs to a charbroiler. Cook 10 minutes per side basting frequently with sauce. Serve.

Serves 6

Fun Food Facts

Kansas City, Missouri Barbeque

Barbeque isn't barbeque unless somewhere the recipe has its original roots from Kansas City. Ask anyone in the Kansas City restaurant business about barbeque and you will quickly find that they have the best. So it is of little wonder that whatever you choose to have as barbeque you know it is going to be good. Just follow the rules and you won't have to make the journey to Kansas City.

Use the best ingredients. This the first rule of all cooking, not only for food ingredients, but all ingredients, including the charcoal. Woods of mesquite, hickory, alder or apple are best suited to barbecuing and grilling. Using charcoal made from these woods are more preferable than using other oil base type charcoal. Charcoal alone, provides a mild smoke flavour and thus is preferred for lamb, seafood and fish. For a stronger smoke taste for beef, pork and game meats, use wood chips of the same type as the charcoal. When using wood chips, soak them in water for a half hour or longer before using them. Then place them evenly over the charcoal for short term cookery with plenty of smoke for that "just right" flavour.

Use a covered grill so all the smoke flavour will penetrate into the food and not escape into the air before it has seasoned the food. Plan ahead, meaning follow your recipe and be sure to begin your fire at least 40 minutes before you want to cook the items. Use only a grill which has been cleaned well and oiled in the same manner.

Allow food ingredients to come to room temperature before grilling them. Use a hot fire to seal meats quickly then transfer them to a cooler part of the grill to finish their cooking. Always cook fish and seafood on the cooler part of the grill. They require no sealing. Cook meats which have more fat than others over a drip pan placed directly upon the coals. Having followed these simple rules you'll cook far better than the weekend chef ever thought he\she could.

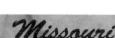

Missouri

Carolina Scallops

Ingredients:

18	18	sliced maple bacon
1 ½ lbs	675 g	large sea scallops
⅓ cup	80 ml	olive oi!
3 tbsp	45 ml	lemon juice
3 tbsp	45 ml	white wine
1 tsp	5 ml	salt
1 tsp	5 ml	cracked black pepper
2 tsp	10 ml	fresh chopped oregano

Sauce:

1 cup	250 ml	fish stock
¼ cup	60 ml	white wine
4 tsp	20 ml	green onions
1 tsp	5 ml	cornstarch
1 tbsp	15 ml	cold water
½ cup	125 ml	whipping cream
¼ tsp	1 ml	salt
¼ tsp	1 ml	pepper
2	2	egg yolks
16	16	green seedless grapes

Preparation:

Cut the bacon slices in half and wrap around the scallops. Skewer with bamboo skewers that have been soaked in water for 20 minutes. Place skewers in a shallow baking pan.

Combine remaining ingredients. Pour over scallops. Marinate refrigerated and covered for 4 hours.

Grill the skewers over medium heat for five minutes per side. Serve at once.

Sauce:

Combine the stock, wine and green onion in a sauce pan. Bring to a boil reduce to half volume. Strain, return the liquid to pan.

Mix cornstarch with the cold water and blend into sauce. Reheat and whisk in the cream, salt and pepper.

Blend the egg yolk with a little cooled sauce. Whisk into the sauce and remove from heat.

Stir in the grapes. Use as required.

Serves 4

 Fun Food Facts

Scallops

Named for the apostle St. James, the Coquille St. Jacques would be a taste he may never have experienced due to his stand of religion. The apostle Peter however, once released from such laws might have enjoyed the mollusk sautéed in a little butter, white wine, mushrooms and green onions. Today, there are more than 75 known recipes for Coquille St. Jacques, all of which we may enjoy. Coquille however, is not the only way to serve the scallop. Poached in court bouillon, battered and deep fried, served cold in salad, scallops can be enjoyed wherever a seafood is called for in the recipe.

Salmon with Cilantro Pesto

Ingredients:

Sauce:

1 ½ cups	375 ml	fresh chopped, packed, cilantro
6	6	minced garlic cloves
⅓ cup	80 ml	toasted pinenuts
⅔ cup	170 ml	grated Parmesan cheese
1 tsp	5 ml	salt
½ tsp	3 ml	pepper
½ cup	125 ml	olive oil

Fish:

4-6 oz	4-170 g	salmon fillets
2 tbsp	30 ml	olive oil
½ tsp	3 ml	salt
½ tsp	3 ml	white pepper

Preparation:

Sauce:

Combine all the ingredients in a food processor, except the oil. Blend until well incorporated. Slowly add the oil until a thick mayonnaise type sauce is formed. Reserve until required.

Fish:

Brush the fillets with oil and season with salt and pepper. Grill the fillets over medium heat for 5-6 minutes per side. Serve with a dollop of sauce on each fillet.

Serves 4

California

Gourmet Catfish

Ingredients:

8-4 oz	8-120 g	catfish fillets
2	2	eggs
¼ cup	60 ml	milk
½ cup	125 ml	flour
1 ½ cups	325 ml	bread crumbs
1 tbsp	15 ml	paprika
1 tsp	5 ml	oregano
1 tsp	5 ml	thyme
1 tsp	5 ml	sage
1 tsp	5 ml	garlic powder
1 tsp	5 ml	onion powder
1 tsp	5 ml	black pepper
1 tsp	5 ml	marjoram
1 tsp	5 ml	chili powder
2 cups	500 ml	safflower oil
3 tbsp	45 ml	butter
3 tbsp	45 ml	flour
½ cup	125 ml	chicken stock (see page 210)
½ cup	125 ml	heavy cream
½ cup	125 ml	champagne

Preparation:

Wash the catfish and pat dry.

In a mixing bowl, combine the eggs and the milk. Place the flour in a second bowl and the bread crumbs in a third. Blend the seasonings into the bread crumbs.

Dust the catfish with the flour; dip into the eggs and dredge in the bread crumbs.

Heat the oil to 325°F (160°C). Fry the catfish to golden brown in small batches being sure that the fish is cooked thoroughly. Cooking time is dependent on the size of the fish pieces.

Reserve hot until all fish is cooked.

While the fish is cooking, melt the butter in a sauce pan. Add the flour and stir into a paste (roux) cooking over low heat.

Add chicken stock, cream and champagne. Whisk all the ingredients together.

Simmer for 10 minutes over medium heat.

Plate the fish and smother with sauce. Serve.

Serves 4

Idaho Trout Almandine
with Idaho Biarritz Potatoes

Ingredients:

4-8 oz	4-175 g	trout
⅓ cup	80 ml	milk
⅓ cup	80 ml	flour
⅓ cup	80 ml	butter
2 tbsp	30 ml	fresh parsley
2 tbsp	30 ml	lemon juice
⅓ cup	80 ml	toasted almond slices

Potatoes:

6	6	large potatoes
1 tbsp	15 ml	butter
⅓ cup	80 ml	light cream
1 tsp	5 ml	salt
½ tsp	3 ml	white pepper
1 cup	250 ml	diced smoked ham
½ cup	125 ml	finely diced green bell pepper
2 tbsp	30 ml	chopped parsley

Preparation:

Trout:

Dip the trout in the milk; dust with flour.

Heat the butter in a large skillet. Sauté the trout in the butter for 5 minutes per side. Remove the fish to a heated platter.

Add the parsley, lemon juice and almonds. Cook for 1 minute. Pour sauce over trout and serve at once.

Potatoes:

Pare and dice the potatoes. Boil in salted water in a large kettle until tender. Drain and transfer to a mixer. Whip the potatoes with butter, cream, salt and pepper.

Stir in the ham, bell pepper and parsley.

Transfer to a serving bowl. Serve very hot.

Serves 4

 Fun Food Facts

Trout

All over the world, every weekend, men can be found with long rods, dangling lines in rivers and lakes in search of the trout. Next to salmon, rainbow trout remains the favourite of restaurant patrons. Whether sautéed in a little butter or stuffed with seafood, trout is always sure to please the fish lover. A small 12", 8 oz (30 cm- 225 g) dressed trout will serve one person. Nutritionally, one dressed trout contains 268 calories, 46.6 grams of protein, 0 grams of carbohydrates, 15 grams of fat, 130 milligrams of cholesterol, 61 milligrams of sodium, 0 grams of fibre. Other kinds of trout include Brook, Brown, Cutthroat, Dolly Varden, Golden and Lake. Trout are known as truite in France, truchas in Spain, forel in Holland, ørret in Norway, trutas in Brazil, öring in Sweden, kitjolohi in Finland, pstragów in Poland, pisztráng in Hungary, and forellen in Germany.

Nebraska Moose

Ingredients:

3 cups	750 ml	miniature marshmallows
½ cup	125 ml	light cream
3 oz	80 g	semi-sweet chocolate
2 tbsp	30 ml	blackberry juice
2 cups	500 ml	whipping cream
2	2	egg whites
1 ½ cups	375 ml	blackberries

Preparation:

In a double boiler melt the marshmallows with the cream and chocolate. Stir in the blackberry juice. Remove from the heat and cool.

Whip the cream and fold in all but ½ cup (125 ml) into cooled mixture. Whip the egg whites stiff and fold into mixture. Fold in 1 cup (250 ml) of the blackberries. Pour into 6 serving dishes or parfait dishes. Chill for 3 hours before serving.

Garnish with the remaining whipping cream and berries.

Smoked Canadian Black Cod

Ingredients:

1 cup	250 ml	riesling white wine
2 cups	500 ml	water
10	10	black peppercorns
1	1	bay leaf
1	1	sprig parsley
½ tsp	3 ml	thyme
½ tsp	3 ml	marjoram
½ tsp	3 ml	basil
1	1	small diced Spanish onion
2	2	pared, diced carrots
2	2	diced celery stalks
1	1	lemon, cut in half
4-6 oz	4-170 g	black cod fillets Sablefish

Preparation:

In a large stock pot or Dutch oven combine the wine and water.

Tie the peppercorns, bay leaf, parsley and herbs together in a cheesecloth and place in the pot. Add the vegetables and lemon. Bring to a boil. Reduce heat and simmer for 10 minutes.

Place the fillets in the pot and coddle very gently, simmering for 15 minutes. Remove to serving plates and serve at once with Herb Butter, fresh steamed carrots, broccoli and a rice pilaff.

Serves 4

Herb Butter

¼ cup	60 ml	butter
½ tsp	3 ml	chives
½ tsp	3 ml	parsley
½ tsp	3 ml	chervil
½ tsp	3 ml	tarragon
½ tsp	3 ml	shallots
1 tbsp	15 ml	whipping cream

Place the ingredients in a blender and process until very smooth.

Yields ⅓ cup (80 ml)

Fun Food Facts

Black Cod

Black cod may be somewhat difficult to find, but if you plan ahead and special order it, the purveyor will be able to supply you with it. The Sablefish of the North Pacific Ocean is often referred to as Canadian or Alaskan Cod. Its appearance (a member of the Anoplopomatidae family) is much like that of cod and thus its "nickname". Because of its heavy oil content, it is most commonly found smoked. Poaching or steaming is certainly the best method of serving it.

Veal Chops Creole Style

Ingredients:

12	12	small veal chops
¼ tsp	1 ml	each of thyme, basil, oregano, salt, cayenne pepper, black pepper, white pepper
½ tsp	3 ml	paprika
1 tsp	5 ml	chili powder
1 ½ cups	375 ml	fine dry bread crumbs
2	2	eggs
¼ cup	60 ml	milk
½ cup	125 ml	flour
¼ cup	60 ml	olive oil
2 cups	500 ml	hot Creole Sauce

Preparation:

Trim the chops of any excess fat.

In a mixing bowl, blend the seasonings with the bread crumbs. Blend the eggs with the milk.

Dust the chops in the flour; dip into the eggs and dredge through the bread crumbs.

Heat the oil in a large skillet and fry the chops for 8 minutes or less depending on their size. Plate the chops and smother with Creole Sauce. Serve at once.

Serves 6

Creole Sauce

Ingredients:

3 tbsp	45 ml	safflower oil
3	3	finely diced onions
2	2	finely diced green bell peppers
3	3	finely diced celery stalks
20	20	peeled, seeded and chopped tomatoes
2 tsp	10 ml	salt
2 tsp	10 ml	paprika
1 tsp	5 ml	each of garlic powder, onion powder, cayenne pepper
½ tsp	3 ml	each of white pepper, black pepper
1 tsp	5 ml	basil leaves
½ tsp	3 ml	each of oregano leaves, thyme leaves
6	6	diced green onions
1 bunch	1 bunch	chopped parsley

Preparation:

Heat the oil in a large sauce pan. Sauté the onion, green pepper and celery until tender. Add the tomatoes and seasonings. Simmer gently until the desired thickness has been achieved (about 4 hours).

Add the green onion and parsley. Simmer 15 minutes longer. Sauce is ready for use.

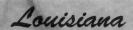

P.E.I. Mussels

Ingredients:

48	48	fresh mussels
2 tbsp	30 ml	butter
2	2	minced garlic cloves
1	1	finely diced onion
1	1	finely diced celery stalk
1 cup	250 ml	white wine
2 cups	500 ml	stewed tomatoes
1 tsp	5 ml	Worcestershire sauce
½ tsp	3 ml	salt
½ tsp	3 ml	basil leaves
¼ tsp	1 ml	cracked black pepper

Preparation:

Scrub and debeard the mussels.

Heat the butter in a sauce pan. Add the garlic, onion and celery. Sauté until tender. Add the remaining ingredients and simmer for 15 minutes.

Add the mussels and continue to simmer an additional 10 minutes. Serve.

Serves 6

Prince Edward Island

Montana Swirled Cheesecake Supreme

Ingredients:

1 cup	250 ml	graham cracker crumbs
1 tbsp	15 ml	granulated sugar
1 tbsp	15 ml	melted butter
32 oz	900 g	softened, cream cheese
1 cup	250 ml	granulated sugar
1 tbsp	15 ml	flour, all purpose
4	4	eggs
4 oz	120 g	melted, Semi-sweet chocolate
1 cup	250 ml	sour cream
1 tsp	5 ml	vanilla extract
21 oz	605 g	cherry pie filling

Preparation:

Combine crumbs, sugar and butter, press onto the bottom of a 9" (23 cm) springform pan. Bake in a preheated 325°F (170°C) oven for 10 minutes.

Combine the cream cheese, sugar and flour. Mix at medium speed on electric mixer until well blended. Add eggs, one at a time, mixing well after each addition. Divide the batter in two and combine the chocolate in one half. Divide the sour cream and vanilla and blend equal amounts into the two halves. Pour the white batter over crust, then pour the chocolate batter on top and swirl with a fork.

Bake at 450°F (220°C) for 10 minutes. Reduce temperature to 250°F (140°C), continue baking for 1 hour. Cool, chill before removing rim of pan. Top with pie filling just before serving.

VARIATION: Substitute 1½ cups (375 ml) finely chopped nuts and 2 tbsp (30 ml) granulated sugar for graham cracker crumbs and sugar.

Serves 10

Fun Food Facts

Chocolate

Chocolate is the product of the cacao bean. First discovered by the natives of Latin America who made a beverage from the bean. Brought back to Europe by the great Spanish explorer Christopher Columbus in 1502, it was received with little interest, after all he also had all that gold. It wasn't until Cortez experienced Montezumas wonderful beverage that the bean got the respect that it deserved, for it too was to become as valuable as the gold. (Nestle, Cadbury, Hershey and Mars families have all gained their wealth through chocolate). The Spanish managed to keep chocolate a secret until 1606 when an Italian visitor, Carletti, stumbled on their hidden delight. He returned home to Italy with the recipe where it quickly spread throughout Europe. First to Austria, then France, eventually to England where it became the beverage of the nobility. Soon it was to find its way back to America where Dr. John Baker put up the money to refine the bean and not long thereafter the substance we know as Bakers chocolate became available. Development of unsweet, semi-sweet, milk and many others came quickly. Today, the finest chocolate will be that which we get to consume. Good quality chocolate may come from America, Germany, Switzerland, but the best must be that of Belgium.

Maine Lobster & Salmon Mousse

Ingredients:

1 tbsp	15 ml	unflavoured gelatin
¼ cup	60 ml	white wine
¾ cup	180 ml	chicken broth (see page 210)
¼ cup	60 ml	mayonnaise
½ tsp	3 ml	salt
½ tsp	3 ml	paprika
½ tsp	3 ml	white pepper
2 tsp	10 ml	grated lemon peel
1 ¾ cups	440 ml	flaked cooked salmon
¾ cup	180 ml	heavy cream
⅓ cup	80 ml	fincly ground saltinc crackers
1 cup	250 ml	minced cooked lobster meat
1 ½ cups	375 ml	Apricot Raspberry Sauce

Preparation:

Soften the gelatin in the wine in a sauce pan. Add the broth and bring to a boil. Cool tc room temperature.

In a mixing bowl combine the mayonnaise, salt, paprika, pepper and lemon peel. Fold in two thirds of the broth. Stir in the salmon, cream and crackers.

In a second mixing bowl, mix the lobster with the remaining broth.

Pour half the salmon mixture into 6-1 cup (250 ml) molds and allow to set.

Spread the lobster mixture on top of the salmon and allow to set. Pour the remaining salmon mixture on top of the lobster and allow to set.

Chill 5-6 hours or overnight; unmold. Place on a serving platter and cover with sauce. Serve.

Serves 6

Apricot Raspberry Sauce

Ingredients:

¾ lb	345 g	peeled, stoned apricots
1 lb	454 g	fresh raspberries
½ cup	125 ml	apple juice
2 tbsp	30 ml	lemon juice
¼ cup	60 ml	sugar

Preparation:

Place the apricots and raspberries in a food processor; purée. Press through a sieve (to remove seeds) into a sauce pan.

Blend in the remaining ingredients and simmer into a thick sauce. Serve over fruit, cakes, ice cream or with souffles.

Wisconsin Cheese Lasagna

Ingredients:

1 lb	454 g	lasagna noodles
2	2	beaten eggs
8 oz	225 g	cream cheese
8 oz	225 g	grated Cheddar cheese
8 oz	225 g	grated Havarti cheese
8 oz	225 g	Ricotta cheese
1 ½ cups	375 ml	grated Parmesan cheese
2 tbsp	30 ml	butter
2 tbsp	30 ml	flour
1 cup	250 ml	milk
1 cup	250 ml	chicken stock (see page 210)
3 cups	750 ml	Tomato Sauce

Preparation:

Prepare the pasta as directed. Blanch the pasta sheets in a large kettle of boiling salted water. Drain the sheets and reserve in cold water.

Blend the eggs with the cheeses. Reserve ½ cup (125 ml) of Parmesan. Chill.

Heat the butter in a sauce pan. Add the flour and cook for 2 minutes. Add the milk and chicken stock. Simmer to a thin sauce.

In a large buttered baking dish, place a thin layer of tomato sauce. Top this with a layer of noodles. Spread a layer of white sauce on the noodles topped by a layer of tomato sauce. Spread onto this a layer of cheese topped by another layer of sauces. Repeat this until complete. Be sure to finish with a layer of tomato sauce. Sprinkle with remaining Parmesan.

Cover with foil and bake in a preheated 400°F (200°C) oven for 25 minutes. Remove the foil and continue to bake for 8 minutes more. Serve.

Serves 8-10

Tomato Sauce

Ingredients:

2 tbsp	30 ml	olive oil
2	2	minced garlic cloves
1	1	diced green bell pepper
1	1	diced onion
2	2	diced celery stalks
4 oz	120 g	sliced mushrooms
1 tsp	5 ml	salt
½ tsp	3 ml	pepper
1 tsp	5 ml	basil leaves
½ tsp	3 ml	each of oregano leaves, thyme leaves, paprika
¼ tsp	1 ml	cayenne pepper
3 lbs	1.5 kg	peeled, seeded, and chopped tomatoes

Preparation:

In a sauce pan heat the oil. Sauté the garlic, green pepper, onion, celery and mushrooms until tender. Add the seasonings and tomatoes. Simmer for 3 hours or until desired thickness. Use as required.

Turkey Fillets Creole

Ingredients:

1 ½ lbs	675 g	turkey breast
2	2	diced Spanish onions
2	2	diced green bell peppers
1	1	diced red bell pepper
3 tbsp	45 ml	safflower oil
½ tsp	3 ml	each of basil, oregano, thyme, paprika, garlic powder, onion powder, chili powder
¼ tsp	1 ml	each of black pepper, white pepper, cayenne pepper
1 tsp	5 ml	salt
1 tbsp	15 ml	Worcestershire sauce
3 cups	750 ml	crushed tomatoes
½ cup	125 ml	chopped green onions
2 tbsp	30 ml	chopped parsley

Preparation:

Cut the turkey in ¾" (19 mm) wide strips.

In a large Dutch oven, fry the turkey, onions and peppers in the oil until the turkey is cooked through. Add the seasoning, Worcestershire and tomatoes. Reduce heat and simmer for 1 ¼ hours.

Add the green onion and parsley. Simmer for 5 minutes longer. Serve over noodles or rice.

Serves 6

Louisiana

Niagara Pear Salad

Ingredients:

4	4	Bartlett, Bosc or Anjou pears
2 tbsp	30 ml	lemon juice
2 tbsp	30 ml	balsamic vinegar
2 tbsp	30 ml	Madeira
2 tbsp	30 ml	Dijon mustard
2	2	egg yolks
¾ tsp	4 ml	salt
½ tsp	3 ml	cracked black pepper
2 tsp	10 ml	fresh chopped basil
¼ cup	60 ml	grape seed oil*
¼ cup	60 ml	walnut oil*
2	2	large bunches watercress
½ cup	125 ml	crumbled, feta cheese
½ cup	125 ml	pecan pieces

Preparation:

Wash the pears. Remove the core through the blossom end of the fruit. Slice thinly from the blossom end to ¼" (7 mm) from the stem end to cause the pear to fan open. Sprinkle each pear with lemon juice to prevent the fruit from oxidizing. Place on a chilled serving plate.

In small mixing bowl blend together the vinegar, Madeira, mustard, egg yolks, black pepper, basil, and oils.

Garnish the pears with the watercress. Ladle the dressing over the pears and watercress. Sprinkle with cheese and pecans. Serve at once.

Serves 4

* Grape seed and walnut oils are available through specialty food stores.

 Fun Food Facts

Pears

Next to apples, pears are the easiest fruit to store for the winter months, simply place them off the floor and keep in a cool room between 40°F and 50°F. Depending on your recipes, choose the pear that suits most. Bosc pears are very good for poaching and presenting whole. Bartletts or Chrétien are the most popular eating pear. Other good cooking pears are Anjou, Bosc, and the Conference. If you poach the pear in a water sugar liquid, be sure to keep the liquid as it will make an excellent pear syrup when reduced.

Ontario

Tourtière Québecoise

Ingredients:

3 tbsp	45 ml	butter
2	2	finely diced onions
3	3	minced garlic cloves
2 cups	500 ml	peeled, seeded and diced tomatoes
¾ lb	345 g	lean ground pork
¾ lb	345 g	finely diced beef
1 cup	250 ml	beef stock (see page 42)
2	2	bay leaves
¼ tsp	1 ml	each of allspice, cinnamon, nutmeg
1 tsp	5 ml	salt
½ tsp	3 ml	pepper
⅓ cup	80 ml	fine bread crumbs
1 quant.	1 quant.	double crust pie dough
3 tbsp	45 ml	milk
1	1	egg

Preparation:

In a large skillet, heat the butter and sweat the onion and garlic. Add the tomatoes. Cook covered for 3 minutes. Add the pork and cook thoroughly. Add beef, stock, bay leaves and seasonings. Cover and simmer for 30 minutes. Uncover and continue to simmer until most of the liquid has evaporated. Stir in the bread crumbs. Cool mixture to room temperature.

Preheat the oven to 400°F (200°C).

Divide pie dough in half. Roll out each half. Line a 10" (25 cm) pie shell with one part. Fill with the mixture and cover with the remaining pastry. Crimp edges and cut a 1" (2.5 cm) hole in top. Make a tin foil chimney and fit into hole. Mix milk with the egg and brush over pastry.

Bake for 10 minutes then reduce the heat to 350°F (180°C). Continue to bake for 25 minutes. Rest the pie for 20 minutes before cutting or cool and chill. Serve.

Serves 8

Double Crust Pie Dough

Ingredients:

1 ½ cups	375 ml	sifted, all purpose flour
½ tsp	3 ml	salt
½ cup	125 ml	shortening
4-5 tbsp	60-75 ml	water

Preparation:

Sift the flour and salt together into a mixing bowl. Cut shortening into flour with a pastry cutter or fork until pastry forms walnut size. Add the water and toss. Use only enough water to bind the pastry. Divide pastry in two and chill covered. Use as directed.

Virginia Honey Glazed Ham

Ingredients:

4 ½ lbs	2 kg	Virginia ham
½ cup	125 ml	peach preserves
¼ cup	60 ml	liquid honey
¼ tsp	1 ml	ground cinnamon
¼ tsp	1 ml	ground cloves
¼ tsp	1 ml	white pepper
2 tbsp	30 ml	lemon juice
1 tbsp	15 ml	cornstarch

Preparation:

Preheat the oven to 325°F (160°C).

Score the ham with 2" (5 cm) deep criss-cross cuts. Place into a roasting pan. Roast the ham for 2 hours.

In small sauce pan, combine the preserves, honey and spices. Heat slowly to a boiling point. Blend the lemon juice and cornstarch together and add to the sauce. Simmer until thick. Pour the sauce over the ham and continue to roast for an additional 30 minutes; basting every 7-10 minutes.

Serve the ham on a hot serving platter with sweet root vegetables and fruit.

Serves 8

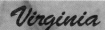

Virginia

Oregon Apple Cake

Ingredients:

½ cup	125 ml	butter
¾ cup	180 ml	brown sugar
½ tsp	3 ml	ground cinnamon
2 cups	500 ml	sliced apples
½ cup	125 ml	golden seedless raisins
½ cup	125 ml	toasted sliced almonds
1 ½ cups	375 ml	sifted flour
1 ½ tsp	8 ml	baking powder
¾ cup	180 ml	granulated sugar
3	3	egg yolks
¼ cup	60 ml	heavy cream
¼ cup	60 ml	apple juice
1 tsp	5 ml	grated lemon zest

Sauce:

3 oz	80 g	butterscotch chips
¾ cup	180 ml	confectioners sugar
¼ cup	60 ml	boiling water
1 cup	250 ml	whipping cream
1	1	egg white
1 tsp	5 ml	vanilla extract

Preparation:

Preheat oven to 350°F (180°C).

Grease a 9" (23 cm) springform pan lined with waxed paper.

Melt the butter and drizzle 2 tbsp (30 ml) on the bottom of the pan. Combine the brown sugar and cinnamon together. Sprinkle ¼ cup (60 ml) of the brown sugar on the bottom of the pan. Cover with the apple slices, raisins and almonds. Sprinkle with the remaining sugar. Drizzle an additional 4 tbsp (60 ml) of the melted butter over the sugar.

Blend the flour, baking powder and sugar together in small mixing bowl. In a second mixing bowl beat the egg yolks with the remaining butter.

Blend the cream and apple juice together. Add to the eggs alternating with flour in equal thirds. Pour over the apples and bake for 45 minutes. Turn out onto a serving platter and serve with the sauce.

Sauce:

In a double boiler, melt the butterscotch. Stir in the sugar and water. Remove from the heat; cool.

Whip the cream and fold into the butterscotch. Whip the egg whites and fold into the mixture along with vanilla.

French Canadian Pea Soup

Ingredients:

1 lb	454 g	chic peas
1	1	ham bone
3 ½ qts	3.5 L	water or chicken broth (see page 210)
3	3	finely diced leeks
3	3	finely diced celery stalks
2	2	finely diced carrots
½ lb	225 g	diced ham
		salt only if required
½ tsp	3 ml	white pepper

Preparation:

Soak the chic peas in water overnight or for 8 hours. Place into a large kettle with the ham bone and cover with the water. Bring to a boil. Reduce to a simmer and add the vegetables. Simmer for 3½-4 hours.

Discard bone. Add the ham and simmer for 15 minutes more. Taste; adjust seasonings. Serve very hot.

Serve with Tourtière Québecoise, (see page 36).

Serves 10

Beef Broth or Stock

Ingredients:

2 ¼ lbs	1 kg	Meaty beef bones or veal bones**
¼ cup	60 ml	olive oil
10 cups	2.5 L	cold water
2	2	coarsely chopped celery stalks
2	2	coarsely chopped large carrots
1	1	coarsely chopped onion
1	1	Bouquet garni*
1 tsp	5 ml	salt

Preparation:

Place the bones in a roaster and cover with oil. Bake in a preheated 350°F (180°C) oven for 1 hour or until the bones are well browned. Transfer to a large kettle or Dutch oven.

Add the water and remaining ingredients; bring to a simmer. Simmer uncovered for 3-4 hours, skimming any scum or grease that may rise to the top.

Remove the meat (reserve and use as required), bones (discard), bouquet (discard) and vegetables (discard). Strain though a cheesecloth or fine sieve.

Chill the stock and remove any fat from the surface.

Allow stock to chill for 24 hours before using. Use for soups and sauces, or as required.

Yields 6 cups (1 ½ L)

* Bouquet Garni for soup is: 2 sprigs fresh thyme, 2 sprigs marjoram, 6 peppercorns, 1 bay leaf, 6 sprigs parsley, 1 leek, tied together in a cheesecloth (J-Cloth works well).

** For veal stock do not brown the meat bones.

Florida Grilled Portobello Soup

Ingredients:

1 lb	454 g	Portobello mushrooms
3 tbsp	45 ml	garlic flavoured grilling oil
2	2	minced, garlic cloves
1	1	lemon, juice only
1 tsp	5 ml	salt
½ tsp	3 ml	each of cracked black pepper, thyme leaves, oregano leaves
3 tbsp	45 ml	butter
3 tbsp	45 ml	flour
1 cup	250 ml	orange juice
3 cups	750 ml	beef broth (see page 42)
1 tbsp	15 ml	finely julienne orange peel

Preparation:

Trim and brush the mushrooms. Place into a large mixing bowl.

Blend the oil, garlic cloves, lemon juice, salt, black pepper, thyme and oregano. Pour over the mushrooms and marinate for 2 hours. Cook over medium coals for 5 minutes per side. Remove from grill and slice.

Heat the butter in a large sauce pan. Add the mushrooms and cook for 5 minutes. Sprinkle with the flour and cook over low heat for an additional 2 minutes. Add the orange juice and beef broth. Simmer until soup has slightly thickened.

Pour soup into bowls. Garnish with orange peel and serve.

Serves 6

Fun Food Facts

Edible Mushrooms

The use of mushrooms in culinary preparation goes as far back as recorded recipes and no doubt far beyond that. Select mushrooms based on how they look and smell. Fresh mushrooms will not appear withered and have an earthly odour. They should be rich in its natural color and conform to the basic shapes of its family. Never eat a mushroom from the wild unless you have absolute knowledge as to what you are choosing. Many mushrooms and toadstools are highly toxic.

Some of the edible varieties are:

Button mushrooms - are the worlds most common and most cultivated mushrooms. They are generally sold fresh in grocers produce section. Look for the mushrooms with the round button like head. Its proper name is "Agaricus bisporus" it is by far easier to remember "button mushrooms".

Enoki - are long slender mushrooms that have a slight nutty flavour. Available fresh, they are best used in that state. Enoki are especially good when garnishing salads.

Shiitake - has a meaty flavour and is umbrella in shape. Great as a side dish or within stir fried dishes. Also known as Oak Mushrooms as they tend to grow on Oak trees. Their main production is within the Orient, however, they are widely available fresh throughout the world.

Morels - are rich in flavour, dark in color and conical in shape. They are used in all forms of cooking with the exception of desserts.

Truffles - are very rich in flavour. These are usually quite expensive and difficult to find fresh. Try a speciality grocer. Truffles are dug out from beneath the ground by specially trained animals (pigs and dogs). Walnut in size, a minimal amount will provide a special richness in soups, salads, sauces and with grilled meats or fish. Truffles are available in three varieties fresh or tinned; Piemont whites, Summer or St. Jean, and Perigord.

Portobello - are large umbrella shapes with a very rich earthly meaty flavour. Excellent in all cuisines. It can be used on its own as appetizers or stuffed as an entree.

Many other varieties of mushrooms are available in the grocers produce section, fresh or dried, depending on the season.

Hoosier Corn Chowder

Ingredients:

½ lb	225 g	diced bacon
1	1	finely diced, large onion
3	3	finely diced, large carrots
3	3	finely diced celery stalks
4 tbsp	60 ml	butter
4 tbsp	60 ml	flour
4 cups	1 L	chicken broth (see page 210)
1 ½ cups	375 ml	cream
2 cups	500 ml	fresh sweet corn
		salt and pepper to taste

Preparation:

In a large kettle, fry the bacon. Add the onion, carrots and celery. Sauté until tender. Drain all excess fat. Add the butter and flour. Cook over low heat for 3 minutes. Pour the chicken broth over and simmer until thick. Add the cream and corn and continue to simmer for 10 minutes. Check for seasoning and serve.

Serves 8

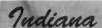

Indiana

D.C. Cherry Torte

Ingredients:

1 cup	250 ml	flour
¼ tsp	1 ml	salt
3 tbsp	45 ml	cocoa powder
2 tbsp	30 ml	safflower oil
1 cup	250 ml	milk
¼ cup	60 ml	soda water
1	1	egg
½ tsp	3 ml	vanilla extract
6 cups	1.5 L	stoned, pitted cherries cut in half
3 cups	750 ml	Chocolate Cherry Ice Cream

Topping:

4 cups	1 L	stoned, pitted and diced cherries
3 cups	750 ml	granulated sugar
2 tsp	10 ml	vanilla extract

Preparation:

Sift the flour, salt and cocoa powder together. Blend in the oil, milk and soda water. Beat the egg and add to the liquid. Stir in the vanilla. Beat until a smooth thin batter is formed.

To cook the crêpes, spread about 3 tbsp (45 ml) of batter in a lightly buttered hot skillet. Cook about 1½ minutes, turn the crêpes and cook 1 minute over medium heat. Turn out and allow to cool to room temperature.

Place a crêpe on a shallow pie plate. Spread with cherries and softened ice cream. Continue until all the crêpes are used. Freeze for 2 hours or until ready to serve.

Topping:

Place the cherries in a sauce pan. Add the sugar and vanilla. Heat over low heat until a boiling point is reached. Reduce heat and simmer until the sauce is thick and clear. Reserve warm.

Slice the crêpe torte. Place on chilled serving plate. Smother with sauce and serve at once.

Serves 6

Chocolate Cherry Ice Cream

Ingredients:

3 cups	750 ml	light half & half cream
2 tbsp	30 ml	flour
2 tbsp	30 ml	water
3	3	egg yolks
1 cup	250 ml	granulated sugar
1 ½ tsp	8 ml	vanilla extract
4 oz	120 g	melted Semi-sweet chocolate
1 ½ cups	375 ml	stoned, pitted cherries

Preparation:

In a double boiler, scald the cream. Blend the flour with the water and add to the cream. Beat the egg yolks with sugar. Slowly add to the cream, extract and chocolate. Cook, stirring constantly until mixture thickens. Remove from heat. Cool. Chill. Freeze according to the directions of your ice cream maker. Add the cherries during the final 5 minutes of the churning process. Freeze until required.

Washington D.C.

Braised Texas Ribs

Ingredients:

2 ¼ lbs	1 kg	racks of standing ribs (prime rib bones)
2 cups	500 ml	flour
½ tsp	3 ml	garlic powder
½ tsp	3 ml	onion powder
½ tsp	3 ml	salt
½ tsp	3 ml	black pepper
¼ tsp	1 ml	each of thyme, oregano, chili powder, paprika, white pepper, cayenne pepper
1	1	minced garlic clove
¼ cup	60 ml	soy sauce
½ tsp	3 ml	ground ginger
¼ cup	60 ml	brown sugar
¼ cup	60 ml	sherry
¾ cup	180 ml	water

Preparation:

Cut the ribs into desired serving portions.

Blend the flour with the seasonings; dust the ribs with flour. Brown in a preheated 350°F (180°C) oven.

Mix the garlic, soy, ginger, sugar, sherry and water together and pour this mixture over the ribs. Cover the ribs. Reduce the temperature of the oven to 300°F (150°C) and bake for 2 hours.

Serve with Spanish Rice

Serves 6

Spanish Rice

Ingredients:

8	8	diced bacon slices
1	1	finely diced, large, Spanish onion
1	1	finely diced, green bell pepper
2	2	celery stalks
2 cups	500 ml	chicken stock (see page 210)
1 cup	250 ml	long grain rice
2 cups	500 ml	peeled, seeded and chopped tomatoes
2 tsp	10 ml	chili powder
½ tsp	3 ml	salt
¼ tsp	1 ml	each of pepper, paprika

Preparation:

In a large sauce pan, fry the bacon. Add the vegetables and sauté until tender.

Add the chicken stock, rice, tomatoes and seasonings. Cover. Bring to a boil. Reduce to a simmer and cook until liquid is absorbed. Serve.

Serves 6

Tampa Bay Barbecued Shrimp

Ingredients:

3 tbsp	45 ml	butter
3 tbsp	45 ml	oil
1	1	minced onion
1	1	minced, garlic clove
⅔ cup	170 ml	tomato catsup
⅔ cup	170 ml	orange brandy
½ cup	125 ml	cider vinegar
½ cup	125 ml	orange juice
½ cup	125 ml	orange juice concentrate
⅓ cup	80 ml	light molasses
1 tbsp	15 ml	Worcestershire sauce
½ tsp	3 ml	thyme leaves
½ tsp	3 ml	basil leaves
½ tsp	3 ml	chervil
½ tsp	3 ml	oregano leaves
½ tsp	3 ml	garlic powder
½ tsp	3 ml	cracked black pepper
½ tsp	3 ml	white pepper
½ tsp	3 ml	paprika
½ tsp	3 ml	salt
¼ tsp	1 ml	Tabasco™ sauce
½ tsp	3 ml	liquid smoke flavouring
2 ½ lbs	1 kg	tiger prawns or very large shrimp
1 quantity	1 quantity	court boullion (see page 416)
3 tbsp	45 ml	melted butter

Preparation:

Heat the butter and oil in a sauce pan. Add the onion and garlic. Sauté until tender. Stir in the catsup, brandy, vinegar, orange juice, concentrate, molasses, Worcestershire, herbs, spices, Tabasco,™ and liquid smoke. Bring to a boil. Reduce heat and simmer until sauce is very thick. Cool.

Peel and devein the prawns. Bring the court bouillon to a boil and simmer the prawns until cooked. Toss the prawns in the barbecue sauce and serve.

Or, brush the prawns with melted butter. Grill over medium coals for 10 minutes, brushing often with sauce.

Serves 6

Florida

Atlantic Salmon Montmorency

Ingredients:

1 ¼ cups	310 ml	bing cherries - fresh or tinned, pitted
¼ cup	60 ml	cherry brandy
3 tbsp	45 ml	cherry liquid or apple juice
1 tbsp	15 ml	lemon juice
2 tbsp	30 ml	granulated sugar
6-6 oz.	6-170 g	Salmon fillets
2 tbsp	30 ml	melted butter

Preparation:

Heat the cherries in the cherry brandy over low heat until very tender. Press through the sieve into a sauce pan.

Add the cherry juice, lemon juice and sugar. Simmer until thick.

Place the fish on a baking sheet and brush with butter. Bake in a preheated 375°F (180°C) oven for 8 minutes.

Plate the fish and smother with sauce. Serve.

Serves 6

Maryland

Chicago's Best Steak

Ingredients:

6-8 oz	6-225 g	Striploin steaks
6 tbsp	90 ml	lemon pepper
1 tbsp	15 ml	each of ground thyme, ground oregano, basil leaves
2 tbsp	30 ml	each of Hungarian paprika, chili powder
2 tsp	10 ml	granular garlic
½ tsp	3 ml	each of white pepper, black pepper, ground coriander
⅛ tsp	pinch	each of cayenne pepper, ground cumin
1 tsp	5 ml	granulated sugar
3 tbsp	45 ml	olive oil

Salad:

½ lb	225 g	bacon
10 oz	300 g	spinach
1 ½ cups	375 ml	mushrooms
⅓ cup	80 ml	freshly grated Parmesan cheese
2	2	grated hard cooked eggs

Dressing:

4 tsp	20 ml	Dijon mustard
2 tsp	10 ml	granulated sugar
¼ cup	60 ml	white wine vinegar
2 tsp	10 ml	Worcestershire sauce
1 tsp	5 ml	seasoned salt
½ cup	125 ml	olive oil
2	2	chopped green onions

Preparation:

Trim the steaks of any excess fat and the strip of grizzle along the top edge. This will prevent the steak from curling during cooking.

Blend the herbs, spices and sugar together. Brush the steaks with the oil and sprinkle with the seasonings. Grill the steaks over medium heat until your desired doneness is achieved.

Salad:

Dice the bacon and fry until crisp. Drain; reserving the drippings.

Wash the spinach and trim the leaves. Tear into bite size pieces. Place on serving plates. Top with the bacon, mushrooms, cheese and eggs.

Dressing:

Heat 3 tbsp (45 ml) of the bacon drippings in a sauce pan. Add the mustard and sugar and bring to a boil. Whisk in the vinegar, Worcestershire and salt.

Slowly add the oil, stirring constantly. Stir in the green onions. Pour sauce over the salad and serve at once.

Illinois

Everglades Gator Kebabs

Ingredients:

2 lbs	900 g	boneless alligator meat*

Marinate:

4 tbsp	60 ml	peanut oil
1 ½ tbsp	23 ml	ground Brazilian nuts
½ tsp	3 ml	ground ginger
1 ½ tsp	8 ml	ground coriander
¼ tsp	1 ml	each of cayenne, garlic powder
½ tsp	3 ml	each of black pepper, onion powder
2 tsp	10 ml	molasses
4 tsp	20 ml	lime juice
4 tsp	20 ml	lemon juice
3 tbsp	45 ml	hot water

Sauce:

½ cup	125 ml	crunchy style peanut butter
1	1	finely chopped onion
1 cup	250 ml	thick, coconut milk
1 tbsp	15 ml	demerara sugar
1 tsp	5 ml	cayenne pepper
1 tbsp	15 ml	soy sauce
3 tbsp	45 ml	chopped cilantro
2 tsp	10 ml	Worcestershire sauce

Preparation:

Soak bamboo skewers in water for 20 minutes. Cut the Alligator meat into ½" (12 mm) cubes. Skewer the alligator meat. Place in a large shallow pan.

Marinate:

In a mixing bowl blend the ingredients together. Pour over the skewered alligator. Marinate, covered, in the refrigerator for 3½-4 hours.

Grill the skewers over high heat for 10-12 minutes, or until meat is cooked through. Brush frequently with marinate.

Sauce:

In a blender or food processor blend all the ingredients together. Serve as a dipping sauce along side the kebabs.

Serves 6

* Alligator meat is available through specialty food store but must be ordered in advance.

Southern Fried Chicken

Ingredients:

4 ½ lbs	2 kg	chicken cut into pieces
4	4	eggs
¾ cup	180 ml	milk
1 ½ cups	375 ml	flour
3 cups	750 ml	bread crumbs
1 tbsp	15 ml	paprika
1 tsp	5 ml	oregano
1 tsp	5 ml	thyme
1 tsp	5 ml	sage
1 tsp	5 ml	garlic powder
1 tsp	5 ml	onion powder
1 tsp	5 ml	black pepper
1 tsp	5 ml	marjoram
1 tsp	5 ml	chili powder
4 cups	1 L	safflower oil

Preparation:

Wash the chicken and pat dry.

In a mixing bowl, combine the eggs and the milk. Place the flour in a second bowl. In a third bowl, blend seasonings and bread crumbs.

Dust the chicken with the flour; dip into the eggs; dredge in the bread crumbs.

Heat the oil to 325°F (160°C). Fry the chicken in small batches until golden brown, being sure that the chicken is cooked thoroughly. Cooking time is dependent on the size of the chicken pieces.

Reserve hot until all chicken is cooked.

Serve with Broccoli Soufflé.

Serves 6

Broccoli Soufflé

Ingredients:

3 tbsp	45 ml	butter
3 tbsp	45 ml	flour
1 ¼ cups	310 ml	milk
1 cup	250 ml	Swiss cheese
⅓ cup	80 ml	Parmesan cheese
½ tsp	3 ml	salt
¼ tsp	1 ml	pepper
6	6	large, separated, room temperature eggs
1 cup	250 ml	steamed broccoli florets

Preparation:

Preheat the oven to 375°F (190°C).

In a sauce pan heat the butter. Add the flour and cook for 2 minutes over low heat. Stir in the milk and simmer until sauce thickens. Stir in the cheeses, salt and pepper. Remove from the heat. Cool.

Butter a 2½ quart (2.5 L) soufflé dish.

In a mixing bowl beat the egg yolks. Whisk the eggs into the sauce, then fold in the broccoli.

Whip the egg whites until stiff. Fold into the mixture. Pour mixture into the soufflé dish. Bake for 40 minutes or until soufflé rises high. Serve at once, (quickly).

Serves 4

Georgia

Sirloin Tip Rotisserie

Ingredients:

4 ½ lbs	2 kg	sirloin tip roast
6	6	garlic cloves
1 cup	250 ml	olive oil
½ cup	125 ml	red wine
1 cup	250 ml	onion slices
1	1	bay leaf
1 tbsp	15 ml	granulated sugar
1 tsp	5 ml	garlic powder
1 tbsp	15 ml	Worcestershire sauce
1 tbsp	15 ml	soy sauce
4 drops	4 drops	Tabasco™ sauce
¼ cup	60 ml	lemon juice

Preparation:

Cut 12 small incisions evenly around the roast. Slice the garlic cloves in half and insert a half in each incision. Place the roast in a shallow roasting pan.

Blend the remaining ingredients together. Pour into a sauce pan. Bring to a boil and remove from heat. Cool. Pour over roast and marinate for 8 hours.

Insert the rotisserie spit through roast and roast over medium low heat for 1 ½-2 hours. Baste with marinate frequently. Carve and serve.

Serves 8

Kentucky

California Tuna & Shark Kebabs

Ingredients:

1 lb	454 g	large cubed tuna
1 lb	454 g	large cubed shark
½ cup	125 ml	apricot nectar
1 tbsp	15 ml	lemon juice
1 tbsp	15 ml	lime juice
¼ cup	60 ml	olive oil
1 tbsp	15 ml	Worcestershire sauce
½ tsp	3 ml	salt
½ tsp	3 ml	thyme leaves
1 tbsp	15 ml	chopped cilantro
2	2	cubed, green bell peppers
1	1	cubed, yellow bell pepper
12	12	mushrooms
12	12	cherry tomatoes
1	1	cubed, Spanish onion
1	1	thick sliced zucchini

Preparation:

Cut the fish into ¾" (19 mm) cubes. Place the cubes in a mixing bowl.

Blend the apricot, lemon, lime, oil, Worcestershire, salt, thyme and cilantro. Pour the marinate over the seafood. Marinate in the refrigerator for 12 hours or overnight.

Soak bamboo skewers for 20 minutes in water. Alternate onto skewers the fish, peppers, mushrooms, tomatoes, onions and zucchini. Grill over medium heat on a broiler for 8-10 minutes; brushing with marinate. Serve.

Serves 6

 Fun Food Facts

Tuna

Albacore tuna is the most popular of the commercial tuna sold. It is rich dark and should be cooked like beef in the way you prefer it; rare, medium or well done. Bigeye, Blackfin, Bluefin and Bonito are all very good and each is preferred in different countries. Bonito is especially favoured by the Japanese and is often the type sold in sushi bars. The average nutritional information of 4 ounces is 163 calories, 26.5 grams of protein, 0 carbohydrates, 5.6 grams of fat, 43 milligrams of cholesterol, 44 milligrams os sodium, 0 grams of fibre.

Pecan Torte

Ingredients:

Cake:

12	12	eggs, separated
1 cup	250 ml	granulated sugar
½ lb.	225 g	finely ground pecans
⅓ cup	80 ml	flour
½ tsp	3 ml	salt
1 tsp	5 ml	rum extract
1 ½ cups	375 ml	fine bread crumbs

Filling:

1 cup	250 ml	whipping cream
2 tbsp	30 ml	confection sugar
½ tsp	3 ml	rum extract
1 cup	250 ml	finely ground pecans

Topping:

2	2	eggs
½ cup	80 ml	melted, butter
1 tsp	5 ml	rum extract
4 cups	1 L	confectioners sugar

Preparation:

Cake:

Preheat the oven to 350°F (180°C).

Beat the egg yolks until light and creamy. Gradually add the sugar beating until very thick. Stir in the pecans and flour; blend thoroughly.

Whip the egg whites with the salt until soft peaks form. Fold in the rum extract. Fold the egg whites into the batter. Stir in the bread crumbs.

Grease a 10" (30 cm) springform pan. Fold the batter into the pan and bake for 45 minutes. Cool for 15 minutes. Turn out onto a cooling rack. Cut into two rounds.

Filling:

Whip the cream until light. Gradually add the sugar and rum. Fold in the pecans. Spread onto the bottom layer of cake. Place top layer of cake over filling.

Topping:

Beat the eggs until thick and foamy. Add the butter beating until thick. Fold in the extract and gradually add the sugar (frosting should a thin spreading consistency). Spread over the cake, covering top and sides. Cover sides with chopped pecans. Decorate with whole pecans.

Arizona

Tennessee Sour Mash Ribs

Ingredients:

Sauce:

3 tbsp	45 ml	butter
3 tbsp	45 ml	oil
1	1	minced onion
1	1	garlic clove, minced
⅔ cup	170 ml	tomato catsup
⅔ cup	170 ml	Sour Mash Whiskey
½ cup	125 ml	cider vinegar
½ cup	125 ml	peach juice
½ cup	125 ml	peach syrup
⅓ cup	80 ml	light molasses
I tbsp	15 ml	Worcestershire sauce
½ tsp	3 ml	thyme leaves
½ tsp	3 ml	basil leaves
½ tsp	3 ml	chervil
½ tsp	3 ml	oregano leaves
½ tsp	3 ml	garlic powder
½ tsp	3 ml	cracked black pepper
½ tsp	3 ml	white pepper
½ tsp	3 ml	paprika
½ tsp	3 ml	salt
½ tsp	3 ml	liquid smoke flavouring

Ribs:

10 lbs	4.4 kg	Danish or baby back pork ribs
½ tsp	3 ml	thyme leaves
½ tsp	3 ml	oregano leaves
½ tsp	3 ml	basil
½ tsp	3 ml	savory
½ tsp	3 ml	sage
1 tsp	5 ml	pepper
1 tsp	5 ml	paprika
1 tsp	5 ml	chili powder
1 tsp	5 ml	salt

Preparation:

Sauce:

Heat the butter and the oil in a sauce pan. Add the onion and garlic. Sauté until tender. Stir in the remaining ingredients and bring to a boil. Reduce heat and simmer until sauce is very thick. Cool.

Ribs:

Cut the ribs into 5 bone sections. Combine the seasonings and sprinkle over ribs. Bake in a 350°F (180°C) oven for 1½ hours. Grill over medium coals for 10 minutes, brushing frequently with sauce. Brush one final time with sauce. Serve.

Serves 8

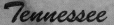

California Fire Shrimp

Ingredients:

¾ cup	180 ml	seedless golden raisins
3 tbsp	45 ml	balsamic vinegar
1 ½ tsp	8 ml	red chili flakes
4	4	garlic cloves
½ tsp	3 ml	salt
½ cup	125 ml	crushed tomatoes
6 oz.	170 ml	plum preserves
½ cup	125 ml	apple juice
2 tbsp	30 ml	demerara sugar
⅓ cup	80 ml	soy sauce
1 tbsp	15 ml	finely chopped ginger
2 ¼ lbs	1 kg	peeled, deveined, Jumbo shrimp
3 tbsp	45 ml	red pepper grilling oil

Preparation:

In a food processor purée the raisins, vinegar, chili flakes, garlic, salt, tomatoes, preserves, apple juice and sugar. Transfer to a mixing bowl and add the soy and ginger.

Wash the shrimp and place into a large bowl. Pour the marinate over the shrimp and marinate for 2-3 hours.

Heat the oil in a large skillet. Drain the shrimp reserving the marinate. Cook the shrimp for 5-7 minutes. Add the marinate and simmer for 3 minutes. Serve at once.

Serves 6

 Fun Food Facts

Balsamic Vinegar

An Italian vinegar of Modena. It is made from the unfermented juice of cooked and concentrated white grapes, aged through a process of transferring the liquid through different aromatic wooden barrels such as chestnut, juniper, red oak and others. The vinegar must be aged no less than 10 years by Modena law and many are aged for 50 or more years. To some the vinegar is more valuable than money, and a small bottle of the black gold can sell for as much as $100.00 US.

Other vinegars include;

Raspberry Vinegar,
Apple Cider Vinegar,
Red Wine Vinegar,
White Wine Vinegar,
Tarragon Vinegar,
Chili Vinegar,
Sherry Vinegar.

 *California*

Redwood Salmon

Ingredients:

1	1	redwood or cedar plank, ¾" x 1" x 8" (19mm x 2.5cm x 20cm)
1	1	minced garlic clove
1 tsp	15 ml	cracked black pepper
½ tsp	3 ml	coarse ground salt
2 tbsp	30 ml	herb flavoured olive oil
4-6 oz	4-170 g	Salmon fillets

Preparation:

Soak the plank under water for 8 hours.

In a mixing bowl blend the garlic, pepper, salt and oil. Brush onto salmon fillets.

Place the plank on your outdoor grill (heated to medium heat.) Once the edges of the plank appear dry, but not burned, place the fillets onto the centre of the plank. Close the lid of the grill and cook for 10-12 minutes depending on the thickness of the salmon.

Serve at once with fresh potato and or pasta salads. Serve with Insalata D'Indivia

Serves 4

Note: Keep a spray bottle of water handy. Check the fish while cooking and spray the edges of the plank to prevent burning.

Insalata D'Indivia

Ingredients:

1 head	1 head	endive lettuce
⅓ cup	80 ml	olive oil
1	1	minced garlic clove
2 tbsp	30 ml	lemon juice
2 tsp	10 ml	fresh chopped mint
¼ tsp	1 ml	salt
⅛ tsp	pinch	pepper
2	2	chopped hard cooked eggs
⅓ cup	80 ml	crisp cooked bacon bits
⅓ cup	80 ml	freshly grated Romano cheese
16	16	cherry tomatoes

Preparation:

Thoroughly wash the lettuce. Trim and chop into bite size pieces.

Blend the oil, garlic, lemon and seasonings. Pour over the lettuce and place in a serving bowl. Sprinkle with egg, bacon and cheese, garnish with tomatoes. Serve at once.

Serves 6

Northern California

Blueberry Crusted Ice Box Cream Pie

Ingredients:

1 ½ tbsp	23 ml	soft butter
2 cups	500 ml	fresh blueberries - divided
½ cup	125 ml	granulated sugar - divided
1	1	envelope unflavoured gelatin
⅔ cup	170 ml	whipping cream - divided
1	1	egg
24 oz	375 g	cream cheese at room temperature
¼ cup	60 ml	icing sugar

Preparation:

Generously butter a 9" (23 cm) pie plate. Gently press about 1½ cups (375 ml) blueberries into the butter to line the pie plate. Sprinkle with 2 tbsp (30 ml) granulated sugar.

Sprinkle the gelatin into ⅓ cup (80 ml) of cream in a medium sauce pan to soften. Stir in the egg and the remaining ⅓ cup (80 ml) granulated sugar. Place over medium heat, stirring constantly until mixture thickens slightly and comes to a boil.

Beat the cream cheese until smooth. Slowly add the gelatin mixture, beating until well blended. Beat the remaining ⅓ cup (80 ml) whipping cream until stiff. Fold into cream cheese mixture. Pour mixture into blueberry shell and chill 3-4 hours. At serving time sprinkle with remaining blueberries and sifted icing sugar.

Northern Ontario

Cajun Scallops
with Chili Pepper Mayonnaise

Ingredients:

Mayonnaise:

2	2	egg yolks
1 cup	250 ml	safflower oil
1 tbsp	15 ml	lemon juice
¼ tsp	1 ml	salt
1 tbsp	15 ml	chili powder
3 drops	3 drops	Tabasco™ sauce

Scallops:

1 lb	454 g	large scallops
½ tsp	3 ml	oregano leaves
½ tsp	3 ml	thyme leaves
½ tsp	3 ml	basil leaves
½ tsp	3 ml	cayenne pepper
½ tsp	3 ml	black pepper
½ tsp	3 ml	onion powder
½ tsp	3 ml	garlic powder
1 tsp	5 ml	paprika
1 tsp	5 ml	chili powder
1 tsp	5 ml	salt
1 ½ cups	375 ml	flour
¾ cup	180 ml	milk
2 cups	500 ml	safflower oil

Preparation:

Mayonnaise:

Place the egg yolks in a blender. With the machine running very slowly; add the oil until a thick sauce is formed. Add the lemon juice, salt, chili powder and Tabasco.™ Turn machine off. Pour sauce in a bowl and serve with the scallops.

Scallops:

Wash and pat dry the scallops.

Blend all the seasonings into the flour. Dip the scallops in the milk; dust with the seasoned flour.

Heat the oil in a large pan to 375°F (190°C) and fry the scallops (a few at a time) for 3-4 minutes until golden brown. Serve at once with the mayonnaise.

Serves 6

Fun Food Facts

Safflower Oil

When given the choice of safflower or peanut oil, choose safflower. Safflower has a high smoking point which makes it perfect for deep frying, as does peanut oil. However, safflower is tasteless and what is cooked within it means the flavour of the item is what is preserved and not peanuts. In addition safflower tends not to transfer flavours of other items cooked therein. Safflower is also an excellent oil to use when blending oils for salad dressings; ⅓ safflower to ⅔ olive oil will make a wonderful blend for use in dressing of greens.

Louisiana

Bisque d'Écrevisse Cardinal

Ingredients:

5 lbs	2 kg	crayfish
10 cups	2.5 L	water
4 tbsp	60 ml	butter
1	1	finely diced medium onion
1	1	minced garlic clove
1	1	finely diced celery stalk
4 tbsp	60 ml	flour
1 cup	250 ml	peeled, seeded, diced tomatoes
3 oz	80 ml	tomato paste
⅓ cup	80 ml	sherry
½ tsp	3 ml	salt
¼ tsp	1 ml	pepper
1 cup	250 ml	whipping cream

Preparation:

Place the crayfish in a large kettle. Cover with the water. Bring to a boil and boil for 30 minutes. Remove the crayfish and allow to cool. Remove the tail meat from the crayfish. Reserve the meat. Return the shells to the water.

Simmer the crayfish shells until the water has reduced to 4 cups (1 L). Strain and reserve the broth. Discard the shells.

In a large sauce pan heat the butter. Sauté the onion, garlic and celery until tender. Sprinkle with flour and cook for 2 minutes over low heat.

Pour the crayfish broth over the vegetables. Add the tomatoes, tomato paste, crayfish tails, sherry, salt and pepper. Simmer for 15 minutes. Transfer the soup to a blender and purèe. Return to the pot and continue to simmer for 5 minutes.

Whip in the cream and simmer for an additional 10 minutes. Serve very hot.

Serves 6

 Fun Food Facts

Crayfish

Also known as crawfish and crawdad's, these are small lobster like fresh water crustaceans. They are shrimp like in flavour and favourites in Louisiana, Scandinavia, France and other European countries. In Louisiana the crayfish is prized for the Crawdad boil. A court bouillon is made highly seasoned with peppers, herbs and spices. The crayfish is then boiled for 20 minutes before they are served very hot. Crayfish must go through a purging before they are ready to cook. Store purchased fish should have already gone through this. For fresh caught crayfish, simply place live crayfish in water for 3 days changing the water every 12 hours. They will purge themselves.

Louisiana

Cane River Salad

Ingredients:

2 heads	2 heads	Belgian endive
1/3 cup	80 ml	olive oil
1	1	minced garlic clove
2 tbsp	30 ml	lemon juice
2 tsp	10 ml	fresh chopped mint
1/4 tsp	1 ml	salt
1/8 tsp	pinch	pepper
2	2	chopped hard cooked eggs
1/3 cup	80 ml	crisp cooked bacon bits
1/3 cup	80 ml	freshly grated Romano cheese

Preparation:

Thoroughly wash the Belgian endive. Seperate the leaves and arrange on a serving plate.

Blend the oil, garlic, lemon and seasonings. Pour over the lettuce place in a serving bowl. Sprinkle with egg, bacon and cheese. Serve at once.

Serves 6

Louisiana

Chicken Jambalaya

Ingredients:

Sauce:

1 ½ lbs	670 g	diced boneless chicken
2 tbsp	30 ml	safflower oil
2 tbsp	30 ml	butter
½ lb	225 g	andouille sausage
½ cup	125 ml	diced onions
2	2	minced garlic cloves
3 tbsp	45 ml	chopped parsley
1 ½ cups	375 ml	diced green bell pepper
2	2	diced celery stalks
2 cups	500 ml	peeled, seeded, chopped tomatoes
1 tsp	3 ml	white pepper
1 tsp	3 ml	black pepper
1 tsp	3 ml	oregano leaves
1 tsp	3 ml	basil
1 tsp	3 ml	thyme leaves
1 tsp	3 ml	garlic powder
1 tsp	3 ml	onion powder
1 tsp	3 ml	chili powder
2 tsp	10 ml	Worcestershire sauce
3 drops	3 drops	Tabasco™ sauce
2 ½ cups	625 ml	water
1 cup	250 ml	raw long grain rice

Preparation:

In a Dutch oven or large kettle, sauté the chicken in the oil and butter. Add the sausage and vegetables. Continue to sauté until vegetables are tender. Stir in the remaining ingredients. Reduce heat, cover and simmer on low heat for 40-45 minutes. Serve with fresh steamed broccoli.

Serves 6

 Fun Food Facts

Andouille Sausage

Andouille Sausage is a highly seasoned pure pork sausage used extensively in Louisiana Cajun and Creole cookery. Its origins are from France. If you can't find Andouille, a hot Italian, or a spicy Spanish Chorize may be substituted. It would be nearly impossible for anyone to list the various sausages of the world. Germany has 1,500 varieties alone. Why not find those you enjoy then search and find some more.

Butter Pecan Torte

Ingredients:

1 ½ cups	375 ml	pastry flour
2 tsp	10 ml	baking powder
¼ tsp	1 ml	salt
⅓ cup	80 ml	butter
¾ cup	180 ml	granulated sugar
2	2	eggs
½ cup	125 ml	milk
1 tsp	5 ml	vanilla
½ cup	125 ml	pecan meats, broken

Preparation:

Sift the flour, baking powder and salt together, twice.

Cream the butter and the sugar until very light and fluffy. Add the eggs beating well after each. Incorporate the flour and milk in thirds into the cream mixture. Stir in the vanilla and nuts.

Pour into a 8" (20 cm) springform pan which has been buttered and floured. Bake in a preheated 350°F (180°C) oven for 45 minutes or until an inserted toothpick comes out clean.

Transfer the cake to a cooling rack. Cool for 10 minutes. Turn cake out and cool completely. Frost with Praline Frosting.

Serves 4

Praline Frosting
Pralines
Ingredients:

1 cup	250 ml	granulated sugar
½ cup	125 ml	cream
2 tbsp	30 ml	butter
2 cups	500 ml	pecan meats, broken

Preparation:

In a heavy sauce pan bring to a boil the sugar, cream, butter and pecans. Using a candy thermometer boil to the soft ball stage or 238°F (113°C). Remove from heat. Cool to warm beating until very creamy. Spread onto a buttered sheet of wax paper. Allow to cool and harden then crush and stir into frosting.

Frosting
Ingredients:

1 cup	250 ml	brown sugar
½ cup	125 ml	boiling water
2	2	egg whites
1 tsp	5 ml	vanilla

Preparation:

In a heavy sauce pan, cook the sugar and water to 244°F (116°C) on a candy thermometer or to the soft ball stage. Remove from heat and cool. Whip the egg whites to stiff. Beat in the syrup in a slow thin stream. Add the vanilla and stir in the pralines. Spread on Butter Pecan Torte.

Arizona

Coconut Beer Shrimp

with Jalapeño Marmalade

Ingredients:

1 ¼ cups	310 ml	flour
½ tsp	3 ml	baking powder
¼ tsp	1 ml	baking soda
1 tsp	5 ml	salt
1 cup	250 ml	beer
2 cups	500 ml	vegetable oil
1 lb	454 g	large peeled and deveined shrimp
¼ cup	60 ml	coconut flakes
1 cup	250 ml	jalapeño marmalade

Preparation:

In a mixing bowl sift together 1 cup (250 ml) flour, baking powder, soda and salt. Slowly add the beer. Whisk briskly and let stand for 1 hour. Fold in the coconut.

Heat the oil to 375°F (190°C).

Dust the shrimp with the remaining flour, dip into the batter. Fry in the oil for 2½ - 3 minutes or until golden brown. Serve at once with the Jalapeño Marmalade on the side.

Serves 6

Jalapeño Marmalade

Ingredients:

¾ lb	345 g	oranges
¼ cup	60 ml	lemon juice
3 cups	750 ml	water
8	8	jalapeños
6	6	coriander seeds
1 ½ lbs	675 g	granulated sugar

Preparation:

Wash the oranges and cut in half. Squeeze all the juices from the oranges and reserve the juice, seeds and pith.

Place the juice in a large sauce pan, and add the lemon juice and water.

Slice the jalapeños in half, remove seeds and dice fine.

Tie the orange seeds, pith and coriander in a cheesecloth. Add to the pan. Slice the orange rind into julienne strips. Add to the pan, heat and simmer until volume is reduced by two thirds.

Add the sugar and stir until it has been dissolved. Bring to a boil, and boil for 12 minutes, add the jalapeños, boil 3 minutes longer.

Remove any scum and let stand 15 minutes. Pour into clean, sterile jars, cool to warm and seal. Label with production date.

Yields 4 cups (1 L)

La Crème Dubarry au Caviar

Ingredients:

2 ½ cups	625 ml	cauliflower florets
4 cups	1 L	chicken stock (see page 210)
3 tbsp	45 ml	butter
3 tbsp	45 ml	flour
2 cups	500 ml	cream
4 tbsp	60 ml	caviar - red

Preparation:

Place the cauliflower in a large sauce pan and cover with the chicken stock. Simmer for 30 minutes. Strain, reserving the liquid and cauliflower.

Purée the cauliflower in a food processor or pass through a food mill. Return the cauliflower to the broth.

In a small sauce pan heat the butter and add the flour. Cook for 2 minutes over low heat. Add the cream and cook into a thick sauce.

Whip the sauce into the soup. Reheat to very hot.

Serve the soup with 1 tbsp (15 ml) of caviar sprinkled over the top.

Serve with fresh homemade biscuits

Serves 6

Old Fashion Cheddar Biscuits

Ingredients:

2 cups	500 ml	bread flour
2 tsp	10 ml	baking powder
⅛ tsp	pinch	salt
2 tbsp	30 ml	butter
1 cup	250 ml	grated medium Cheddar
¾ cup	180 ml	milk

Preparation:

Sift the flour, baking powder and salt together. Cut in the butter and cheese. Gradually add the milk until a soft dough is formed.

Turn out on a lightly floured surface and knead slightly (30 seconds). Roll dough into a square ¼" thick. Cut into biscuits with a round biscuit cutter or into even squares.

Place on a ungreased baking sheet. Bake in a preheated 400°F (200°C) oven for 15-18 minutes.

Yields 12 Biscuits

Buttermilk Honey Biscuits

Ingredients:

2 cups	500 ml	bread flour
2 tsp	10 ml	baking powder
¼ tsp	1 ml	baking soda
½ tsp	3 ml	salt
¼ cup	60 ml	shortening
½ cup	125 ml	buttermilk
¼ cup	60 ml	liquid honey

Preparation:

Sift the flour, baking powder, baking soda and salt together. Cut in the shortening until a coarse dough is formed.

Stir in the buttermilk and honey, knead forming a soft dough. Roll the dough into a ½" (12 mm) thick square. Cut with a floured cutter. Bake for 15-18 minutes in a preheated 400°F (200°C) oven.

Yields 12 Biscuits

Louisiana

Peach and Almond Salad

Ingredients:

10 oz	300 g	spinach, washed and trimmed
8	8	large, sliced mushrooms
1 cup	250 ml	grated Gruyère cheese
1 cup	250 ml	red seedless grapes
1 ½ cups	375 ml	fresh peach slices
¼ cup	60 ml	toasted almonds
1 cup	250 ml	mayonnaise
½ cup	125 ml	orange juice concentrate
¼ tsp	1 ml	ground cinnamon

Preparation:

Tear the spinach into bite size pieces and place on chilled serving plates. Top with mushrooms, cheese, grapes, peach slices and almonds.

In a mixing bowl, blend together the mayonnaise, juice and cinnamon. Serve with the dressing on the side.

Serves 6

Fun Food Facts

Limited Cheese Glossary

Abbey St. Benoit:
a firm interior ripened cheese that has great potential in cooking and desserts.

Belpaese (bell-pa-za):
comes in a circular cake two inches high and is used for culinary purposes as well as for desserts. Belpaese has a drab silvery surface with a yellow interior.

Blue:
a cylindrical cheese 6" (15 cm) in diameter, 4.5" (11.25 cm) in height. Comes in a foil with a green mould interior. Made with cow's milk, this cheese can be used in canapes, desserts or in cooking. When imported, it is called Bleu.

Brick:
a semi-soft rectangular cheese with a yellowish brown surface and a creamy yellow interior.

Brie (bree):
a creamy circular cheese 2-3" (5 cm -7 cm) high, with a soft mould ripened brown surface and a creamy yellow interior. It is used for cooking and desserts.

Cacio-cavallo (casse-e-o-ka-vallo):
a hard cheese shaped like a gourd or ten pin with a clay colored surface and a light colored interior. It can be used for culinary delights when grated.

Camembert (kam-am-bert):
a soft circular cheese 6.5" (16 cm) in diameter and 1.5" (4 cm) in height. It has a grey mould surface, with a creamy yellow interior. It is used on cheese trays and for desserts.

Cheddar:
a hard cheese, generally circular or cylindrical shaped, with a waxed-yellow brown surface, and a light yellow interior. It can come processed and has cooking use or can be used in a variety of desserts.

Cream:
comes in various shapes with a soft, smooth texture. It has a creamy color and is made with minimum 30% milk fat. It can be used on salads, sandwiches or for dessert.

Potage Alligator au Sherry

Ingredients:

2 tbsp	30 ml	butter
2 tbsp	30 ml	safflower oil
1 lb	454 g	diced alligator meat*
1	1	finely diced onion
2	2	finely diced carrots
2	2	finely diced celery stalks
2 quarts	2.5 L	chicken stock (see page 210)
2 cups	500 ml	cooked rice
½ cup	125 ml	cream sherry

Preparation:

In a large kettle heat the butter and the oil. Brown the alligator meat; remove and reserve.

Add the vegetables and sauté until tender. Return the meat to the kettle and cover with the chicken stock. Reduce heat and simmer uncovered for 1½ hours. Skim soup for any impurities that rise to the top.

Add the cooked rice and sherry. Simmer for 15 minutes longer. Serve.

Serves 8

* Alligator meat may be a little hard to find. Try special ordering it through your butcher or seafood supplier.

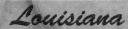

Louisiana

Cilantro Pasta

with Blackened Chicken in Ancho Chile, Garlic Sauce

Ingredients:

1 quantity	1	Cilantro Pasta
1 lb	454 g	boneless chicken breast - strips
½ tsp	3 ml	each of oregano, basil, thyme, onion powder
1 tsp	5 ml	garlic powder
¼ tsp	1 ml	each of cayenne pepper, black pepper, white pepper
1 tsp	5 ml	chili powder
1 tsp	5 ml	salt
4 tbsp	60 ml	olive oil
3	3	minced ancho chilies
3	3	minced garlic cloves
2 cups	500 ml	tomato purée

Preparation:

Process the pasta as directed. Cut into desired shape.

Blend all the seasoning together. Reserve 1 tbsp (15 ml) of seasoned blend.

Dust the chicken with the seasonings. Heat 3 tbsp (45 ml) of oil in a skillet to very hot. Fry the chicken, a few strips at a time, for 2 minutes per side. Once complete reserve hot.

Heat the remaining oil in a sauce pan. Sauté the chili and garlic, add the tomato purée and remaining seasoning. Simmer for 20 minutes.

Cook the pasta al dente in a large kettle of boiling salted water. Drain the pasta and toss with sauce. Top with chicken strips and serve.

Cilantro Pasta

Ingredients:

2	2	beaten eggs
1 tsp	5 ml	safflower oil
½ cup	125 ml	chopped cilantro leaves
2 cups	500 ml	semolina flour
		ice water only if required

Preparation:

Blend the eggs, oil and cilantro together. Add the flour and slowly knead into a soft ball (add small amounts of ice water if required). Knead the dough for 15 minutes and allow to rest for an additional 15 minutes. Roll out the dough. Lightly dust with flour; fold in three; and roll out again. Repeat 6 to 8 times.

Pass the dough through the pasta machine setting the rollers gradually down until you reach the desired thickness. The result should be a smooth sheet of dough to process as you require.

Pass through a pasta machine, or cut by hand to desired size. If processed by hand, simply roll the dough and cut into thin strips for noodles (fettucini) or into wider strips for lasagna, cannelloni, ravioli, etc.

Process as any of our recipes direct.

Note: Use only enough flour to prevent sticking while rolling.

Serves 6

Classic Crème Caramel
with Pecan Chocolate Dipped Strawberries

Ingredients:

3 ¾ cups	940 ml	milk
1 ¾ cups	440 ml	vanilla sugar
5	5	eggs
4	4	egg yolks
1 tbsp	15 ml	vanilla

Strawberries:

24	24	fresh large strawberries
4 oz	120 g	semi - sweet chocolate - grated
1 tbsp	15 ml	butter - melted
1 ½ cups	375 ml	pecan pieces chopped fine

Preparation:

Scald the milk and allow to cool 20 minutes. In a sauce pan, melt ¾ cup (180 ml) of sugar and cook until dark brown; stirring constantly. Take care not to scorch. Pour into a warm mold covering the bottom and the sides. Beat the eggs and egg yolks with the remaining sugar. Slowly whip in the milk and vanilla. Pour into the sugar lined mold. Place mold in a second pan filled halfway with hot water. Bake for 45 minutes in a 325°F (160°F) oven. Cool. Chill. To serve invert onto a rimmed serving platter. Top with a strawberry.

Strawberries:

Wash the berries then dry them. In a double boiler melt the chocolate and stir in the butter. Dip the strawberries in the chocolate then into the nuts. Place on a sheet of wax paper. Allow to harden before removing to a platter. Do not refrigerate.

Serves 6

 Fun Food Facts

Pecans

The nut is grown extensively in the southern United States and is a native of that country, widely accepted as an essential ingredient to flavour confections. It is a principal ingredient in Cajun\Creole cuisine. It is related to the hickory nut and the English walnut. Some of the most popular pecan dishes include pralines, pecan pie, pecan ice cream and praline cheesecake.

Louisiana

Chef K's Stuffed Shrimp

Ingredients:

18	18	tiger shrimp
4 tbsp	60 ml	butter
1 ¾ cups	440 ml	flour
1 ½ cups	375 ml	milk
2 ½ cups	625	cooked crab meat
½ tsp	3 ml	each of oregano leaves, thyme leaves, basil leaves, cayenne pepper, black pepper, onion powder, garlic powder, salt, paprika
2	2	eggs
2 cups	500 ml	fine dry bread crumbs
3 tbsp	45 ml	olive oil

Sauce:

3 tbsp	45 ml	butter
3 tbsp	45 ml	flour
½ cup	125 ml	chicken stock (see page 210)
½ cup	125 ml	heavy cream
½ cup	125 ml	champagne
1 cup	250 ml	rehydrated sun dried tomatoes
1	1	bunch chopped arugula

Preparation:

Peel and devein the shrimp. Slice down the centre three quarters through. Flatten with a meat mallet. Place on a baking sheet.

Heat the butter in a sauce pan. Add 4 tbsp (60 ml) flour. Reduce heat and cook for 2 minutes. Add 1 cup (250 ml) of milk. Cook, stirring until a very thick sauce is formed. Cool to room temperature.

Stir in the crab meat. Place 2 tbsp (30 ml) of filling on each shrimp. Chill for 2 hours.

Blend the seasoning with the remaining flour. Beat the eggs in the remaining milk. Dust the shrimp with the seasoned flour; dip in the egg milk mixture and dredge in the bread crumbs. Brush with the oil.

Bake in a preheated 350°F (180°C) oven for 15 minutes. Plate the shrimp and serve with the sauce.

Sauce:

Melt the butter in a sauce pan. Add the flour and stir into a paste (roux) cooking over low heat.

Add chicken stock, cream and champagne. Simmer for 10 minutes over medium heat. Stir in the tomatoes and arugula and simmer for 5 additional minutes.

Serves 6

Manhattan Clam Chowder

Ingredients:

3 tbsp	45 ml	butter
1	1	peeled, coarsely diced, large Spanish onion
3	3	peeled, coarsely diced, large carrots
3	3	coarsely diced celery stalks
4	4	peeled, coarsely diced, large potatoes
2 cups	500 ml	chopped fresh clams
2 ½ cups	625 ml	seeded, peeled, diced, tomatoes
4 cups	1 L	fish or chicken broth (see page 000 or 210)
1 ½ tsp	8 ml	Worcestershire sauce
¼ tsp	1 ml	Tabasco™ sauce
¼ tsp	1 ml	cracked black pepper
½ tsp	3 ml	each of oregano, thyme, basil
1 ½ tsp	8 ml	salt

Preparation:

In a large kettle heat the butter over low heat. Add the onion, carrots and celery. Sauté until tender. Add the potatoes and clams. Continue to sauté for an additional 10 minutes.

Stir in the tomatoes. Add the broth and the remaining ingredients. Simmer for 35 minutes.

Serves 6-8

New York

New York Style Cheesecake

Ingredients:

Crust:

3 ½ cups	875 ml	graham cracker crumbs
1 tbsp	15 ml	cinnamon
¼ cup	60 ml	melted butter

Filling:

2 ¾ lbs	1250 ml	cream cheese
2 cups	500 ml	granulated sugar
1 ½ cups	375 ml	heavy cream
2 tbsp	30 ml	lemon juice
1 tbsp	15 ml	vanilla
4	4	eggs - room temperature
1 ½ cups	375 ml	sour cream

Preparation:

Crust:

Fit a 6" baking cardboard collar around a 10" spring form pan. Combine crust ingredients. Press into the bottom and sides of the buttered spring-form pan. Chill. Preheat the oven to 325°F (160°C).

Filling:

Beat the cream cheese and sugar until smooth. Add the cream, lemon juice and vanilla. Beat until well blended. Add the eggs one at a time, beating well after each addition. Stir in the sour cream.

Pour mixture into prepared shell and bake in the oven until the centre is set, about 90 minutes. Turn off the oven and prop door open slightly.

After about 30 minutes, transfer to a rack to cool. Chill overnight. Serve with fresh fruit or fruit sauce.

Serves 12

 Fun Food Facts

Limited Cheese Glossary (cont'd)

Gorgonzola:
a cylindrical shaped semi-soft cheese with an earthly colored surface and a yellow with green mould inside. It can be used in cooking or desserts.

Gouda:
a semi-hard, coming in a ball shape with a flared top and bottom. It also has a red coated surface with a creamy yellow interior. It can be used on cheese trays, in cooking or in desserts.

Gruyère (grew-yare):
a hard circular cheese with triangular portions. This cheese is wrapped in foil with a light yellow interior. It has cookery use and can also be used in desserts.

Guetost (yea-toast):
a semi-hard cubical and rectangular cheese with light brown color. This semi-sweet cheese has cooking and dessert use.

Le Moine:
a semi-soft cake shaped cheese in the Swiss tradition. An excellent cheese for cooking and dessert use.

Grilled Atlantic Salmon

with Two Sauces

Ingredients:

Sauce 1:

2 cups	500 ml	finely chopped roasted sweet red bell peppers
⅓ cup	80 ml	hot chicken broth (see page 210)
1 ¼ tsp	8 ml	each of salt, chili powder
¼ tsp	1 ml	each of black pepper, white pepper, basil, oregano leaves, thyme leaves, basil leaves, Hungarian paprika

Sauce 2:

1 ½ tbsp	23 ml	butter
1 ½ tbsp	23 ml	flour
⅔ cup	170 ml	chicken broth (see page 210)
⅔ cup	170 ml	half & half cream
¼ cup	60 ml	freshly grated Parmesan cheese

Salmon:

6-6 oz	6-170 g	Salmon fillets or Salmon steaks
1 tbsp	15 ml	pepper grilling oil
1 tsp	5 ml	salt
½ tsp	3 ml	each of cracked black pepper, basil leaves, oregano leaves, thyme leaves, Hungarian paprika

Preparation:

Sauce 1:

Place the red peppers, chicken broth and spices in a food processor; purée. Pour into a sauce pan. Simmer over low heat until sauce thickens. Press through a sieve into a mixing bowl.

Sauce 2:

Heat the butter in a sauce pan. Add the flour and cook for 2 minutes over low heat. Stir in the chicken broth and cream. Reduce heat and simmer until thickened. Stir in the cheese and simmer for 2 more minutes.

Salmon:

Wash and trim the salmon. Remove any bones. Brush with the oil. Blend the herbs and spices together and sprinkle on the salmon. Grill over a hot grill for 5 minutes per side.

Place the red pepper sauce on a serving plate top with a salmon fillet. Pour a small amount of the cream sauce over the salmon and serve. This dish is especially good served with a orzo pilaff and fresh asparagus.

Serves 6

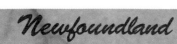

Newfoundland

Prairie 3 Cheese Buckwheat Linguine

Ingredients:

1 cup	250 ml	buckwheat flour
½ cup	125 ml	semolina flour
1 tsp	3 ml	salt
1	1	beaten, extra large egg
¼ cup	60 ml	ice cold milk
		ice water, only if required
⅓ cup	80 ml	Gorgonzola cheese
1 cup	250 ml	Mascarpone cheese
⅓ cup	80 ml	grated Romano cheese
½ cup	125 ml	half & half cream

Preparation:

Sift the flours and salt together. Place into a mixing bowl. Slowly blend in the egg. Add the milk and the water (only if required) slowly until a smooth soft dough is formed.

Knead the dough for 15 minutes and allow to rest for an additional 15 minutes. Roll out the dough. Lightly dust with flour, fold in three, and roll out again. Repeat 6 to 8 times.

Pass the dough through the pasta machine setting the rollers gradually down until you reach the desired thickness. The result should be a smooth sheet of dough. Cut into linguine. Cook pasta al dente in a large kettle of boiling salted water. Drain.

Blend the cheeses with the cream. Toss the hot noodles through the cheese sauce. Serve.

Serves 6

 Fun Food Facts

Cheese

Beer Bash:

When serving a dark bock-type beer, serve a good selection of Cheddars, from mild to the sharp. MacLaren's Imperial is especially good with the rich smooth dark beer.

When serving lager or ale, a good selection of any of the following will show off your creative ability and will please your guests. Especially during those play-off games. Begin with Brick, Brie, Camembert, Tiny Dame Havarti. Follow with Swiss/Emmental, Lemoine, St. Benoit, Gouda, Cheddar sharp (old), Monterey Jack, Port Salut, Blue. You'll steal the cheers from the game and direct them towards yourself.

Alberta

New York Bistro Veal Chops

Ingredients:

4 tbsp	60 ml	butter
⅓ cup	80 ml	chopped green onions
1 cup	250 ml	red wine
½ cup	125 ml	cream style sherry
¼ tsp	1 ml	crushed rosemary
¼ tsp	1 ml	marjoram
2 tbsp	30 ml	flour
½ cup	125 ml	veal or beef stock (see page 42)
1 tbsp	15 ml	lemon juice
4 tbsp	60 ml	chopped parsley
6-6 oz	6-180 g	veal chops

Preparation:

Heat 2 tbsp (30 ml) of butter in a sauce pan. Sauté the green onions for 3 minutes. Add the wine, sherry, rosemary and marjoram. Bring to a boil, reduce heat and simmer to ¾ cup (180 ml) of liquid. Strain through a fine sieve.

In a second sauce pan heat the remaining butter. Add the flour and cook over low heat for 8 minutes or until hazelnut in colour. Add the strained sauce, beef stock and lemon juice. Continue to simmer for an additional 7 minutes. Sprinkle with parsley.

Broil the chops to the desired doneness. Place on serving plates. Pour sauce over the chops and serve with a root vegetable sauté.

Serves 6

New York

Wild Mushroom Buffalo Steak Stroganoff

Ingredients:

1 lb	454 g	buffalo tenderloin
2 tbsp	30 ml	safflower oil
2 tbsp	30 ml	butter
2 cups	500 ml	sliced wild mushrooms
2 tbsp	30 ml	flour
¾ cup	180 ml	beef broth (see page 42)
1 tsp	5 ml	Worcestershire sauce
2 tbsp	30 ml	soy sauce
2 tbsp	30 ml	tomato paste
1 tsp	5 ml	salt
1 tsp	5 ml	cracked black pepper
1 tsp	5 ml	Hungarian paprika
¼ tsp	1 ml	oregano leaves
¼ tsp	1 ml	white pepper
¼ tsp	1 ml	basil leaves
¼ tsp	1 ml	thyme leaves
¼ cup	60 ml	sherry
¼ cup	60 ml	sour cream
4 cups	1 L	hot cooked egg noodles

Preparation:

Trim the tenderloin and cut into large cubes.

Heat the oil in a large skillet and sauté the tenderloin to desired doneness.

While steak cooks, heat the butter in a sauce pan. Sauté the mushrooms. Sprinkle with flour and cook over medium heat for 3 minutes. Add the broth, Worcestershire, soy sauce, tomato paste, spices, herbs and sherry. Reduce heat and simmer until very thick. Stir in the sour cream. Continue to simmer for 5 minutes.

Place noodles on serving plates.

Stir the steak into the sauce and ladle over noodles.

Serves 4

Fun Food Facts

Buffalo Meat

North American plains buffalo is no longer an endangered species. It is a prized meat much like beef, yet better. Buffalo meat has 85% less fat than beef, 25% more protein and 50% more thiamin (Vitamin B-1). It contains no drugs, hormones or chemicals. It is completely natural. Wherever beef is required, buffalo meat may be exchanged. This meat is obtainable in most countries through a butcher by special order.

Alberta

Nova Scotia Lobster Salad

Ingredients:

4 cups	1 L	fish broth or court bullion (see page 416)
2-1 ½ lbs	2-680 g	Lobsters
⅓ cup	80 ml	olive oil
1	1	minced garlic clove
2 tbsp	30 ml	lemon juice
2 tsp	10 ml	fresh chopped mint
¼ tsp	1 ml	salt
⅛ tsp	pinch	pepper
1	1	large head romaine lettuce
2	2	chopped hard cooked eggs
⅓ cup	80 ml	crisp cooked bacon bits
⅓ cup	80 ml	freshly grated Romano cheese

Preparation:

Bring the fish stock to a rapid boil. Cook the lobster in the boiling stock for 3 minutes after it floats to the top. Remove the lobster and allow to drain. Cool. Chill. Cut the lobster in half and remove the tail and claw meats. Reserve the shell. Cut the meats into bite size pieces and place into a mixing bowl.

Blend the oil, garlic, lemon and seasonings. Pour over the lobster meats.

Thoroughly wash the lettuce. Trim and chop into bite size pieces. Place onto serving plates. Top the lettuce with a lobster shell that has been drained from the marinate; reserve the marinate. Fill the shell with the lobster meats.

Pour the marinate over the lobster and lettuce. Sprinkle with egg, bacon and cheese. Serve at once.

Serves 4

 Fun Food Facts

Lobster

The king of crustaceans, lobster is the global favourite. Lobster provides the most return for the dollar spend on seafood as it yields more edible meat than any other type of shellfish. The Maine or American lobster is known by many other names globally such as Homard in France, Hummer in Germany, Denmark, Sweden and Norway. In Italy it is Astice, Bogavante in Spain, Hummar of Iceland, Levagante in Greece and Iseebi of Japan. 1½ lb (675 g) of lobster meat in the shell contains 136 calories, 28.2 grams of protein, .8 grams of carbohydrates, 1.4 grams of fat and 143 milligrams of cholesterol. Other types of lobster are Rock, Scampo (a smaller version) and Spiny lobsters. Chicken (1 lb 454 g), Quarters 1½ lbs 675 g. Large (2¼ lb - 1 kg). Jumbo (over 2¼ lb -1 kg).

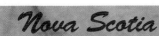

B.C. Apple Cake

Ingredients:

Cake:

3	3	eggs
1 ½ cups	375 ml	oil
2 cups	500 ml	granulated sugar
3 cups	750 ml	all purpose, flour
1 tsp	5 ml	baking soda
1 tsp	5 ml	salt
1 tsp	5 ml	vanilla extract
1 cup	250 ml	pecans
3 cups	750 ml	cored, peeled, diced apples

Icing:

4 oz	120 g	butter
1 cup	250 ml	packed brown sugar
¼ cup	60 ml	milk

Preparation:

Mix all cake ingredients together and pour into 9" x 13" (23 cm x 32 cm) oblong pan. Bake at 350°F (180°C) for 45 minutes or until inserted toothpick comes out clean.

Cook icing ingredients in small saucepan for 2½ minutes. Poke holes in the cake, then pour icing over the cake.

Serves 6

British Columbia

Vancouver Cioppino

Ingredients:

3 tbsp	45 ml	butter
1	1	sliced red bell pepper
1	1	sliced green bell pepper
1	1	sliced small onion
1	1	minced garlic cloves
1 tbsp	15 ml	chopped fresh parsley
2 cups	500 ml	peeled, seeded, chopped tomatoes
4 cups	1 L	fish broth
2 cups	500 ml	white wine
¼ lb	120 g	peeled and de-veined shrimp
½ lb	225g	sliced artic char
¼ lb	120 g	green mussels
¼ lb	120 g	clams, in shell
¼ lb	120 g	king crab claws
1	1	bouquet garni*

Preparation:

In a large Dutch oven or kettle, heat the butter. Add the vegetables and sauté until tender. Add the parsley, tomatoes, broth and wine. Bring to a boil. Reduce heat and simmer for 10 minutes.

Add the fish, seafood and bouquet garni. Cover and simmer for 15 minutes. Discard the bouquet garni. Serve the stew with fresh french bread.

Serves 6

* A bouquet garni is: thyme leaves, basil sprig, marjoram, bay leaf and five peppercorns tied together in a cheesecloth. (J-Cloth works well.)

 Fun Food Facts

Alaska King Crab

Also known as the Japanese crab and Russian crab, these principally are caught in the icy water of the North Pacific. The largest of the crab family, king crabs can weight up to 20 lbs (9 kg). The most common meat chosen from the crab is the claws and legs. Other types of crabs are: Calico, Dungeness, Green, Jonah, Lady oyster, Reds, Rock, Snow, Spider, Stone and Tanner.

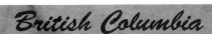 *British Columbia*

Chicken Fried Steak

Ingredients:

6-4 oz	6-120 g	top round steaks
2	2	eggs
¼ cup	60 ml	milk
1 cup	250 ml	fine bread crumbs
¼ tsp	1 ml	salt
¼ tsp	1 ml	pepper
¼ tsp	1 ml	basil
¼ tsp	1 ml	thyme leaves
¼ tsp	1 ml	chili powder
¼ tsp	1 ml	onion powder
¼ tsp	1 ml	oregano
¼ tsp	1 ml	paprika
⅓ cup	80 ml	flour
¼ cup	60 ml	safflower oil
2 cups	500 ml	Country Gravy

Preparation:

Pound the steaks with a meat mallet to tenderize.

Blend the eggs with the milk. Mix the bread crumbs together with the seasonings.

Dust the steaks with flour; dip them into the egg wash; dredge the steaks through the bread crumbs.

Heat the oil in a large skillet. Fry the steaks for 3 minutes per side. Serve with gravy on the side.

Serves 6

Country Gravy

Ingredients:

4 tbsp	60 ml	butter
3 tbsp	45 ml	flour
1 cup	250 ml	milk
1 cup	250 ml	chicken broth (see page 210)
½ tsp	3 ml	salt
¼ tsp	1 ml	cracked black pepper

Preparation:

In a sauce pan heat the butter. Add the flour and cook over low heat for 2 minutes. Whisk in the milk, broth, salt and pepper. Reduce heat and simmer until smooth.

Yields 2 Cups (500 ml)

 Fun Food Facts

Chicken Fried Steak

Called chicken fried steak because of the coating that is applied to the meat and then fried like one would for Southern fried chicken. Found to be popular at the turn of the century when beef reigned as the meat of choice. Chicken fried steak is still a popular choice in the southern United States today. Try chicken fried chicken too, by substituting a boneless chicken breast instead of a round steak and follow the balance of the recipes.

 Texas

Buffalo Chicken Wings

Ingredients:

2 ¼ lbs	1 kg	chicken wings
4 cups	I L	oil
¼ cup	60 ml	butter
5 tbsp	75 ml	Franks-Durkees™ red hot cayenne pepper sauce
1 bunch	1 bunch	celery
1 cup	250 ml	blue cheese crumbled
1 cup	250 ml	mayonnaise

Preparation:

Trim and separate the wing bone from the drumette. Heat the oil to 375°F (190°C). Fry the wings, a few at a time, for 10 minutes. Be sure to maintain oil at set temperature. Reserve hot in the oven.

Melt the butter in a sauce pan and add the hot sauce. Use less for mild; more for hot. Place chicken wings in a serving bowl. Pour sauce over and toss to coat.

While wings are cooking cut the celery into sticks. Blend the blue cheese with the mayonnaise. Serve as a dip for both the celery and wings.

Serves 4

Salt Lake City Barbecued Ribs

Ingredients:

3 tbsp	45 ml	butter
3 tbsp	45 ml	oil
1	1	minced onion
1	1	minced, garlic clove
⅔ cup	170 ml	tomato catsup
⅔ cup	170 ml	orange brandy
½ cup	125 ml	cider vinegar
½ cup	125 ml	orange juice
½ cup	125 ml	orange juice concentrate
⅓ cup	80 ml	light molasses
1 tbsp	15 ml	Worcestershire sauce
½ tsp	3 ml	thyme leaves
½ tsp	3 ml	basil leaves
½ tsp	3 ml	chervil
½ tsp	3 ml	oregano leaves
½ tsp	3 ml	garlic powder
½ tsp	3 ml	cracked black pepper
½ tsp	3 ml	white pepper
½ tsp	3 ml	paprika
½ tsp	3 ml	salt
¼ tsp	1 ml	Tabasco™ sauce
½ tsp	3 ml	liquid smoke flavouring
4 ½ lbs	2 kg	baby back ribs
2 tsp	10 ml	seasoned salt

Preparation:

Heat the butter and oil in a sauce pan. Add the onion and garlic. Sauté until tender. Stir in the catsup, brandy, vinegar, orange juice, concentrate, molasses, Worcestershire, herbs, spices, Tabasco,™ and liquid smoke. Bring to a boil. Reduce heat and simmer until sauce is very thick. Cool.

Trim the ribs of any excess fat. Place them on a shallow baking sheet. Sprinkle with seasoned salt. Bake in a preheated 300°F (160°C) oven for 2 hours.

Transfer ribs to a hot grill, brush with sauce, grill 10 minutes. Brush heavily with sauce before serving.

Serves 6

Utah

Latin America

Say "Latin American food" to a person who is not from Latin America and they think Taco's, Burrito's, etc. But say it to someone from Latin America and their mouth begins to water with thoughts of Pollo al Ajo (Garlic and Thyme Chicken) or Croquetas de Cerdo (Pork Croquettes). Now you're talking their language. You are talking about the food of the people.

On one trip to the Yucatan Peninsula (a tourist paradise) we had visited most of the restaurants along the hotel row and found all displeasing when it came to both food and service. They thought that an American would want American food, but not us. Quickly tiring of that kind of food, we hailed a cab and my associate, (who spoke prefect Spanish) told the cabby to take us where he would go and eat. He drove for some time and finally pulled to a closed restaurant. "No problem senior" the cab driver said and went into the restaurant and convinced the owner to open just for us. Needless to say, we found true paradise. Tender chicken simmered in a bittersweet chocolate sauce, giant shrimp sautéed with a secret spice blend then finished with a tomato, banana sauce. Why would anyone want to leave paradise with that kind of food nearby? We thanked the owner, tipped him heavily and returned to Canada knowing that for just a moment we experienced something few who travel there will. We experienced what true Latin America is like, wonderful.

This chapter attempts to bring to you a taste of what Latin America offers. These are nations who have given the world their abundance; tomatoes, cacao, chilies, bell peppers, and much more. Sample their giving spirit when you share a bowl of Latin America Bean Soup with a friend, or that Spicy Yucatan Shrimp at your next dinner party, (he gave me the recipe for the world to enjoy).

Enjoy siesta time with a rich Columbia coffee and a wonderful slice of Enrrollado De Bizcochuelo (Caramel Sponge Roll). Want something light at the end of the night? Try what the Peruvians enjoy, a rich coffee pie with Kahlua and rum it's sure to put you at ease, but it doesn't come in decaffeinated. When you can't go to the people, then bring their foods to you and enjoy.

Sherry Rabbit Soup

Ingredients:

2 tbsp	30 ml	butter
2 tbsp	30 ml	safflower oil
1 lb	454 g	diced rabbit meat
1	1	finely diced onion
2	2	finely diced carrots
2	2	finely diced celery stalks
2 quarts	2.5 L	chicken stock (see page 210)
2 cups	500 ml	cooked rice
½ cup	125 ml	cream sherry

Preparation:

In a large kettle, heat the butter and the oil. Brown the rabbit meat; remove and reserve.

Add the vegetables and sauté until tender. Return the meat to the kettle. Cover with the chicken stock. Reduce heat and simmer for 1½ hours; uncovered. Skim soup for any impurities that rise to the top.

Add the cooked rice and sherry. Simmer for 15 minutes. Serve.

Serves 4

Mexico

Ensalada Latina

Ingredients:

1	1	head bibb lettuce
1	1	bunch green onions
3	3	celery stalks
4	4	large radishes
1	1	red bell pepper
1	1	small cucumber
1	1	small jicama, peeled
½ cup	125 ml	brushed, sliced mushrooms
1 ½ cups	375 ml	broccoli florets
1 ½ cups	375 ml	cauliflower florets
24	24	cherry tomatoes
1 ½ cups	375 ml	olive oil
1	1	minced garlic clove
3 tbsp	45 ml	minced onion
2 tbsp	30 ml	minced red pimiento
2 tbsp	30 ml	sugar
2 tsp	10 ml	Worcestershire sauce
1 tsp	5 ml	each of salt, dry mustard, paprika
½ tsp	3 ml	each of thyme leaves, basil leaves, oregano leaves, marjoram leaves, chervil
¼ cup	60 ml	lemon juice
¼ cup	60 ml	white vinegar

Preparation:

Wash and tear the lettuce into bite size pieces. Place into a large serving bowl.

Coarsely dice the onions, celery, radishes, pepper, mushrooms, cucumber and jicama. Add to the lettuce. Mix in the remaining vegetables.

Blend all the remaining ingredients together thoroughly. Serve along the side of the salad.

Serves 6

Potato Jalapeño Cheese Biscuits

Ingredients:

¾ cup	180 ml	cold mashed potatoes
3	3	fresh, seeded and finely dices jalapeño peppers
¼ cup	60 ml	freshly grated Parmesan cheese
1 cup	250 ml	bread flour
3 tbsp	45 ml	baking powder
1 tsp	5 ml	salt
2 tbsp	30 ml	butter
½ cup	125 ml	cold milk

Preparation:

Blend the potatoes and jalapeño peppers with the cheese.

Sift together the flour, baking powder and salt. Cut the butter into the flour and stir in the potatoes. Work the dough into a course meal incorporating the flour and the potatoes completely. Stir in the milk making a soft dough.

Turn the dough out onto a lightly dusted flour surface. Roll out to ½" (12 mm) thick. Cut into even squares. Place on a ungreased baking sheet and bake for 12-15 minutes in a preheated 400°F (200°C) oven.

Yields 12 Biscuits

Mexico

Pincho Moruno

Ingredients:

1 ½ lbs	675 g	beef tenderloin
2 tsp	10 ml	granulated sugar
1 tsp	5 ml	black pepper
1 tsp	5 ml	minced garlic
1 tsp	5 ml	onion powder
½ cup	125 ml	garlic vinegar
½ cup	125 ml	red wine
1 cup	250 ml	olive oil
½ tsp	3 ml	chopped basil
½ tsp	3 ml	dried thyme leaves
½ tsp	3 ml	dried marjoram leaves
1 tsp	5 ml	salt

Preparation:

Trim the tenderloin and cut it into 1" (2.5 cm) cubes. Skewer the meat with bamboo skewers. Place them into a shallow pan.

Blend the remaining ingredients together forming a marinate. Pour the marinate over the beef. Marinate refrigerated and covered for 6-8 hours. Drain; reserve marinate.

Grill skewered meat over medium heat until desired doneness; brushing frequently with marinate.

Serves 6

Latin Ginger Fruit Salad

Ingredients:

1	1	pineapple
1	1	large papaya
2	2	bananas
2 cups	500 ml	strawberries
2 cups	500 ml	sliced peaches
2 cups	500 ml	watermelon balls
2 cups	500 ml	honeydew melon balls
6 oz	180 g	trimmed, washed spinach leaves
½ cup	125 ml	safflower oil
¼ cup	60 ml	lime juice
¼ cup	60 ml	lemon juice
3 tbsp	45 ml	honey
2 tbsp	30 ml	grated ginger
1 tsp	5 ml	salt

Preparation:

Pare and dice the pineapple and papaya, place into a mixing bowl. Slice the bananas. Add the strawberries, melon balls and peaches to the salad. Chop the spinach and stir into the salad.

Blend the oil with the remaining ingredients and pour over the salad. Serve on chilled plates.

Serves 6-8

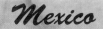

Mexico

Spicy Tomato Capellini

Ingredients:

2 quantities	2 quantities	Tomato Pasta Dough
1	1	minced garlic clove
2 tbsp	30 ml	pinenuts
1 tbsp	15 ml	fresh chopped basil leaves
1 tsp	5 ml	marjoram
3 tbsp	45 ml	chopped parsley
1 cup	250 ml	seeded, diced red peppers
2 tsp	10 ml	chopped chipotle chilies
2 tsp	10 ml	orange zest
3 oz	90 g	freshly grated Romano cheese
¼ cup	60 ml	olive oil

Preparation:

In a food processor, process the garlic and pinenuts until very fine. Add basil, marjoram, parsley, peppers, chilies, orange zest and cheese; process into a purée. Slowly add the oil and continue to process into a mayonnaise like sauce.

Cook the pasta al dente in 4 quarts (4 L) of boiling salted water. Drain.

Toss the sauce through noodles. Place on hot plates. Serve.

Tomato Pasta Dough

Ingredients:

2	2	eggs
¼ cup	60 ml	tomato paste
1 tbsp	15 ml	olive oil
2 cups	500 ml	semolina flour
		ice water only if required

Preparation:

Blend the eggs, tomato paste and oil together. Place in a mixing bowl. Slowly add the flour. Knead into a smooth ball (add ice water if required).

Knead the dough for 15 minutes and allow to rest for an additional 15 minutes. Roll out the dough. Lightly dust with flour, fold in three, and roll out again. Repeat 6 to 8 times.

Pass the dough through the pasta machine setting the rollers gradually down until you reach the desired thickness. The result should be a smooth sheet of dough ready to process as you require.

Pass through a pasta machine, or cut by hand to desired size. If processed by hand, simply roll the dough and cut into thin strips for noodles (fettucini) or into wider strips for lasagna, cannelloni, ravioli, etc.

Process as any of our recipes direct.

Note: Use only enough flour to prevent sticking while rolling.

Serves 6

Caramel Sponge Roll

Ingredients:

Cake:

5	5	eggs - separated
⅔ cup	170 ml	sugar
¼ tsp	1 ml	salt
½ cup	125 ml	pastry flour
3 tbsp	45 ml	butter - melted
1 tsp	5 ml	vanilla
½ cup	125 ml	confectioners sugar

Filling:

1 ¼ cups	310 ml	brown sugar
½ cup	125 ml	white granulated sugar
1 ⅓ cups	330 ml	corn syrup
⅓ cup	80 ml	butter
1 cup	250 ml	condensed milk
½ tsp	3 ml	vanilla

Preparation:

Cake:

Whip the eggs to soft peaks.

Combine the egg yolks with the sugar in a double boiler. Heat to about 140°F (60°C). Remove from heat. Beat until mixture holds soft peaks. Combine the salt with the flour and fold into mixture. Fold in the butter and vanilla 1 tbsp (15 ml) at a time. Fold in the egg whites. Pour into a wax paper lined 15" x 10" (30 cm x 22 cm) pan.

Bake in a preheated oven 350°F (180°C) for 18 minutes.

Remove from oven and turn out onto a wax paper surface dusted with confectioners sugar. Remove the wax paper on the cake. Quickly pour the filling over the cake. Trim the edges even. Roll the cake. Wrap with the wax paper until cool. Remove wax paper once cool and dust with confectioners sugar. Serve.

Filling:

Combine the sugars and corn syrup together. Heat in a heavy saucepan. Boil to 245°F (118°C) on a candy thermometer.

Add the butter, milk, and vanilla. Return to 230°F (110°C) on the thermometer.

👑	*Fun Food Facts*

Eggs

Many people wonder what is the equivalent in eggs when a recipe calls for a measure of eggs. Well here's a tip:

5 large eggs equal 1 cup (250 ml),

4 large egg whites equal ½ cup (125 ml),

6 large egg yolks is the equivalent of ½ cup (125 ml).

Argentina Bean Soup

Ingredients:

8 oz	225 g	navy beans
8 cups	2 L	chicken stock (see page 210)
2 cups	500 ml	tomato juice
¼ lb	125 g	diced bacon
1	1	finely diced Spanish onion
2	2	finely diced celery stalks
2	2	minced garlic cloves
2	2	finely diced carrots
¼ cup	60 ml	tomato paste
½ tsp	3 ml	each of paprika, oregano, thyme, pepper
1 tbsp	15 ml	chili powder
1 tsp	5 ml	salt
¼ tsp	1 ml	black pepper

Preparation:

Soak the beans in cold water for 6-8 hours. Drain. Place the beans in a large kettle; cover with chicken stock. Simmer the beans for 2½ hours. Add the tomato juice.

Sauté the bacon in a skillet. Add the onion, celery, garlic and carrots. Continue to sauté until all are tender. Drain the excess fat. Add the bacon and vegetables to the soup.

Stir in the tomato paste and seasonings. Continue to simmer for 1 hour. Serve very hot.

Serves 6

Latin Barbequed Beef for Sandwiches

Ingredients:

¼ cup	60 ml	flour
1 tsp	5 ml	basil
½ tsp	3 ml	each of thyme leaves, chervil, salt
5 lbs	2.2 kg	baron of beef
2 tbsp	30 ml	each of Worcestershire sauce, dry mustard
1	1	each of chopped onion, bay leaf
2	2	each of chopped carrots, chopped celery stalks
1 cup	250 ml	each of red wine, beef broth or water

Sauce:

3 tbsp	45 ml	olive oil
2 tbsp	30 ml	each of minced onion, minced green peppers, minced celery
3	3	each of minced garlic clove, seeded and diced jalapeño peppers
¼ cup	60 ml	white wine
1 tbsp	15 ml	chili powder
2 tsp	10 ml	paprika
¼ tsp	1 ml	black pepper
½ tsp	3 ml	each of oregano leaves, ground cumin, hickory smoked salt
3 tbsp	45 ml	brown sugar
1 ¼ cups	310 ml	tomato purée

Preheat the oven to 325°F (160°C). Mix the flour, mustard and seasonings together, rub into the roast. Pour Worcestershire over.

Surround roast with the vegetables and bay leaf. Pour in the red wine and water. Bake to desired doneness, basting often.

Slice thinly, place in the barbeque sauce and serve on your favourite bread.

Sauce:

Heat the oil in a sauce pan. Add the onion, green peppers, celery, garlic, and jalapeños and sauté until tender. Blend in the remaining ingredients. Bring sauce to a boil, reduce heat and simmer for 20 minutes.

SERVES 6-8

Peruvian Pork Croquettes

Ingredients:

¼ cup	60 ml	butter
1 ¼ cups	310 ml	flour
½ tsp	3 ml	salt
½ tsp	3 ml	pepper
½ tsp	3 ml	oregano
½ tsp	3 ml	paprika
½ tsp	3 ml	white pepper
½ tsp	3 ml	thyme
1 ¼ cups	310 ml	milk
1	1	minced garlic clove
1 tbsp	15 ml	lime zest
2 tbsp	30 ml	grated onion
2 cups	500 ml	ground pork, cooked
1	1	egg
3 cups	750 ml	fine seasoned bread crumbs
3 cups	750 ml	oil

Preparation:

Heat the butter in a sauce pan over low heat. Add ¼ cup (60 ml) of the flour and cook for 2 minutes.

Add the seasonings and 1 cup (250 ml) of the milk. Simmer into a very thick sauce. Stir in the garlic, lime, onion and pork. Cool to room temperature and refrigerate for 3 hours.

Heat the oil in a shallow pan to 350°F (180°C).

Shape the mixture into 6 large croquettes. Mix the egg with the remaining milk. Dust the croquettes in the remaining flour; dip into the egg mixture; then roll into the bread crumbs. Fry each side for 3 minutes. Serve at once with the sauce on the side.

Croquette Sauce

Ingredients:

3 tbsp	45 ml	olive oil
3 tbsp	45 ml	flour
⅔ cup	160 ml	chicken broth (see page 210)
⅔ cup	160 ml	light cream
⅓ cup	80 ml	tomato catsup
2 tsp	10 ml	Worcestershire sauce
1 tsp	5 ml	paprika
1 tsp	5 ml	chili powder
1 tsp	5 ml	salt
3 drops	3 drops	Tabasco™ sauce
1 tbsp	15 ml	lemon juice

Preparation:

Heat the oil in a sauce pan. Add the flour and cook for 2 minutes over low heat. Whisk in the broth and cream and simmer until thick. Whisk in the remaining ingredients. Continue to simmer for 2 additional minutes. Remove from the heat. Use as required.

Serves 6

Peru

Spicy Yucatan Shrimp

Ingredients:

½ cup	125ml	safflower oil
1	1	minced Spanish onion
1	1	finely diced green bell pepper
1	1	finely diced celery stalk
2	2	minced garlic cloves
2 tsp	10 ml	minced red chilies
1 cup	250 ml	crushed tomatoes
1 cup	250 ml	mashed bananas
½ tsp	3 ml	salt (optional)
½ tsp	3 ml	cayenne pepper
1 tsp	5 ml	oregano
¼ tsp	1 ml	white pepper
¼ tsp	1 ml	black pepper
2 ¼ lbs	1 kg	jumbo shrimp

Preparation:

Heat the oil in a sauce pan. Add the onion, bell pepper, celery, garlic and chilies. Sauté until tender. Add the tomatoes, bananas and seasonings. Simmer for 15-20 minutes.

Peel and devein the shrimp. Place the shrimp in a large casserole dish. Cover with the sauce. Cover casserole dish with foil wrap. Bake in a preheated 350°F (180°C) oven for 15 minutes.

Uncover and bake for 15 additional minutes. Transfer to a serving plate. Serve at once.

Serves 6

Peru

Avocado Crab and Chicken Salad

Ingredients:

½ lb	125 g	cooked crab meat
½ lb	125 g	cooked chicken meat
3	3	chopped green onions
1	1	finely diced celery
¼ cup	60 ml	finely diced green bell pepper
¼ cup	60 ml	finely diced red bell pepper
1 cup	250 ml	plain yogurt
1 tbsp	15 ml	lemon juice
½ tsp	3 ml	salt
¼ tsp	1 ml	fresh cracked black pepper
1 tsp	5 ml	granulated sugar
1 tsp	5 ml	dill weed
1 tsp	5 ml	sweet basil
6	6	large avocados
2 cups	500 ml	alfalfa sprouts
6	6	lettuce leaves
1 tbsp	15 ml	chopped cilantro

Preparation:

Finely dice the meats and place into a mixing bowl. Mix in the vegetables.

Blend the yogurt, lemon, and seasonings together.

Peel the avocados then cut them in half; discarding the pit.

Pour half the dressing onto the salad and blend well. Fill the avocado cavity with salad.

Place the alfalfa and lettuce onto chilled plates to form nests.

Place an avocado in each nest. Spoon over each a little dressing. Sprinkle with cilantro and serve.

Serves 6

Thick Barbeque Sauce

Ingredients:

4 tbsp	60 ml	catsup
4 tbsp	60 ml	dry white wine
1 tbsp	15 ml	olive oil
2	2	garlic cloves, blanched and puréed
1 tbsp	15 ml	Worcestershire sauce
1 tsp	5 ml	horseradish
1 tbsp	15 ml	chopped fresh basil
		few drops Tabasco sauce, salt and freshly ground pepper

In a food processor, combine the ingredients and blend. Use as required.

Clementine Orange Chocolate Mousse

Ingredients:

3 cups	750 ml	miniature marshmallows
½ cup	125 ml	light cream
3 oz	80 g	semi-sweet chocolate
2 tbsp	30 ml	orange juice concentrate
1 ½ cups	375 ml	whipping cream
2	2	egg whites
1 cup	250 ml	clementine orange segments

Preparation:

In a double boiler, melt the marshmallows with the cream and chocolate. Stir in the orange juice. Remove from the heat; cool.

Whip the cream and fold into cooled mixture. Whip the egg whites stiff and fold into mixture. Fold in the orange segments. Pour into 6 serving dishes or parfait dishes. Chill for 3 hours before serving.

Serves 6

Peru

Roasted Grilled Bell Peppers with Pesto

Ingredients:

2	2	red bell peppers
2	2	green bell peppers
2	2	yellow bell peppers
¾ cup	180 ml	olive oil
1 cup	250 ml	fresh chopped basil
2	2	minced garlic cloves
1 cup	250 ml	chopped, roasted, and salted macadamia nuts
¼ cup	60 ml	fresh grated Parmesan cheese

Preparation:

Place the peppers on a baking sheet and roast in a 400°F (200°C) oven until the skins blister. Place in a paper bag and allow to steam for 20 minutes. Remove from bag and peel away the skin. Cut into quarters. Remove seeds.

In a food processor or blender, blend ¼ cup (60 ml) of oil, basil, garlic, nuts and cheese. With the machine running, slowly pour in the remaining oil.

Grill the quartered peppers over medium heat for 6 minutes. Place on serving plates and top with sauce. Serve.

Serves 6

Crab Chalupas

Ingredients:

8	8	corn tortillas
3 cups	750 ml	crab meat
2 cups	500 ml	refried beans
3 cups	750 ml	shredded lettuce
2	2	chopped tomatoes
1 cup	250 ml	grated Cheddar cheese
		Guacamole
		Picante Sauce

Preparation:

Heat the oven to 375°F (190°C).

Place the tortillas on baking sheets and bake for 3 minutes or until crisp.

Place the crisp tortillas on serving plates. Spread with crab and beans. Top with lettuce, tomatoes and cheese. Serve with the Guacamole and Picante Sauces.

Guacamole

2	2	pared, diced large ripe avocados
1	1	seeded, diced and peeled tomato
3 tbsp	45 ml	grated onion
1	1	minced garlic clove
3	3	minced, canned chilles
1 tbsp	15 ml	lime juice
¾ tsp	4 ml	salt
¼ tsp	1 ml	pepper

Combine all the ingredients together in a food processor and purée.

Picante Sauce

6	6	large tomatoes
2 cups	500 ml	stewed tomatoes
1	1	finely diced Spanish onion
3 tbsp	45 ml	vinegar
3 tbsp	45 ml	granulated sugar
¼ cup	60 ml	lime juice
1 tsp	5 ml	salt
10	10	seeded, diced jalapeños

Combine all the ingredients together in a sauce pan. Heat to a boil. Reduce heat and simmer until thick.

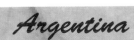

Argentina

Consommé Olenka

Ingredients:

⅔ cup	170 ml	twice ground chicken
1 tsp	5 ml	grated onion
¼ tsp	1 ml	pepper
¼ tsp	1 ml	basil
¼ tsp	1 ml	thyme
¼ tsp	1 ml	oregano
¼ tsp	1 ml	paprika
½ tsp	3 ml	salt
1	1	egg white
⅛ cup	30 ml	whipping cream
6 cups	1.5 L	chicken broth (see page 210)
¾ cup	180 ml	peas
2	2	pared finely diced carrots
1 cup	250 ml	green beans, trimmed, blanched
3 oz	90 g	Enoki mushrooms

Preparation:

In a mixing bowl combine the chicken, onion, seasonings, egg white and cream. Press through a fine sieve and roll into small balls.

Bring 2 cups (500 ml) of the broth to a boil. Drop the balls in the broth. Reduce heat and simmer for 10 minutes. Remove the meat balls.

Bring the remaining broth to a boil. Reduce to a simmer and add the peas, carrots and beans. Simmer for 10 minutes. Add the chicken balls and continue simmering for an additional 5 minutes. Garnish with Enoki mushrooms. Serve soup very hot.

Serves 6

Chicken Jalapeño Pie

Ingredients:

1 ¼ lbs	570 g	ground chicken
½ cup	125 ml	safflower oil
1 cup	250 ml	cornmeal
1 tbsp	15 ml	granulated sugar
1 tsp	5 ml	salt
½ tsp	3 ml	black pepper
½ tsp	3 ml	baking soda
1 cup	250 ml	milk
2	2	beaten eggs
1 ¼ cups	310 ml	creamed corn
3	3	finely diced jalapeños peppers
1	1	finely diced Bermuda onion
2 cups	500 ml	grated Cheddar cheese

Preparation:

Preheat the oven to 350°F (180°C).

In a large skillet brown the chicken in 2 tbsp (30 ml) of the oil, drain and reserve.

Sift the cornmeal, sugar, salt, pepper and baking soda together into a mixing bowl. Add the remaining oil, eggs, milk, creamed corn, jalapeños, onions and cheese.

Spread half the mixture in a 8" x 10" (20 cm x 25 cm) casserole dish. Top with chicken. Spread with the remaining mixture. Bake in the oven for 40-50 minutes. Serve at once hot with a side soup or salad.

Serves 6

Peru

Crepas Fajitas

Ingredients:

1 ½ lbs	675 g	flank steak
3	3	sliced garlic cloves
2	2	sliced Spanish onions
2	2	minced serrano chilies
¼ cup	60 ml	chopped cilantro
⅓ cup	80 ml	lime juice
¼ cup	60 ml	lemon juice
3 tbsp	45 ml	butter
2 tbsp	30 ml	safflower oil
1	1	sliced green bell pepper
1	1	sliced red bell pepper
1	1	sliced yellow bell pepper
3 oz	90 g	sliced mushrooms
1 tsp	5 ml	salt
1 tsp	5 ml	Worcestershire sauce
1 tbsp	15 ml	chili powder
24	24	crêpes (see page 312)
½ cup	125 ml	sour cream
1 cup	250 ml	guacamole (see page 146)
1 cup	250 ml	Salsa sauce

Preparation:

Slice the steak into very thin strips. In a casserole dish layer the steak, garlic, 1 onion, chilies and cilantro. Pour the citrus juices over mixture. Cover and refrigerate for 3-4 hours. Drain thoroughly.

In a large skillet, heat the butter and oil. Sauté the remaining onion together with the peppers and mushrooms. Season the vegetables with a little salt and the Worcestershire sauce. Transfer to a very hot serving plate and reserve hot.

Cook the steak over a hot grill for 3-4 minutes seasoning with the chili powder and remaining salt. Transfer to a second hot plate.

Serve the steak, vegetables, crêpes, sour cream, guacamole and salsa separately, allowing your guest to "fix em" up how they prefer.

NOTE: If you choose to use shrimp or lobster do not marinate. Chicken however may follow the same recipe.

Serves 6

Salsa

1 lb	454 g	peeled and seeded tomatoes
1	1	Spanish onion
3	3	crushed garlic cloves
1	1	bunch chopped cilantro
2	2	jalapeño peppers
1	1	green bell pepper
2 tbsp	30 ml	lime juice
½ tsp	3 ml	salt

Chop the tomatoes and mince the onion. Place in a mixing bowl along with the garlic and cilantro.

Seed the jalapeños and dice fine. Blend into the tomatoes. Stir in the lime juice and salt.

Argentina

Spicy Chicken with Coconut

Ingredients:

1 ½ lbs	675 g	chicken pieces
1 tsp	5 ml	each of salt, paprika, pepper
6 tbsp	90 ml	butter
1	1	diced Spanish onion
1	1	minced garlic clove
¾ cup	180 ml	blanched, grated almonds
1 tsp	5 ml	crushed red chilies
½ tsp	3 ml	thyme leaves
1	1	bay leaf
¼ cup	60 ml	lemon juice
¼ cup	60 ml	honey
1 ¾ cups	410ml	coconut milk or condensed milk
1 cup	250 ml	shredded fresh coconut

Preparation:

Sprinkle the chicken pieces with salt, paprika and pepper.

Heat the butter in a large skillet. Fry the onion with the chicken to brown. Add the remaining ingredients. Cover. Reduce heat and simmer for 45 minutes.

Serve with rice pilaff.

Serves 6

Coconut Almond Rice Pilaff

Ingredients:

3 tbsp	45 ml	butter
1 ½ cups	375 ml	converted rice
2 ½ cups	625 ml	chicken broth (see page 210)
½ cup	125 ml	coconut milk
¾ cup	180 ml	chopped parsley
¾ cup	180 ml	finely diced celery
½ cup	125 ml	finely diced scallions
⅓ cup	80 ml	shredded coconut
½ cup	125 ml	blanch slivered almonds

Preheat the oven to 375°F (190°C).

Heat the butter in a skillet. Add the rice and toss to cook until rice is golden brown. Place into a 2 quart casserole dish.

In a sauce pan bring the chicken broth and coconut milk to a boil. Pour over the rice. Bake in the oven for 20 minutes.

Stir in the parsley, celery, scallion, coconut and almonds. Return to the oven and bake for an additional 15 minutes.

Serves 6

Sweetened Condensed Milk

Can't find sweetened condensed milk, try this:

1 cup	250 ml	powdered milk
⅔ cup	160 ml	granulated sugar
⅓ cup	80 ml	boiling water
3 tbsp	45 ml	melted butter

Combine the ingredients in a food processor. Blend until smooth.

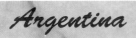

Argentina

Ebony and Ivory Strawberries

Ingredients:

25	25	fresh large strawberries
4 oz	120 g	grated white chocolate
4 oz	120 g	grated semi-sweet chocolate
2 tbsp	30 ml	butter

Preparation:

Wash and hull the berries; dry them.

Prepare 2 double boilers. In one, melt the white chocolate. In the other, melt the dark chocolate. Stir in 15 ml (1 tbsp) of butter in each.

Dip one of the berries in the white chocolate. With a spoon, drizzle dark chocolate over it. Place it on a sheet of waxed paper to harden. Dip another berry in the dark chocolate and drizzle with white chocolate. Repeat and alternate until all the berries are dipped.

Serves 6

Argentina

Colombian Green Bean Salad

Ingredients:

1 lb	454 g	green beans
1	1	large Spanish onion
4	4	large tomatoes
½ cup	125 ml	olive oil
4 tbsp	60 ml	lime juice
1 tbsp	15 ml	fresh oregano (or 1 tsp (5 ml) dry)
1 tsp	5 ml	cracked black pepper
1 tsp	5 ml	salt
2	2	hard boiled eggs

Preparation:

Trim the beans and blanch in boiling salted water for 5 minutes. Chill in ice water. Drain completely.

Slice the onions and place into a large mixing bowl. Add the beans. Cut the tomatoes into quarters and add to the beans.

Mix the oil, lime juice and seasonings and pour over the salad. Marinate the salad for 15 minutes. Grate the eggs and sprinkle over the salad before serving.

Serves 6

Colombia Corn Bread

Ingredients:

¾ lb	375 g	sausage meat
2 cups	500 ml	cornmeal
½ cup	125 ml	flour
1 tbsp	15 ml	baking powder
1 tsp	5 ml	baking soda
1 tsp	5 ml	salt
2 tsp	10 ml	granulated sugar
2	2	beaten eggs
3	3	seeded and diced jalapeño peppers
1	1	medium onion, finely diced
1 ¼ cups	310 ml	creamed corn
2 cups	500 ml	buttermilk
½ cup	125 ml	grated Cheddar cheese

Preparation:

Preheat the oven to 400°F (180°C).

In a skillet fry the sausage meat, drain and reserve 3 tbsp (45 ml) of the fat.

In a mixing bowl, sift together the cornmeal, flour, baking powder, baking soda, salt and sugar.

In a second mixing bowl blend the eggs, jalapeños, onion, corn, buttermilk and cheese. Fold in the dry mixture, sausage meat and reserved fat.

Pour batter into a 10″ (25 cm) iron skillet, bake in the oven for 25 minutes.

Serves 6

Colombia

Garlic and Chicken Empanadas

Ingredients:

Crust:

⅓ cup	80 ml	ice cold water
1	1	large egg
2 tsp	10 ml	vinegar
3 cups	750 ml	flour
6	6	minced garlic cloves
⅓ cup	80 ml	cold butter
⅓ cup	80 ml	cold shortening (lard)
1 tsp	5 ml	salt
2	2	egg whites

Filling:

3 tbsp	45 ml	butter
1	1	minced large Spanish onion
2	2	minced garlic cloves
¼ tsp	1 ml	each of allspice, cinnamon, cloves
1 tbsp	15 ml	salt
¾ lb	335 g	boneless, skinless chicken, coarsely diced
2 tsp	10 ml	oregano

Preparation:

Crust:

Blend the water, egg and vinegar together. Place the flour and garlic in a mixing bowl. Cut in the butter and shortening. Add the salt. Blend in the liquid. Blend the dough until a coarse mixture is formed.

Filling:

Heat the butter in a skillet. Add the onion and garlic and sauté until tender. Add the remaining ingredients and continue to cook over low heat for 15 minutes. Cool to room temperature.

Preheat the oven to 425°F (210°C).

Roll the pastry out on a floured surface. Cut into 2" (5 cm) rounds. Place 1 tbsp. (15 ml) of the filling on each round. Fold the round in half and crimp the edges to seal. Brush the pastry with the egg whites. Place on a greased baking sheet. Bake for 15-20 minutes or until golden brown.

Yields 16

Fun Food Facts

Butter

Butter, derived from the churning of cream, is usually found as two types; salted (not generally recommended for baking) and sweet (unsalted). Whipped butter is also available today and is considered "light, lite" butter. Water, cream and or air is whipped into the butter. When heated this butter will separate from the water causing a poor final product.

Nachos Con Salsa Fresca

Ingredients:

4	4	medium tomatoes
4	4	minced garlic cloves
1	1	small cucumber
½ cup	125 ml	finely diced celery
¼ cup	60 ml	finely diced onion
½ cup	125 ml	cilantro, packed
2	2	jalapeño peppers, seeded & diced
2 tbsp	30 ml	lemon juice
1 tbsp	15 ml	granulated sugar
½ tsp	3 ml	salt
½ tsp	3 ml	basil
1 lb	454 g	nacho chips
2 cups	500 ml	grated Monterey Jack cheese

Preparation:

Coarsely chop the tomatoes; drain well.

Pare, seed and finely dice the cucumber.

Mix the tomatoes, cucumber, garlic, celery, onion and cilantro together and refrigerate for 1 hour.

Stir the jalapeño peppers into the vegetables. Add the lemon juice, sugar, salt and basil.

Place the nacho chips on a large, ovenproof serving platter. Sprinkle with cheese. Place under the oven broiler until cheese is melted. Serve at once with salsa.

Serves 6

Guatemala

Colombian Cilantro Carrot Soup

Ingredients:

6	6	large carrots
4 cups	1 L	water
¼ cup	60 m	grated onion
4 tbsp	60 ml	butter
3 tbsp	45 ml	flour
3 cups	750 ml	chicken stock (see page 210)
2 cups	500 ml	light cream
1 tsp	5 ml	salt
¼ tsp	1 ml	white pepper
⅛ tsp	pinch	cayenne pepper
2 tbsp	30 ml	cilantro (coriander)

Preparation:

Pare and chop the carrots. Boil the carrots in the water until tender. Drain and purée the carrots in a food processor.

Sauté the onion in the butter. Sprinkle with flour and cook for 2 minutes over low heat. Add the chicken stock, cream and carrot purée. Simmer for 3 minutes. Stir in the seasonings. Simmer for 5 minutes longer. Sprinkle with cilantro and serve.

Serves 6

Spanish Caesar Salad

Ingredients:

1	1	garlic clove
2	2	egg yolks
1 tsp	5 ml	dry mustard
2 tsp	10 ml	granulated sugar
⅛ tsp	pinch	cayenne pepper
1 ½ cups	375 ml	olive oil
3 tbsp	45 ml	lemon juice
¼ cup	60 ml	buttermilk
⅓ cup	80 ml	freshly grated Parmesan cheese
2 tbsp	30 ml	minced chives
3	3	seeded, finely diced jalapeño peppers
½ tsp	3 ml	cracked black pepper
2	2	heads, washed Romaine lettuce
⅓ cup	80 ml	cooked diced bacon
⅓ cup	80 ml	croutons

Preparation:

Place the garlic, egg yolks, mustard, sugar and cayenne in a blender or food processor. With the machine running, very slowly, add the oil in a thin stream until mixture reaches the consistency of mayonnaise.

Stir in the lemon juice, buttermilk, cheese, chives, jalapeños and pepper.

Cut the lettuce into bite size pieces and place into a large bowl. Cover lettuce with dressing and toss to coat.

Serve the salad on chilled plates. Garnish with bacon and croutons.

Serves 6

Colombia

Panamanian Tarragon Chicken

Ingredients:

1 tbsp	15 ml	olive oil
1-3 lbs	1.1 kg	chicken
8 oz	225 g	thin strips of sliced ham
2	2	sliced onions
2	2	coarsely diced celery stalks
3	3	coarsely diced carrots
1 cup	250ml	chicken broth (see page 210)
1 tbsp	15 ml	chopped fresh tarragon
2 tbsp	30 ml	butter
2 tbsp	30 ml	flour

Preparation:

Rub the oil over the chicken. Place in a earthenware cocotte (casserole dish). Place uncovered in a preheated 350°F (180°C) oven. Bake for 30 minutes.

Add the ham, onion, celery, carrots, broth and tarragon. Cover and continue to bake for 1 hour. Remove from oven. Strain the broth and carve chicken.

Return the chicken to the cocotte and reserve warm with the vegetables.

Heat the butter in a sauce pan. Stir in the flour and pour in 2 cups (500 ml) of the strained broth. Simmer until sauce thickens. Pour over chicken and vegetables. Serve in the cocotte.

Serves 6

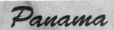

Panama

Guatemalan Cheesecake

with Pineapple Walnut Topping

Ingredients:

Crust:

1 cup	250 ml	flaked coconut
1 cup	250 ml	ground, roasted filberts
⅓ cup	80 ml	granulated sugar
¼ cup	60 ml	melted butter

Filling:

1 ½ lbs	680 g	cream cheese
1 cup	250 ml	granulated sugar
¼ cup	60 ml	coconut cream nectar*
1 cup	250 ml	whipping cream
1 ½ cups	375 ml	crushed pineapple, well drained
3	3	eggs
2 tsp	10 ml	rum extract

Topping:

1 cup	250 ml	pineapple juice
1 cup	250 ml	brown sugar
6 tbsp	90 ml	cornstarch
6 tbsp	90 ml	pineapple gelatine
1 cup	250 ml	boiling water
3 cups	750 ml	pineapple chunks
1 cup	250 ml	walnut pieces
1 ½ cups	375 ml	shredded, toasted coconut

Preparation:

Crust:

Combine all the ingredients together. Press into a greased 9" (23 cm) springform pan. Refrigerate 10 minutes. Bake in a preheated 350°F (180°C) oven for 7 minutes.

Filling:

Cream the cheese with the sugar until very smooth. Blend in the coconut cream, cream and pineapple. Beat in the eggs, 1 at a time. Add the rum flavouring and blend well. Pour into shell. Bake at 350°F (180°C) for 90 minutes.

Transfer to a cooling rack. Cool. Chill for 8 hours.

Topping:

In a sauce pan, combine the juice, sugar, cornstarch and gelatine. Bring to a boil. Stir in the boiling water. Continue to cook until sauce thickens.

Add the pineapple chunks and walnut pieces. Cool. Spread over chilled cake. Sprinkle with toasted coconut. Serve.

Serves 8

* Available in speciality food stores.

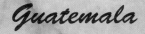

Guatemala

Honduran Spiced Beef
in Red Wine Mushroom Sauce

Ingredients:

2 ¼ lbs	1 kg	sirloin, sliced into thin strips
3 tbsp	45 ml	butter
3 tbsp	45 ml	safflower oil
4 oz	120 g	sliced mushrooms
3 tbsp	45 ml	finely diced carrots
3 tbsp	45 ml	finely diced celery
¼ cup	60 ml	flour
½ cup	125 ml	red wine
2 cups	500 ml	beef broth (see page 42)
3 tbsp	45 ml	tomato paste
1 tsp	5 ml	black pepper
1 tsp	5 ml	garlic powder
1 tsp	5 ml	onion powder
1 tsp	5 ml	white pepper
1 tsp	5 ml	oregano
1 tsp	5 ml	thyme
1 tsp	5 ml	basil
1 tsp	5 ml	salt
1 tbsp	15 ml	chili powder

Preparation:

In a large Dutch oven or kettle, sauté the beef in the butter and oil. Add the vegetables and continue to cook until tender. Sprinkle with flour. Reduce the heat and cook for 5 minutes.

Add the wine, broth, tomato paste and seasonings. Simmer covered for 50 minutes.

Serve over noodles.

Serves 6

Spanish Eggplant Casserole

Ingredients:

4	4	slices, diced bacon
1	1	diced red Bermuda onion
1	1	seeded, diced green bell pepper
3 cups	750 ml	diced eggplant
1 tsp	5 ml	salt
½ tsp	3 ml	cracked black pepper
1 tbsp	15 ml	chili powder
1 ¼ cups	310 ml	tomato purée
1 cup	250 ml	chicken broth (see page 210)
½ cup	125 ml	bread crumbs
1 ¼ cups	310 ml	grated Monterey Jack cheese

Preparation:

Preheat the oven to 350°F (180°C).

In a skillet fry the bacon until crisp; remove the meat and reserve. Add the onion and pepper to the fat and sauté until tender, drain excess fat.

Place the eggplant into a greased 8" x 10" (20 cm x 25 cm) casserole dish. Mix in the onion and peppers and sprinkle with the seasonings.

Blend the tomato purée with the chicken broth and pour over the casserole.

Blend the bread crumbs with the reserved bacon. Sprinkle the cheese over the casserole and top with bread crumbs.

Bake in the oven for 25-30 minutes. Serve at once, hot.

British Honduras

Spanish Pepper and Seafood Salad

Ingredients:

2	2	garlic cloves, pounded into a paste
2	2	egg yolks
½ tsp	3 ml	salt
pinch	pinch	pepper
½ tsp	3 ml	Dijon mustard
1 cup	250 ml	olive oil
4 tsp	20 ml	wine vinegar
16	16	cherry tomatoes
1	1	julienne sliced red bell pepper
1	1	julienne sliced yellow bell pepper
1	1	julienne sliced green bell pepper
2	2	diced jalapeño peppers
1	1	sliced Spanish onion
1 cup	250 m	diced cooked lobster
1 cup	250 ml	cooked sea scallops
1 cup	250 ml	cooked large shrimp

Preparation:

In a blender or food processor cream the garlic, egg yolks, salt, pepper and mustard. With the machine running add the oil in a slow thin stream. Add the vinegar; blend.

In a large mixing bowl combine the remaining ingredients. Pour the sauce over and toss to coat. Serve chilled.

Serves 6

Colombia

Chilean Chicken Almond Soup with Red Chilies

Ingredients:

5 tbsp	75 ml	butter
5 tbsp	75 ml	flour
4 cups	1 L	chicken stock (see page 210)
1 ½ cups	375 ml	whipping cream
2 ½ cups	625 ml	diced, cooked chicken
1 tsp	5 ml	crushed red chilies
⅓ cup	80 ml	toasted, sliced almonds

Preparation:

Heat the butter in a large sauce pan. Stir in the flour. Cook for 2 minutes over low heat. Add the chicken stock, cream, chicken and chilies. Bring to a boil; reduce heat and simmer for 20 minutes.

Garnishing with the almonds. Serve.

Serves 6

Corn Bread Pie

Ingredients:

Corn bread

1 ½ cups	375 ml	corn meal
½ cup	125 ml	flour
2 tsp	10 ml	granulated sugar
1 tbsp	15 ml	baking powder
½ tsp	3 ml	baking soda
1 tsp	5 ml	salt
1 cup	250 ml	buttermilk
2	2	beaten eggs
¼ cup	60 ml	safflower oil

Filling:

1 lb	454 g	lean ground beef
1	1	finely diced Spanish onion
1 tbsp	15 ml	chili powder
1 tsp	5 ml	salt
½ tsp	3 ml	each of pepper, basil, thyme, paprika
1 ¼ cups	310 ml	tomato sauce
2 cups	500 ml	chicken broth (see page 210)
1	1	seeded, finely diced green bell pepper
1 ½ cups	375 ml	fresh kernel corn

Preparation:

Corn bread:

In a mixing bowl sift the corn meal, flour, sugar, baking powder, baking soda and salt together.

Mix the buttermilk, eggs and oil together and add to the dry ingredients. Blend until thick but still coarse (lumpy).

Filling:

Preheat the oven to 400°F (200°C).

In a large skillet brown the beef. Add the onions and sauté until tender. Drain any excess fat. Add the seasonings, tomato sauce and chicken broth. Reduce heat and simmer for 10 minutes. Add the green pepper and corn and continue to simmer for an additional 15 minutes.

Spoon the filling mixture into a 9" x 13" (22cm x 32cm) casserole dish. Spoon the corn bread mixture over top. Bake in the oven for 20-25 minutes.

Serves 6

Chile

Chilean Red Pepper Shrimp

Ingredients:

3	3	red bell peppers
½ cup	125 ml	chicken broth (see page 210)
¼ cup	60 ml	white wine
2 ½ tbsp	38 ml	flour
2	2	minced garlic cloves
1 ½ cups	375 ml	heavy cream
2 tsp	10 ml	lime juice
1 tsp	5 ml	crushed red chilies
1 tsp	5 ml	crushed thyme
1 ½ tsp	8 ml	salt
½ tsp	3 ml	each of paprika, black pepper, white pepper, cayenne pepper, basil, oregano
1 tbsp	15 ml	chili powder
2 tbsp	30 ml	olive oil
2 ½ lbs	1 kg	large shrimp, peeled and deveined, skewered

Preparation:

Roast the peppers either over coals or in a very hot oven until the skin blisters. Place in a paper bag and allow to sweat for 20 minutes. Peel the skin, slice and discard the seeds and membranes.

Combine the peppers, chicken broth, wine, flour, garlic in a food processor and blend until very smooth. Transfer to a sauce pan and heat gently. Add the cream, lime juice, chilies, thyme and ½ tsp (3 ml) salt. Simmer 8-10 minutes.

Blend the balance of the salt with the remaining spices and herbs.

Brush the skewered shrimp with the oil and sprinkle with spice blend. Broil the skewered shrimp over medium coals while the sauce simmers.

Place the shrimp onto serving platters. Cover with sauce and serve at once.

Serves 6

Fun Food Facts

Shrimp and Prawns

Why are flamingos pink? Because they have a complete diet of shrimp. The love affair flamingos have with shrimp can't compare with the love affair man has with these crustaceans. Shrimp and prawns are generally considered the same but actually differ very little. Prawns tend to be slightly more slender but have a sweeter tasting meat. Both are sold by count per pound, ie; 6-8 per pound, for tiger prawns and up to 35-50 per pound for large shrimp. This is an average size sold for home use. Shrimp for salad may have a count as high as 200 per pound which of course means these are very tiny. Shrimp require very little cooking and are excellent in all areas of cookery, except desserts. Four ounces of raw shrimp meat contains 120 calories, 23 grams of protein, 1 gram of carbohydrates, 2 grams of fat, 172 milligrams of cholesterol, 168 milligrams of sodium and 0 grams of fibre. Shrimp are best when fresh and quickly boiled in a rich flavoured fish court boullion.

Chile

Chilean Sweet Potato Pie

Ingredients:

1 cup	250 ml	granulated sugar
¼ tsp	1 ml	salt
1 tsp	5 ml	cinnamon
1 tsp	5 ml	nutmeg
½ tsp	3 ml	ground ginger
2 cups	500 ml	sweet potatoes, boiled and mashed smooth
1 cup	250 ml	milk
2	2	beaten eggs
½ quantity	½ quantity	pie dough (see page 30)
2 cups	500 ml	whipped cream

Preparation:

Combine the dry ingredients. Mix into the sweet potatoes. Blend in the milk and eggs.

Roll out the dough and fit into a 9" (23 cm) pie plate. Pour potato mixture into pie shell.

Bake in a 450°F (230°C) oven for 10 minutes. Reduce temperature to 350°F (180°C) and continue to bake for 35 minutes longer. Cool. Chill.

Pipe whipped cream over and serve.

Serves 6

Chile

Red Snapper Ceviche

Ingredients:

2 ½ lbs	1 kg	red snapper
6	6	lemons
6	6	limes
2 tbsp	30 ml	grated ginger
3	3	minced garlic cloves
2	2	minced jalapeño peppers
4	4	thinly sliced scallions
2 tbsp	30 ml	coarse salt
1 tbsp	15 ml	cracked black pepper
¼ cup	60 ml	olive oil
1	1	finely diced red bell pepper
¼ cup	60 ml	chopped cilantro
6	6	lettuce leaves

Preparation:

Fillet the snapper and remove all the skin. Dice into ¼" (.5 mm) cubes.

Cut the lemons and limes in half and juice the fruit. In a large stainless or glass bowl combine the juices, ginger, garlic, peppers, scallions, salt and pepper. Add the fish and marinate refrigerated for 2 hours.

Remove the fish from the marinate and place into a serving bowl. Pour the oil over the fish. Toss in the red pepper and cilantro.

Place the lettuce leaves on chilled plates. Cover with fish and serve.

Serves 6

Spanish Cheese Corn Bread

Ingredients:

1 cup	250 ml	corn meal
½ tsp	3 ml	baking soda
1 tsp	5 ml	salt
¼ cup	60 ml	safflower oil
2	2	beaten eggs
1 cup	250 ml	milk
1 ½ cups	375 ml	creamed corn
2 cups	500 ml	grated Monterey Jack cheese
3	3	seeded and diced jalapeño peppers

Preparation:

Preheat the oven to 350°F (180°C).

Sift the corn meal, baking soda and salt together in a mixing bowl. Add the oil, eggs and milk. Pour ½ the batter into an 8" x 8" (20 cm x 20 cm) greased, baking pan. Top with the creamed corn, cheese and peppers. Cover with the remaining batter. Bake in the oven for 40-50 minutes. Serve hot.

Peru

Brazilian Fiery Pork Steak

with Corn Mango Salsa

Ingredients:

Steaks:

12-5 oz	12-150 g	pork steaks
1 tsp	5 ml	garlic granules
2 tsp	10 ml	black pepper
½ tsp	3 ml	cayenne pepper
½ tsp	3 ml	oregano leaves
½ tsp	3 ml	thyme leaves
½ tsp	3 ml	crushed rosemary
½ tsp	3 ml	basil leaves
½ tsp	3 ml	onion powder
½ tsp	3 ml	salt

Salsa:

3 cups	750 ml	corn kernels
¼ cup	60 ml	water
2 tbsp	30 ml	olive oil
2	2	sliced large garlic cloves
¼ cup	60 ml	diced Spanish onions
4	4	green chilies, roasted, seeded and diced
5	5	large tomatoes, roasted, seeded and diced
1 ¼ cups	375 ml	diced mango
1 tbsp	15 ml	balsamic vinegar
½ tsp	3 ml	granulated sugar
¼ tsp	1 ml	salt
2 tbsp	30 ml	fresh chopped cilantro

Preparation:

Trim the steaks of fat. Blend the seasonings together and rub into steak. Leave steaks for 30 minutes. Cook over medium coals until cooked through.

While steaks are cooking, place the corn into a sauce pan. Add the water and cook covered for 4 minutes. Drain. Place into a mixing bowl.

Heat the oil in a sauté pan and fry the garlic slices until golden brown. Remove the garlic transfer to the corn. Add the onions to the pan and fry until translucent; transfer to the corn. Blend the remaining ingredients into the corn mixture and combine.

Place equal amounts of salsa onto serving plates. Top with two steaks. Serve at once.

Serves 6

Brazil

Brazilian Calypso Coffee Pie

Ingredients:

½ cup	125 ml	butter
1 ¼ cups	310 ml	confectioners sugar
2	2	eggs
1 cup	250 ml	granulated sugar
¼ cup	60 ml	flour
¼ tsp	2 ml	salt
1 cup	250 ml	milk - scalded
¼ cup	60 ml	Kahlua liqueur
¼ cup	60 ml	Dark Rum
¼ cup	60 ml	strong coffee
2 oz	60 g	semi sweet chocolate

Preparation:

Cream the butter. Add the confectioners sugar.

In a separate bowl, beat the eggs. Stir in the granulated sugar, flour, salt, milk, Kahlua, Rum, coffee and chocolate. Cook in a double boiler for 10 minutes. Cool. Whip into the creamed butter. Pour into a prebaked pie shell or graham crumb crust. Refrigerate for two hours. Serve covered with sweetened whipped cream and chocolate shavings.

Graham Cracker Crust

Ingredients:

3 ½ cups	875 ml	graham cracker crumbs
1 tbsp	15 ml	cinnamon
¼ cup	60 ml	melted butter

Preparation:

Combine all ingredients. Press into the bottom and sides of a buttered 9" (23 cm) or 10" (25 cm) springform pan. Chill.

Baked Pie Crust

Ingredients:

⅓ cup	80 ml	ice cold water
1	1	large egg
2 tsp	10 ml	vinegar
3 cups	750 ml	flour
⅓ cup	80 ml	cold butter
⅓ cup	80 ml	cold shortening (lard)
1 tsp	5 ml	salt

Preparation:

Blend the water, egg and vinegar together. Place the flour in a mixing bowl. Cut in the butter and shortening. Add the salt. Blend in the liquid.

Mix into a coarse texture. Divide into two. Place dough on a lightly floured surface. Roll into 12" (30 cm) rounds. Place rounds into two 9" (23 cm) pie plates. Poke the crust with a fork creating holes all over the dough. Fold edges under the bottom round. Crimp edges and cut away excess dough.

Bake in a 400°F (200°C) oven for 10-12 minutes or until golden brown.

Brazil

Empanadillas

Ingredients:

Crust:

⅓ cup	80 ml	ice cold water
1	1	large egg
2 tsp	10 ml	vinegar
3 cups	750 ml	flour
⅓ cup	80 ml	cold butter
⅓ cup	80 ml	cold shortening (lard)
1 tsp	5 ml	salt
2	2	egg whites

Filling:

2 tbsp	30 ml	olive oil
¼ lb	60 g	extra lean ground beef
¼ lb	60 g	lean ground pork
¼ tsp	1 ml	salt
¼ tsp	1 ml	paprika
¼ tsp	1 ml	black cracked pepper
¼ tsp	1 ml	cumin
1 tbsp	15 ml	chili powder
¼ cup	60 ml	minced onion
1	1	minced garlic clove
1	1	minced jalapeño pepper
1 tbsp	15 ml	butter
2	2	hard cooked eggs, chopped
3 tbsp	45 ml	pimento stuffed olives, chopped
3 tbsp	45 ml	seedless raisins
½ cup	125 ml	tomato sauce (see page 262)

Preparation:

Crust:

Blend the water, egg and vinegar together. Place the flour in a mixing bowl. Cut in the butter and shortening. Add the salt. Blend in the liquid. Blend the dough until a coarse mixture is formed.

Filling:

In a skillet heat the oil and brown the meats. Add the seasonings, onion, garlic and jalapeño. Sauté until tender. Drain any excess fat. Add the remaining ingredients and simmer until very thick. Cool to room temperature.

Preheat the oven to 425°F (210°C).

Roll the pastry out on a flour surface, cut into 2" (5 cm) rounds. Place 1 tbsp (15 ml) of meat mixture on each round. Fold the round in half and crimp the edges to seal. Brush the pastry with the egg whites. Place on a greased baking sheet and bake for 15-20 minutes, or until golden brown.

Yields 24

Mexico

Brazilian Garlic & Thyme Chicken

Ingredients:

6-6 oz	6-170 g	boneless chicken breasts, skin on
3 tbsp	45 ml	butter
6	6	minced garlic cloves
1 tsp	5 ml	shredded ginger root
1 tbsp	15 ml	fresh chopped thyme
1	1	minced jalapeño pepper
¼ cup	60 ml	fine dry bread crumbs

Preparation:

Wash the chicken breasts and lay flat on a baking sheet.

Preheat the oven to 350°F (180°C).

In a small mixing bowl blend the butter, garlic, ginger, thyme, jalapeño and the bread crumbs.

With a small knife, gently lift the skin of the chicken from the meat. Stuff equal amounts of the butter filling under the chicken skin. Skewer the ends with tooth picks to seal the ends.

Bake the chicken in the oven for 20-25 minutes, or until golden brown.

Serve with fresh vegetables and rice or Latin Lovers Salad.

Serves 6

Latin Lovers Salad

Ingredients:

1	1	yellow bell pepper
2 cups	500 ml	peeled, seeded and diced tomatoes
3 cups	750 ml	cooked, chilled long grain rice
3 tbsp	45 ml	chopped chives
⅓ cup	80 ml	olive oil
2 tbsp	30 ml	lime juice
2 tbsp	30 ml	balsamic vinegar
1 tsp	5 ml	minced garlic
½ tsp	3 ml	salt
½ tsp	3 ml	fresh cracked black pepper
½ tsp	3 ml	basil
½ tsp	3 ml	thyme
4	4	lettuce leaves

Preparation:

Core the yellow pepper. Remove the seeds and membranes and finely dice.

In a mixing bowl, blend the pepper, tomatoes, rice and chives.

Whip the oil together with the remaining ingredients. Pour over the rice. Marinate for 2 hours refrigerated. Place the washed lettuce leaves on chilled plates. Top with salad. Serve.

Serves 6

Mexican Vegetable Soup

Ingredients:

3 tbsp	45 ml	butter
1	1	finely diced onion
2	2	finely diced celery stalks
2	2	finely diced carrots
3 tbsp	45 ml	flour
2 cups	500 ml	sliced okra
4 cups	1 L	vegetable stock
2 cups	500 ml	peeled, seeded and diced tomatoes
¼ tsp	1 ml	oregano
¼ tsp	1 ml	thyme
¼ tsp	1 ml	basil
¼ tsp	1 ml	garlic powder
¼ tsp	1 ml	onion powder
1 tsp	5 ml	salt
½ tsp	3 ml	black pepper

Preparation:

In a large sauce pan heat the butter. Add the vegetables and sauté until tender. Sprinkle with flour and cook for 2 minutes.

Add okra and vegetable stock. Simmer for 30 minutes. Add the tomatoes and seasonings, continue to simmer for 15 minutes. Serve very hot.

Serves 6

Mexico

Panamanian Barbequed Flank Steak

Ingredients:

2 ¼ lbs	1 kg	flank steak
½ tsp	3 ml	cayenne pepper
½ tsp	3 ml	oregano leaves
½ tsp	3 ml	thyme leaves
½ tsp	3 ml	crushed rosemary
½ tsp	3 ml	basil leaves
½ tsp	3 ml	onion powder
½ tsp	3 ml	salt
1 tbsp	15 ml	chili powder
2	2	minced garlic cloves
3 tbsp	45 ml	lemon juice
3 tbsp	45 ml	lime juice

Sauce:

½ cup	125 ml	tomato catsup
¼ cup	60 ml	molasses
1	1	minced medium onion
¼ cup	60 ml	packed brown sugar
1 tsp	5 ml	chili powder
2 tsp	10 ml	Worcestershire sauce
½ tsp	3 ml	salt
½ tsp	3 ml	thyme leaves
½ tsp	3 ml	oregano leaves
½ tsp	3 ml	basil leaves

¼ tsp	1 ml	paprika
¼ tsp	1 ml	onion powder
¼ tsp	1 ml	garlic powder
¼ tsp	1 ml	Tabasco™ sauce

Preparation:

Trim the steak of any excess fat.

Blend the seasonings with the garlic and rub into the steaks. Place into a large pan. Pour the fruit juices over and allow to marinate for 1 hour.

Thoroughly blend the sauce ingredients together. Pour over the steak and continue to marinate for an additional 2 hours.

Broil over medium heat to desired doneness; brushing frequently with the marinade. Serve with rice and tomatoes.

Serves 6

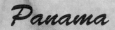

Arroz Con Leche

Ingredients:

1 ½ cups	375 ml	brown sugar
4 cup	1 L	milk
1 tsp	5 ml	vanilla
1 cups	250 ml	raw rice
1 tsp	5 ml	ground cinnamon

Preparation:

Dissolve the sugar in the milk. Add the vanilla and bring to a boil. Add the rice reduce the heat and simmer covered for 35-40 minutes. Pour into serving bowls. Cool. Chill. Serve with a sprinkling of cinnamon.

Garnish with toasted almonds and raisins.

Serves 6

Fun Food Facts

Arroz Con Leche

Arroz Con Leche is excellent served with fresh fruit such as, mango, pineapple, papaya, kiwi, banana and others. Use a medium grain white rice, never use converted rice in this dish.

Chilean Potato Salad

Ingredients:

8	8	large potatoes
¼ lb	115 g	bacon
1 tbsp	15 ml	safflower oil
2 tbsp	30 ml	vinegar
3	3	chopped green onions
5	5	diced radishes
2	2	diced celery stalks
1 cup	250 ml	Blue Cheese Mayonnaise
1 tbsp	15 ml	mustard
3	3	chopped hard cooked eggs
1 tsp	5 ml	salt
½ tsp	3 ml	white pepper
2	2	red bell peppers, roasted, peeled diced

Preparation:

Pare and dice the potatoes. Place in a pot and boil until tender. Drain and rinse under cold water to cool.

Dice the bacon and fry until crisp. Drain and reserve.

Place the potatoes in a large mixing bowl. Sprinkle with the oil and vinegar. Stir in the onions, radishes and celery.

In a small mixing bowl, blend the mayonnaise, mustard, eggs, salt and pepper. Fold ½ the mixture and the bacon into the potatoes. Transfer into a casserole dish. Spread the balance of the mixture on to the top. Broil in the oven until golden brown. Garnish with red peppers. Serve.

Blue Cheese Mayonnaise

Ingredients:

½ tsp	3 ml	prepared mustard
½ tsp	3 ml	granulated sugar
⅛ tsp	pinch	cayenne pepper
1	1	egg yolk
⅔ cup	170 ml	olive oil
1 tbsp	15 ml	lemon juice
½ cup	125 ml	crumbled blue cheese

Preparation:

Blend the mustard, sugar and pepper together.

Beat in the egg yolk thoroughly. Beat in the oil a few drops at a time until the sauce is very thick. Add the lemon juice blending completely. Fold in the blue cheese.

Chile

Mexican Corn Chowder

Ingredients:

¼ cup	60 ml	butter
1	1	diced Spanish onion
4	4	medium potatoes, peeled and diced
2	2	diced, large carrots
3	3	diced, celery stalks
1	1	minced, large garlic clove
4 cups	1 L	corn kernels
¼ cup	60 ml	flour
1 tbsp	15 ml	grated ginger
½ tsp	3 ml	cayenne pepper
½ tsp	3 ml	oregano leaves
½ tsp	3 ml	thyme leaves
½ tsp	3 ml	crushed rosemary
½ tsp	3 ml	basil leaves
½ tsp	3 ml	onion powder
½ tsp	3 ml	salt
4 cups	1 L	chicken stock (see page 210)
2 cups	500 ml	cream
½ cup	125 ml	peas

Preparation:

Heat the butter in a large kettle. Add the onion, potatoes, carrots, celery and garlic. Sauté until onions are translucent. Add the corn and continue to sauté for 5 minutes. Stir in the flour and cook over low for 2 minutes.

Stir in the ginger, seasoning and chicken stock. Simmer for 30 minutes. Add the cream and peas; continue to cook for 5 minutes. Serve at once, very hot.

Serves 6

Fun Food Facts

Limited Cheese Glossary (cont'd)

Liederkranz Brand:
a soft cheese with a strong flavour and rectangular shape. It has a russet surface and a creamy yellow interior. It can be used on cheese trays for desserts.

Limburger:
a semi-soft cheese comes in cubical and rectangular shapes or jars. It has a greyish brown surface and creamy interior. It can be used in sandwiches or in general cooking. It may also be found processed.

Monterey Jack:
a semi-soft circular cake, 10" (25 cm) in diameter, and 2" (5 cm) in height. It has a greyish white surface and a white interior. It can be used in cooking desserts.

Mozzarella:
a semi-soft cheese, cream color with a light nut flavour.

Muenster (mun-stir):
a hard cheese in sausage-link shape with a light brown surface lined with rope marks and a light yellow interior. It has cookery uses.

Mysost:
a semi-hard cubical, light brown cylinder of a cheese that has semi-sweet taste. It has cookery uses.

Costa Rican Bean Soup

Ingredients:

⅓ cup	80 ml	pinto beans
⅓ cup	80 ml	black beans
⅓ cup	80 ml	Flor de Mayo red beans
¼ lb	120 g	diced bacon
2	2	finely diced onions
1	1	finely diced carrot
4 cups	1 L	chicken broth (see page 210)
½ tsp	3 ml	marjoram leaves
½ tsp	3 ml	thyme leaves
½ tsp	3 ml	salt
½ tsp	3 ml	pepper
½ tsp	3 ml	paprika
pinch	pinch	cayenne pepper
1 tbsp	15 ml	chili powder
5 drops	5 drops	Tabasco™ sauce
½ tsp	3 ml	Worcestershire sauce
1	1	bay leaf
⅓ cup	80 ml	sherry
½ cup	125 ml	sour cream
¼ cup	60 ml	finely diced red onion

Preparation:

Soak the beans for 8 hours or overnight in water.

In a large pot or Dutch oven, fry the bacon. Add the vegetables and sauté until tender. Add the beans, chicken broth, seasonings, Tabasco,™ Worcestershire and bay leaf. Cover and simmer for 1½ hours. Discard bay leaf.

Purée the soup in small batches in a food processor or blender. Return to the pot and reheat. Add sherry.

Place in soup bowls and top with sour cream. Garnish with red onion.

Serves 6

 Fun Food Facts

Beans

Beans, legumes or pulses, an ancient discovery for a meatless protein. Daniel, when given a challenge, chose a diet of pulse and water over a diet of meat and wine. The result was men who were stronger and healthier, over a very short period of time. Beans are a high source of vitamin A and C and very rich in protein. Eight ounces of black beans (turtle beans) has 205 calories, 14 grams of protein, 37 grams of carbohydrates, 1 gram of fat, 0 milligrams of sodium, 0 milligrams of cholesterol.

Arroz Con Pollo

Ingredients:

½ tsp	3 ml	each of oregano, thyme, basil
1	1	scotch bonnet pepper, dried, crushed
2	2	minced garlic cloves
1 tsp	5 ml	salt
1 tbsp	15 ml	olive oil
1 tsp	5 ml	vinegar
2 ½ lbs	1 kg	chicken, cut up
¼ cup	60 ml	butter
⅔ cup	160 ml	chopped bacon
1	1	diced, large Spanish onion
1	1	diced green bell pepper
1	1	diced red bell pepper
⅓ cup	80 ml	chopped pitted green olives
1 tsp	5 ml	capers
2	2	tomatoes, peeled, seeded and diced
1 cup	250 ml	crushed tomatoes
2 cups	500 ml	peas
1 cup	250 ml	raw rice
3 cups	750 ml	chicken broth (see page 210)
½ cup	125 ml	pimento, sliced

Preparation:

Crush together the oregano, thyme, basil, scotch bonnet, garlic and salt with the oil and vinegar. Rub onto the chicken.

Heat the butter in large skillet and brown the chicken. Add the bacon and continue to cook for 10 minutes. Add the onions, peppers, olives and capers. Sauté for 5 minutes. Add the tomatoes, peas, rice and chicken broth. Cover and simmer for 30 minutes.

Transfer to a serving dish, garnish with the pimento and serve.

Serves 6

 Fun Food Facts

Capers

A caper is a small bud of the flowering European caper bush, usually found in a brine solution of vinegar and salt. Usually blended in sauce for serving with meats, most commonly lamb, it is a key ingredient in tartar sauce for fish and is often used in steak tartar and Caesar salad. Often the pickled caper is confused with a pickled nasturtium seeds which is larger than the much smaller caper bud.

Leche Asada

Ingredients:

3 ¾ cups	940 ml	milk
1 ¾ cups	450 ml	brown sugar
5	5	eggs
4	4	egg yolks
1 tbsp	15 ml	vanilla

Preparation:

Scald the milk and allow to cool 20 minutes.

In a sauce pan, melt ¾ cup (180 ml) of sugar and cook until dark brown stirring constantly. Take care not to scorch. Pour into a warm mold covering the bottom and the sides.

Beat the eggs and egg yolks with the remaining sugar. Slowly whip in the milk and vanilla. Pour into the sugar lined mold. Place mold in a second pan fill halfway with hot water. Bake for 45 minutes in a 325°F (160°F) oven. Cool. Chill.

To serve, invert on to a rimmed serving platter.

Serves 6

Latin Favourite Drinks

Brezzer

Ingredients:

2 cups	500 ml	honeydew melon
1 ½ cups	375 ml	pineapple chunks
1 cup	250 ml	apple juice

Preparation:

Freeze the melon and pineapple. Once frozen, place into a food processor with the apple juice and purée. Serve at once.

Serves 2

Hot Brezzer

Ingredients:

¼ cup	60 ml	brown sugar
⅓ cup	80 ml	cinnamon sticks
8	8	cloves
3 cups	750 ml	pineapple juice
3 cups	750 ml	white wine

Preparation:

Place all the ingredients in a sauce pan. Bring to a boil. Reduce heat and simmer for 10 minutes. Discard the cinnamon sticks and cloves. Serve very hot in mugs.

British Honduran Papaya Salsa Shrimp

Ingredients:

2 ¼ lbs	1 kg	large shrimp, peeled and deveined
1 tsp	5 ml	garlic granules
2 tsp	10 ml	black pepper
½ tsp	3 ml	cayenne pepper
½ tsp	3 ml	oregano leaves
½ tsp	3 ml	thyme leaves
½ tsp	3 ml	crushed rosemary
½ tsp	3 ml	basil leaves
½ tsp	3 ml	onion powder
½ tsp	3 ml	salt
2 tbsp	30 ml	olive oil
1	1	diced Spanish onion
2	2	minced garlic cloves
1 tbsp	15 ml	minced ginger
4	4	large tomatoes, roasted, seeded
2	2	minced serrano chilies
¾ cup	190 ml	coconut milk
2 cups	500 ml	diced papaya
1 cup	250 ml	diced pineapple

Preparation:

Soak bamboo skewers in water for 20 minutes. Skewer the shrimp.

Mix the garlic, pepper and other seasonings together and sprinkle on the shrimp.

In a sauce pan heat the oil. Add the onion, garlic and ginger. Sauté until onions are translucent. Add the tomatoes, chilies, coconut milk, papaya and pineapple. Reduce heat and simmer until very thick. Transfer to a food processor and purée.

Broil the shrimp for 2½ to 3 minutes per side. Serve with the salsa on the side.

Serves 6

 Fun Food Facts

Papaya

Among the more famous of the discoveries of Latin America, papaya was first discovered in the Caribbean. Now grown the world over in tropic climates. Papayas are melon like fruit that have ability to enhance flavours. A marinate made of papaya was once used to tenderize inferior beef by a now defunct national restaurant chain, it is the enzyme (papain) in many chemical food tenderizers. Papaya is excellent when served fresh. It has a yellow flesh and a melon like taste.

Europe

Someone once said, "there is nothing sadder than a missed opportunity." Nowhere is that more true when one misses the opportunities of experiencing the flavours and cuisines of another country. Nowhere are the culinary opportunities greater than the many countries of the European continent.

If one were to begin their journey in the north and travel south, it would literally take a life time to experience all the varieties of the cuisines of Europe. Every country has contributed immensely to enhancing their cuisines.

Cuisine as we know it today, has its roots in Italy and France. Prior to their intervention food service was basically unrefined and certainly lacking in flavour and very unappetizing. But when a 14 year old girl was given in marriage to a 14 year old heir of the French throne, cuisine and the service thereof changed forever. Catherine de' Medici would travel from Italy with a army of Italian chef's who exchanged their art with the nobility of France. Soon it was very stylish and you were considered very chic if your chef hailed from Italy. Catherine's chefs would introduce to the French refinements for the table, as cheese from Parma, artichoke hearts, sweets such as zabaglione, gelato and other Venetian delights.

The French chefs would soon surpass the Italians, refining their creations, introducing rich sauces, cultivated fish and seafood, becoming the teachers and freely passing their knowledge on to any who would come seeking it. Come they did and still do. France still holds in the hearts and minds of most cooking professionals or otherwise as the place to travel to for refining their skills in the culinary arts.

Still there is much more to Europe than Italy and France. Spain introduced the continent to most of the foods that they enjoy today through the discoveries of their great explorers such as Columbus and Cortez. Germany has brought incredible wines, creams and cheeses into the culinary experience and of course the global celebration of Oktoberfest. This began simply as a party of well wishers for Prince Ludwig of Bavaria on his engagement. The marriage was a success but not nearly as much as the celebration for the party continues with much of the festivities as they had nearly 200 years ago. Great food, great fun and really good beer. From the North seas came fish and seafoods, from Russia caviar, wheat and great beef.

Today, you and your family may continue to experience outstanding cuisine just venturing within the pages of this chapter. Enjoy dishes like Lapin Forestiere (France), Vandermint Torte (Holland), Minestra Di Due Colori (Italy), Nalesniki z Kury z Grzybami "Polish Style Crêpes" (Poland), Schmorbraten (Germany) and many others.

Souvlakia

Ingredients:

1 ½ lbs	680 g	Boneless lamb
1	1	finely diced small onion
2	2	minced garlic cloves
¼ cup	60 ml	olive oil
1 tbsp	15 ml	lemon juice
2 tsp	10 ml	Worcestershire sauce
2 tbsp	30 ml	chopped parsley
2 tsp	10 ml	oregano leaves
1 tsp	5 ml	salt
¼ tsp	1 ml	ground pepper
2	2	firm, large hot house tomatoes

Preparation:

Coarse dice the lamb into 1½" (35 mm) cubes. Place into a large mixing bowl.

In a small mixing bowl combine the onion, garlic, oil, lemon juice, Worcestershire, parsley, oregano, salt and pepper. Pour over the lamb and allow to marinate for 2-3 hours.

Coarsely dice the tomatoes (or use cherry tomatoes). Alternate lamb and tomatoes onto water soaked (20 minute soak) bamboo skewers.

Broil over medium coals for 10-15 minutes, brushing with the marinate.

Serves 6

Greece

Russian Chicken Cutlets
with Mushroom Sauce

Ingredients:

1 ½ lbs	675 g	boneless chicken breasts, enough for 6
2	2	eggs
¼ cup	60 ml	milk
½ cup	125 ml	flour
1 cup	250 ml	seasoned, fine bread crumbs
¼ cup	60 ml	safflower oil

Sauce:

3 tbsp	45 ml	butter
1 ½ cups	375 ml	sliced mushrooms
3 tbsp	45 ml	flour
1 ¼ cups	310 ml	chicken broth
1 ¼ cups	310 ml	half & half cream
½ cup	125 ml	freshly grated Parmesan cheese

Preparation:

Preheat the oven to 350°F (180°C).

Flatten and tenderize each breast into a cutlet with a meat mallet.

Blend the eggs into the milk. Dust each cutlet with flour; dip into the egg wash and dredge with bread crumbs.

Heat the oil in a large skillet and fry each cutlet to golden brown on each side. Place on a baking sheet. Bake for 10 minutes. Serve with sauce.

Sauce:

Heat the butter in a sauce pan. Add the mushrooms and sauté until tender. Sprinkle with flour and cook for 2 minutes over low heat.

Stir in the chicken broth and cream. Reduce heat and simmer until thickened. Stir in the cheese and simmer for 2 more minutes.

Serves 6

Chicken Broth or Stock

Ingredients:

2 ¼ lbs	1 kg	meaty chicken bones
10 cups	2.5 L	cold water
2	2	coarsely chopped celery stalks
2	2	coarsely chopped large carrots
1	1	coarsely chopped onion
1	1	bouquet garni (see page 326)
1 tsp	5 ml	salt

Preparation:

Place the bones in a large kettle or Dutch oven.

Add the water and remaining ingredients; bring to a simmer. Simmer uncovered for 3-4 hours. Skim any impurities or grease that may rise to the top.

Remove the meat (reserve and use as required). Discard bones, bouquet garni and vegetables. Strain through a cheesecloth or fine sieve.

Chill the stock and remove any fat from the surface.

Allow stock to chill for 24 hours before using. Use for soups and sauces or as required.

Yields 6 cups (1.5 L)

Russia

Dutch Apple Torte

Ingredients:

½ cup	125 ml	unsalted butter
1 cup	250 ml	granulated sugar
2	2	eggs
1 ¼ cups	310 ml	apple sauce
2 cups	500 ml	flour
1 tsp	5 ml	baking soda
¾ tsp	4 ml	salt
¾ tsp	4 ml	cinnamon
¾ tsp	4 ml	cloves
¾ tsp	4 ml	nutmeg
¾ tsp	4 ml	allspice
2 ½ cups	625 ml	apples, pared, cored, diced
1 cup	250 ml	seedless golden raisins
1 cup	250 ml	walnut pieces

Sauce:

4	4	eggs
¼ cup	60 ml	sugar
⅛ tsp	pinch	salt
1 ½ cups	375 ml	scalded milk
½ cup	125 ml	apple juice concentrate

Preparation:

Preheat the oven to 350°F (180°C).

Cream the butter with the sugar until very light.

Add the eggs, one at a time. Fold in the applesauce. Sift in the flour, baking soda and spices and add to cream mixture. Gently fold in the apples, raisins and walnut pieces. Pour batter into a 9" x 13" (22cm x 32cm) square cake pan.

Bake for 45 minutes or until an inserted toothpick comes out clean. Remove from oven and cool slightly. Serve warm with the custard sauce.

Sauce:

Beat the eggs with the sugar and salt. Place on top of a double boiler and gradually beat in the scalded milk and apple juice concentrate. Cook for 8-10 minutes until thick, stirring constantly. Cool to room temperature.

Serves 10

Holland

Raspberry Cream Peppered Veal Chops

Ingredients:

3 cups	750 ml	fresh raspberries
¼ cup	60 ml	granulated sugar
¼ cup	60 ml	heavy cream
6-6 oz	6-180 g	veal chops
¼ cup	60 ml	crushed black peppercorns
¼ cup	60 ml	butter

Rice:

1 ½ cups	375 ml	long grain rice
4 cups	1 L	apple juice
¾ cup	180 ml	chopped pitted dates
½ cup	125 ml	toasted sliced almonds

Preparation:

Process 2½ cups (625 ml) of the raspberries in a food processor until smooth. Using a fine sieve, strain raspberries into a sauce pan to remove the seeds, add the sugar. Heat to a boil. Reduce the heat and simmer until liquid yields ½ cup (125 ml). Whip in the cream.

While raspberry juice simmers, pat the peppercorns into the veal chops.

Heat the butter in a large skillet and sauté the veal chops to the desired doneness.

Plate the chops. Pour sauce over the chops garnishing with the remaining raspberries. Serve with the rice.

Rice:

Bring the rice to a boil in the apple juice. Cover and reduce to a simmer. Simmer until liquid has been absorbed.

Stir in the dates and almonds. Serve at once.

Serves 6

 Fun Food Facts

Pepper

The hot sweet spicy taste of pepper cannot be resisted the world over. Some of the finest pepper comes from the island off the African coast of Madagascar. Other good grades can be found in Hungary, Mexico, Brazil and India.

White pepper is less strong. It is derived from the ripe berries outer skin being removed and the seed cleaned and dried. Black pepper is actually the green berries left to dry as they are, resulting in the strong flavour being more bitter than white. Green peppercorns are the unripe berries picked fresh and then tinned. Some can be found dried. They give a special flavour to cuisine sauces for broiled, grilled and boiled meats. Cayenne pepper is a very hot spice derived from capsicums (chili). Use sparingly.

 *Holland*

Beef Croquettes

Ingredients:

2 tbsp	30 ml	butter
4 tbsp	60 ml	flour
1 cup	250 ml	milk
2 cups	500 ml	cooked lean ground beef, fat drained
½ tsp	3 ml	salt
½ tsp	3 ml	paprika
½ tsp	3 ml	chili powder
¼ tsp	1 ml	pepper
1 tsp	5 ml	Worcestershire sauce
2 tsp	10 ml	soy sauce
1 tsp	5 ml	finely chopped parsley
1	1	egg
2 tbsp	30 ml	water
½ cup	125 ml	seasoned flour
1 ½ cups	375 ml	fine bread crumbs
1 cup	250 ml	safflower oil

Salad:

10 oz	300 g	wash and trimmed spinach
8	8	large, sliced mushrooms
1 cup	250 ml	grated Gruyère cheese
1 cup	250 ml	red seedless grapes
1 ½ cups	375 ml	fresh peach slices
¼ cup	60 ml	toasted almonds
1 cup	250 ml	mayonnaise
½ cup	125 ml	orange juice concentrate
¼ tsp	1 ml	ground cinnamon

Preparation:

Heat the butter in a sauce pan. Add the flour and cook over low heat for 2 minutes. Stir in the milk and simmer into a very thick sauce. Stirring constantly, stir in the beef, seasonings, Worcestershire, soy and parsley. Cool to room temperature. Shape into equal size patties.

Blend the egg with the water. Dust each patty with flour; dip into the egg, and coat with bread crumbs.

Heat the oil in a large skillet, fry the patties to golden brown on each side. Serve.

Salad:

Tear the spinach into bite size pieces and place on chilled serving plates. Top with mushrooms, cheese, grapes, peach slices and almonds.

In a mixing bowl, blend together the mayonnaise, juice concentrate and cinnamon. Serve on the side of the salad.

Serves 4

Holland

Baklava

Ingredients:

10	10	sheets phyllo pastry
¾ cup	180 ml	melted butter
1 ½ cups	375 ml	slivered almonds
1 cup	250 ml	honey
¼ cup	60 ml	lemon juice
¼ cup	60 ml	orange juice
½ cup	125 ml	granulated sugar
2 tsp	10 ml	cinnamon

Preparation:

Preheat the oven to 350°F (180°C).

Lay one sheet of pastry on a greased pastry sheet. Brush with butter and sprinkle with almonds. Repeat this process 7 more times. Brush the remaining phyllo layers with butter and place onto the final layer. Score the pastry layers into triangles. Bake for 60-65 minutes.

Combine the honey, juices, sugar and cinnamon in a sauce pan. Bring to boil and boil for 3 minutes. Pour ½ over warm baked baklava.

Slice the pastry and pour the remaining liquid over allowing the liquid to soak into the pastry before serving.

Greece

Bogrács Gulyás

Ingredients:

3 tbsp	45 ml	butter
1	1	sliced onions
2	2	minced garlic cloves
2 tsp	10 ml	salt
1 tsp	5 ml	pepper
1 tbsp	15 ml	paprika
2 ¼ lbs	1 kg	cubed veal
3 tbsp	45 ml	flour
4 cups	1 L	hot beef broth (see page 42)
1	1	bouquet garni*
1 ½ cups	375 ml	diced potatoes
1	1	sprig of fresh marjoram
1 cup	250 ml	sour cream
¼ cup	60 ml	tomato paste
1 tsp	5 ml	caraway seeds

Preparation:

In a large kettle or Dutch oven heat the butter. Add the onions and cook until brown.

Add the garlic, salt, pepper and paprika together. Dust the veal with the seasonings and add to the pot. Cook until brown. Sprinkle with flour and continue to cook for 3 minutes over low heat.

Add the broth and bouquet garni and simmer for 1 ¼ hours.

Add the potatoes and marjoram. Continue to simmer for an additional 30 minutes. Discard the bouquet garni. Stir in the sour cream, tomato paste and caraway seeds. Simmer for 5 minutes longer. Serve at once.

Serves 6

 Fun Food Facts

* A bouquet garni is a bundle of herbs tied in a cheese cloth (j-cloth works great). It will consist of your choice of all or several of the following: Parsley, bay leaf, thyme, marjoram, sage, basil and cloves.

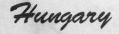

Hungary

Gravlax

Ingredients:

1 ½ lbs	675 g	fresh salmon (centre cut)
8 oz	225 g	dill (fresh only)
½ cup	125 ml	granulated sugar
¼ cup	60 ml	rock salt
1 tbsp	15 ml	cracked black peppercorns
1 tbsp	15 ml	cracked white peppercorns
1	1	lemon sliced

Sauce:

¼ cup	60 ml	Dijon mustard
3 tbsp	45 ml	granulated sugar
2 tbsp	30 ml	white wine vinegar
¼ cup	60 ml	safflower oil
1 tbsp	15 ml	lemon juice
2 tbsp	30 ml	fresh chopped dill

Preparation:

Bone the salmon; retain two equal size fillets.

Coarse chop the dill. Crush the sugar, salt and peppercorns together.

Place one fillet skin side down on a large platter. Coat with half the crushed salt mixture. Cover with the chopped dill. Coat with the remaining crushed salt mixture. Lay the second fillet over the mixture and cover tightly with plastic wrap.

Refrigerate under weight (place a small brick on top) for 72 hours. Remove the plastic wrap and excess moisture every 12 hours. Rewrap and continue to refrigerate.

When marination is complete, lay the fish, skin side down and scrape away the salt and dill. Thinly slice the fish. Serve with the lemon and sauce.

Sauce:

In a small mixing bowl blend all the ingredients thoroughly.

Fun Food Facts

Salt

Once a form of wages for a Roman soldier, salt is now prized for its culinary value. There are five major types of salt used in culinary arts; common table salt, sea salt, kosher salt, rock salt, and a spice blend know as seasoned salt. Common salt is salt which comes from mines. Sea salt is exactly that. Salt obtained from the sea and oceans around the world. Salt Lake City in Utah also supplies excellent salt. Kosher salt is salt used by Orthodox Jews. It is a valued addition to any meats as it will cling to the food it is processed with. Rock salt is used in the making of ice creams. Seasoned salt is used or seasoning many differing dishes. It is a blend of salt, peppers, paprika, chili pepper and various other herbs and spices.

Greek Salad

Ingredients:

4	4	large hot house tomatoes
1	1	large Spanish onion
1	1	small English cucumber, pared
2	2	green bell peppers
24	24	mushrooms, quartered
24	24	black olives
1 cup	250 ml	Feta cheese
½ cup	125 ml	olive oil
2 tbsp	30 ml	lemon juice
2 tbsp	30 ml	white wine vinegar
1 tbsp	15 ml	oregano leaves
2	2	minced garlic cloves
1 tsp	5 ml	salt
½ tsp	3 ml	cracked black pepper

Preparation:

Chop the vegetables into a large dice and place into a large mixing bowl with the olives and Feta cheese.

In a small mixing bowl combine the oil, lemon juice, vinegar, oregano, garlic, salt and pepper. Pour over the salad and allow to marinate for 30 minutes before serving.

Serves 6

Soupa Avgholemona

Ingredients:

4 cups	1 L	chicken stock (see page 210)
1 cup	250 ml	long grain rice
2	2	egg yolks
1 tsp	5 ml	grated lemon rind
3 tbsp	45 ml	lemon juice

Preparation:

Place the stock in a sauce pan. Stir in the rice and cook until the rice is tender.

Stir the egg yolks together with the lemon rind, juice and a little warm stock. Remove soup from heat. Whip in the egg. Serve at once with Greek Salad.

Serves 6

Greece

Moussaka

Ingredients:

⅔ cup	170 ml	melted butter
1	1	minced medium onion
1	1	minced garlic clove
1 ½ lbs	680 g	ground lamb
2 cups	500 ml	crushed tomatoes
2 tsp	10 ml	salt
1 tsp	5 ml	paprika
1 tsp	5 ml	basil
½ tsp	3 ml	each of oregano leaves, thyme leaves, black pepper, cinnamon
3 tbsp	45 ml	red wine
1 tbsp	15 ml	cornstarch
1 ¼ lbs	565 g	eggplants
⅔ cup	170 ml	Feta cheese
⅔ cup	170 ml	Swiss cheese

Sauce:

4 tbsp	60 ml	butter
4 tbsp	60 ml	flour
2 cups	500 ml	milk
½ tsp	3 ml	salt
½ tsp	3 ml	white pepper
pinch	pinch	nutmeg

Preparation:

Place 2 tbsp (30 ml) of butter into a Dutch oven. Add the onion and garlic and sauté until tender. Add the lamb and continue to cook until brown. Add the tomatoes, salt and seasonings. Reduce heat and simmer for 30 minutes.

Mix the cornstarch with the wine and add to the sauce. Simmer until thick. Remove from heat.

Cut the eggplant into 1½" (35 mm) slices, lengthwise. Place on a broiling pan. Brush with the remaining butter and broil for 4 minutes in a preheated oven.

Grease a large casserole dish. Alternate layers of eggplant and lamb sauce. Sprinkle with the cheeses. Bake in a preheated 350°F (180°C) oven for 30 minutes.

Sauce:

Melt the butter in a sauce pan. Add flour and stir into a paste (roux). Cook for 2 minutes over low heat.

Add the milk and stir. Simmer until thickened. Add the seasonings and simmer for 2 additional minutes.

Pour sauce over the eggplant casserole. Bake in a preheated 350°F (180°C) oven for an additional 35 minutes.

Serves 6

Greece

Hungarian Goulash Soup

Ingredients:

½ lb	225 g	cooked beef roast
¼ lb	120 g	cooked pork roast
¼ lb	120 g	smoked ham
3 tbsp	45 ml	butter
3 tbsp	45 ml	oil
1	1	diced Spanish onion
1	1	diced celery stalk
1	1	diced red bell pepper
3 tbsp	45 ml	flour
2 cups	500 ml	peeled, seeded and diced tomatoes
6 cups	1.5 L	rich beef stock (see page 42)
1 tsp	5 ml	caraway seeds

Preparation:

Slice the meats then shred.

Heat the butter and oil together in a large sauce pan. Add the vegetables and sauté until tender. Sprinkle with flour and cook for 5 minutes or until the flour caramelizes.

Stir in the tomatoes and stock. Add the meats and simmer gently for 90 minutes. Sprinkle with caraway and simmer for 5 minutes longer. Serve very hot.

Serves 8

Hungary

Chicken Hotel Style

Ingredients:

4-8 oz	4-225 g	chicken breasts, skin on
12 oz	360 g	highly seasoned sausage meat
4 tbsp	60 ml	melted butter
8 oz	225 g	sliced wild mushrooms
3 tbsp	45 ml	flour
1 ½ cups	375 ml	veal stock (see page 42)
½ cup	125 ml	white wine
¼ tsp	1 ml	Hungarian paprika
¼ tsp	1 ml	salt
¼ tsp	1 ml	white pepper
¼ tsp	1 ml	basil

Preparation:

Preheat the oven to 350°F (180°C).

Carefully run a paring knife under the skin of the chicken to lift it from the meat. Be sure not to cut through. Stuff equal amounts of sausage meat between the chicken meat and the skin. Brush with butter. Place the chicken in a large casserole dish and bake for 15 minutes.

In a sauce pan place the remaining butter and sauté the mushrooms. Spoon the mushrooms over the chicken and continue to bake for 15 minutes.

Sprinkle the flour into the sauce pan and cook over low heat for 5 minutes. Add the stock, wine and seasonings. Simmer for 5 minutes. Pour over the chicken and continue to bake for an additional 10 minutes.

Remove the chicken to serving plates. Smother with the mushroom sauce. Serve with root vegetables.

Serves 4

 Fun Food Facts

Chicken

Chicken is the most popular of land meats and has replaced beef as the meat in demand not only for versatility but also for nutritional concerns. Four ounces of cooked chicken contains: 215 calories, 32.8 grams protein, 0 grams of carbohydrates, 8.4 milligrams of fat, 101 milligrams of cholesterol, 98 milligrams of sodium, 0 grams of fibre.

Choose your chicken according to the recipe, need and budget. Squab; a very young chicken, is average size 1 ½ lbs (675 g). Broil, grill, roast or deep fry. Broiler; the most common size of chicken available. 1½-2¼ lbs (675 g - 1 kg). Boil, grill, roast, deep fry. Use the breasts of the broiler for any dish requiring chicken breasts. Fryer: an older chicken and can be a little tougher, 2¼-3 lbs (1 kg-1.5 kg). Broil, braise, stew, roast. Roaster; over 3 lbs (1.5 kg) Use for braising, poaching or roasting. Fowl; the oldest and largest of the commercial birds. Use for braising or stewing. Capon; a male chicken that has been neutered. 4½-6¾ lbs (2-3 kg). A very flavourful chicken excellent for stuffing and roasting.

France

Polish Chocolate Cake

Ingredients:

2 tbsp	30 ml	cocoa powder
2 cups	500 ml	pastry flour
1 tsp	5 ml	baking soda
¼ tsp	1 ml	salt
½ cup	125 ml	butter
1 ½ cups	375 ml	granulated sugar
2	2	eggs
4 oz	120 g	melted, semi-sweet chocolate
1 cup	250 ml	buttermilk

Frosting:

8 oz	240 g	semi-sweet chocolate
1 cup	250 ml	heavy cream
2 tsp	10 ml	melted butter
2	2	egg yolks
4 cups	1 L	confectioners sugar
1 tsp	5 ml	vanilla

Preparation:

Sift the cocoa, flour, baking soda and salt together, 3 times. Cream the butter and sugar together until very light. Add the eggs, one at a time. Add the chocolate. Incorporate the flour and buttermilk in thirds.

Pour into 2-8" (20 cm) round greased and floured cake pans. Bake in a preheated 350°F (180°C) oven for 35-40 minutes. Cool for 10 minutes. Turn out on a cooling rack. Cool and frost.

Frosting:

In a double boiler melt the chocolate and transfer to a mixing bowl. Blend in the remaining ingredients beating at medium speed until very smooth and light.

 Fun Food Facts

Chocolate

White chocolate, delicious, creamy, melt in your mouth texture, but there is a problem, white chocolate is not really chocolate. White chocolate is a blend of confectioners sugar, flavoring and cocoa butter however at no time does it ever contain chocolate, sorry. However white chocolate can be used in most chocolate recipes with only a change in colour as the noticeable difference.

White chocolate is an American original creation by the Herbert Candy Mansion of Massachusetts. Chocolate would not keep during the hot summer days (before the days of air conditioning), so Herbert created a candy substance that would hold it's integrity in the heat and yet have the smooth melt in your mouth texture of chocolate. So use a good quality white chocolate with confidence, enjoy.

Swimming Crayfish

Ingredients:

Stock:

4 ½ lbs	2 kg	fish trimmings and bones
1	1	diced onion
3	3	large diced carrots
3	3	diced celery stalks
1	1	bouquet garni*
12 cups	3 L	water

Crayfish:

2 ¾ cups	680 ml	ground crayfish meat (reserve tail shells)
1 tbsp	15 ml	grated onion
1 tsp	5 ml	each of pepper, basil, thyme, paprika
1 tsp	5 ml	salt
3	3	egg whites
¼ cup	60 ml	peas
1 oz	30 g	sliced ham

Sauce:

3 tbsp	45 ml	butter
3 tbsp	45 ml	flour
2 cups	500 ml	fish broth
1 cup	250 ml	half & half cream
½ cup	125 ml	freshly grated Parmesan cheese

Preparation:

Stock:

Place the fish trimmings and bones into a large kettle or Dutch oven. Add the vegetables, bouquet garni and water. Heat gently without boiling. Simmer for 2 hours. While stock simmers remove any impurities that may rise to the top.

Strain through a fine sieve. Strain again a second time through a cheesecloth. Return to a pot and bring to a boil. Reduce to 4 cups (1 L).

Crayfish:

In a mixing bowl combine the meat, onion, seasonings and egg white. Press through a fine sieve and shape into small oval shapes. Place 2 peas as eyes; a small piece of ham along the back and insert a reserved shell for the tail.

Place 2 cups (500 ml) of reserved broth in a small pot. Place the crayfish on a plate and insert into the pot so that no moisture gets on the plate. Steam the crayfish for 10 minutes; reserve hot.

Sauce:

Heat the butter in a sauce pan. Add the flour and cook for 2 minutes over low heat. Stir in the broth and cream. Reduce heat and simmer until thickened. Stir in the cheese and simmer for 2 more minutes.

Cover a large serving platter with the sauce. Arrange the crayfish on the sauce. Serve.

Serves 6

* Bouquet Garni for soup is: 2 sprigs fresh thyme, 2 sprigs marjoram, 6 peppercorns, 1 bay leaf, 6 sprigs parsley, 1 leek, tied together in a cheesecloth (J-Cloth works well).

Polish Pork & Cheese Cutlets

Ingredients:

1 lb	454 g	boneless pork loin
½ tsp	3 ml	salt
½ tsp	3 ml	pepper
½ tsp	3 ml	paprika
½ tsp	3 ml	thyme
8	8	slices of thinly sliced Gruyère cheese
¼ cup	60 ml	milk
2	2	eggs
¼ cup	60 ml	flour
½ cup	125 ml	fine dry seasoned bread crumbs
¼ cup	60 ml	oil
3 tbsp	45 ml	butter
3 tbsp	45 ml	flour
1 ¼ cups	310 ml	chicken broth (see page 210)
1 ¼ cups	310 ml	half & half cream
½ cup	125 ml	freshly grated Parmesan cheese

Preparation:

Preheat the oven to 350°F (180°C).

Cut the pork loin into 4 even pieces. Place between two sheets of waxed paper and pound the meat very thin. Season with the seasonings. Place two slices of Gruyére cheese on each cutlet.

Blend the milk with the eggs. Dust the cutlets in the flour; dip into the egg mixture and dredge through the bread crumbs.

Heat the oil in a skillet and fry the cutlets, cheese side up, for 5 minutes. Transfer to a baking sheet and bake in the oven, cheese side up, for 15 minutes.

While the cutlets bake, heat the butter in a sauce pan. Add the flour and cook for 2 minutes over low heat.

Stir in the chicken broth and cream. Reduce heat and simmer until thickened. Stir in the Parmesan cheese and simmer for 2 more minutes.

Place the cutlets on serving plates and smother with sauce. Serve at once.

Serves 4

 Fun Food Facts

Cheese

Can you imagine a four ton cheese! If that's too small, how about a seventeen ton cheese! Personally, I can't image it either. Yet, the four ton cheese was displayed at the Toronto World's Fair at the turn of the century. The seventeen ton cheese was displayed at the World's Fair in 1964-65. It took 3,000 cows to produce 170,000 pounds of milk to produce the Cheddar. Free samples of it were handed out during the fair where so much was left remaining that it was cut into thousands of two-pound blocks and sold as souvenirs.

Minestra Di Due Colori

Ingredients:

1 cup	250 ml	milk
1 ½ tbsp	20 ml	butter
¼ tsp	1 ml	salt
⅛ tsp	pinch	nutmeg
1 ½ cups	375 ml	flour
1	1	egg
1	1	egg yolk
¼ cup	60 ml	freshly grated Parmesan cheese
4 oz	120 g	washed and trimmed spinach
8 cups	2 L	chicken stock (see page 210)

Preparation:

Heat the milk in a sauce pan. Add the butter, salt and nutmeg. Gradually add the flour working it into a smooth paste. Remove from the heat. Beat in the egg and the egg yolk. Stir in the Parmesan cheese. Divide the paste into two.

Steam the spinach. Purée the spinach in a food processor; drain well. Blend the spinach into 1 part of the paste.

Heat the chicken stock to a boil. Drop spoonfuls of green and yellow paste into the soup. Cook until the dumplings float. Serve very hot.

Serves 6

Italy

Italian Mocha Cake

Ingredients:

6	6	eggs, separated
1 cup	250 ml	granulated sugar
2 tbsp	30 ml	lemon juice
1 tsp	5 ml	grated lemon rind
1 tsp	5 ml	instant coffee
2 tbsp	30 ml	hot water
½ cup	125 ml	pastry flour
2 tsp	10 ml	baking powder
¼ tsp	1 ml	salt
16	16	chocolate covered coffee beans

Preparation:

Whip the egg yolks and beat in the sugar, lemon juice and rind. Dissolve the coffee in the hot water. Add to the egg yolks.

Sift together the flour, baking powder and salt. Fold into the egg mixture. Beat the egg whites until soft peaks form. Fold into batter. Do not over mix.

Pour into 2-9" (22 cm) greased and floured round cake pans. Bake in a preheated 350°F (180°C) oven for 20 minutes. Transfer to a cooling rack. Cool for 10 minutes before removing from pans. Cool completely.

Frost and fill with Mocha Cream Frosting. Decorate with chocolate covered coffee beans.

Mocha Cream Filling

Ingredients:

½ cup	125 ml	granulated sugar
¼ cup	60 ml	very strong black coffee
¼ cup	60 ml	coffee liqueur
3	3	egg yolks
½ cup+2 tbsp	155 ml	butter - unsalted

Preparation:

Heat the sugar, coffee and liqueur in a small sauce pan into a thick syrup. Whip the egg yolks. Whip the hot syrup in slowly.

Cream the butter until light and fluffy. Fold into the egg - coffee mixture. Use as required.

 Fun Food Facts

Coffee

A strong coffee blend - 2 tbsp (30 ml) of hot water with 1 tsp (5 ml) of instant coffee. A very strong blend - ¼ cup (60 ml) of boiling water with 1 tbsp (15 ml) of instant coffee. Use as required.

Italian Almond Sole

Ingredients:

Cous Cous:

3 tbsp	45 ml	butter
¼ cup	60 ml	finely diced red bell pepper
¼ cup	60 ml	finely diced green bell pepper
¼ cup	60 ml	finely diced yellow bell pepper
1	1	finely diced small onion
2	2	minced garlic cloves
¼ tsp	1 ml	each of cracked black pepper, white pepper, Hungarian paprika, basil leaves, thyme leaves
1 tsp	5 ml	salt
3 cups	750 ml	chicken broth (see page 210)
1 cup	250 ml	cous cous

Fish:

⅓ cup	80 ml	milk
2	2	eggs
4-6 oz	4-175 g	sole fillets
⅓ cup	80 ml	flour
¾ cup	180 ml	ground almonds
⅓ cup	80 ml	butter
2 tbsp	30 ml	fresh parsley
2 tbsp	30 ml	lemon juice

Preparation:

Cous Cous:

In a sauce pan heat the butter. Sauté the peppers, onion and garlic until tender. Add the seasonings and broth and bring to a boil. Stir in the cous cous and cook until the liquid has been absorbed.

Fish:

In a small mixing bowl mix the milk and eggs.

Dust the sole in the flour; dip into the milk and roll in the almonds to coat completely.

Heat the butter in a large skillet. Sauté the fillets in the butter for 2½ minutes per side. Remove the fish to a heated platter.

Add the parsley and lemon juice to the skillet. Cook for 1 minute. Pour sauce over fillets. Serve at once with the cous cous.

Serves 4

 Fun Food Facts

Onion

It's the vegetable that makes every dish worth crying over. Onions have become a mainstay in every area of cuisine, except that of desserts. Onions are in fact a member of the lily family as are garlic, chives and leeks.

Rolled Stuffed Veal Italian Style

Ingredients:

6-4 oz	6-120 g	provimi veal cutlets
6 oz	170 g	thinly sliced prosciutto
2 oz	60 g	washed, trimmed spinach leaves
1	1	small onion
1	1	carrot
1	1	celery stalk
¼ tsp	1 ml	lemon rind
½ tsp	3 ml	salt
½ tsp	3 ml	basil leaves
½ tsp	3 ml	black pepper
½ tsp	3 ml	thyme leaves
2 cups	500 ml	fine bread crumbs
1	1	egg
3 tbsp	45 ml	oil
3 tbsp	45 ml	butter
4 tbsp	60 ml	flour
1 ½ cups	375 ml	chicken stock (see page 210)
¾ cup	180 ml	heavy cream
2 tbsp	30 ml	chopped parsley

Preparation:

Pound the cutlets very thin. Layer with prosciutto slices and spinach leaves. In a food processor grind the onion, carrot, and celery very fine. Transfer to a mixing bowl and add the lemon, seasonings and bread crumbs, mixing thoroughly. Add the egg to bind. Spread the stuffing over the cutlets. Roll and tie together.

Heat the oil and butter in a sauce pan. Sear the veal on each side then transfer them to a casserole dish. Sprinkle the flour into the skillet. Reduce heat and cook for 2 minutes. Add the chicken stock and cream. Simmer for 5 minutes. Pour the sauce over the veal.

Bake in a preheated 350°F (180°C) oven for 1 hour. Remove the cutlets and untie. Place cutlets on a platter and pour the sauce over. Sprinkle with parsley before serving.

Serves 6

 Fun Food Facts

Prosciutto

Simply, this is the Italian word for ham. However, there are differing types of prosciutto. Prosciutto cotto is a cooked salted ham while prosciutto crudo is a raw air dried salted seasoned ham. Prosciutto crudo is usually the type most people think of when they think of prosciutto sliced very thin and served with melons. Prosciutto originated in Parma. It is made from animals that have been fed chestnut curds and whey from the cows of the same region which produce the cheese we know as Parmesan. Excellent hams also come from San Daniele and Veneto.

Potage Nelusko

Ingredients:

3 tbsp	45 ml	butter
3 tbsp	45 ml	flour
5 cups	1.25L	chicken stock (see page 210)
1 cup	250 ml	whipping cream
2 cups	500 ml	chicken purée
¼ cup	60 ml	hazelnut purée
⅔ cup	170 ml	twice ground raw chicken
1 tsp	5 ml	grated onion
¼ tsp	1 ml	pepper
¼ tsp	1 ml	basil
¼ tsp	1 ml	thyme
¼ tsp	1 ml	paprika
½ tsp	3 ml	salt
1	1	egg white
2 tbsp	30 ml	light cream
⅓ cup	80 ml	hazelnut pieces or almond slices

Preparation:

Heat the butter in a large sauce pan. Stir in the flour and cook for 2 minutes over low heat. Add 3 cups (750 ml) of the chicken stock, cream, chicken and hazelnut purée. Bring to a boil. Reduce heat and simmer for 20 minutes.

While soup is simmering, combine the raw chicken meat, onion, seasonings, egg white and light cream in a mixing bowl. Press through a fine sieve and roll into small balls.

Bring the remaining 2 cups (500 ml) of the broth to a boil. Drop the balls in the broth. Reduce heat and simmer for 10 minutes. Remove the meat balls and transfer into the soup.

Serve in soup bowls. Garnish with the hazelnut pieces or almonds.

Serves 6

Fun Food Facts

Hazelnut

The nut is the fresh or dried fruit or seed of the Hazel Tree. Its name is derived from the celebration of St. Philbert's Day, as this is when the nuts are ready for harvest. To make hazelnut purée, process 2 cups (500 ml) of filberts with 2 tbsp (30 ml) of vegetable oil in a food processor until smooth.

Kummel Suppe

Ingredients:

2 tbsp	30 ml	butter
1	1	finely diced Spanish onion
1	1	finely diced medium carrot
2	2	finely diced celery stalks
2 tbsp	30 ml	flour
1 tsp	5 ml	caraway seeds
5 cups	1.25 L	beef broth (see page 42)
2 cups	500 ml	cooked elbow macaroni

Preparation:

Heat the butter in a large sauce pan. Add the vegetables and sauté until tender. Sprinkle with flour and caraway. Cook until the vegetables and flour turn brown.

Add the broth and simmer until soup slightly thickens. Stir in the macaroni and simmer for 5 minutes. Serve hot.

Serves 4

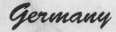
Germany

Grilled Italian Swordfish

Ingredients:

6-6 oz	6-170 g	swordfish steaks
3 tbsp	45 ml	lime juice
2 tbsp	30 ml	olive oil
2 tbsp	30 ml	sour cream
2 tsp	10 ml	granulated sugar
¼ tsp	1 ml	salt
½ tsp	3 ml	oregano
½ tsp	3 ml	thyme leaves
½ tsp	3 ml	cracked black pepper
½ tsp	3 ml	crushed red chili peppers

Preparation:

Wash the steaks and pat dry. Place in a shallow pan.

Combine the remaining ingredients in a small mixing bowl. Pour over the steaks and marinate for 4 hours. Grill steaks for 5 minutes per side, brushing with marinate. Serve with the Potato Cake and your favourite vegetable.

Potato Cake:

Ingredients:

1 lb	454 g	potatoes
2 tbsp	30 ml	butter
4	4	eggs
¼ cup	60 ml	heavy cream
1 cup	250 ml	freshly grated Parmesan cheese
1 cup	250 ml	flour
½ tsp	3 ml	each of salt, chili powder, black pepper, paprika, thyme
2 cups	500 ml	fine bread crumbs
4 cups	1 L	safflower oil

Preparation:

Pare and boil the potatoes. Mash and press through a sieve or process in a food processor until smooth.

Add the butter, 1 egg yolk, cream and cheese; blend until very smooth.

Shape into an even amount of 2" (5 cm) squares. Cool.

Mix the flour with the seasonings. Beat in the remaining eggs.

Dust the potatoes with the flour; dip in the eggs and dredge with bread crumbs.

Heat the oil. Deep fry the potatoes until golden brown.

Serves 4

Italy

Sztufada

Ingredients:

¼ lb	115 g	bacon
2 ¼ lbs	1 kg	beef round
3 tbsp	45 ml	butter
3 tbsp	45 ml	minced onion
2 tsp	10 ml	salt
½ tsp	3 ml	garlic powder
½ tsp	3 ml	onion powder
¼ tsp	1 ml	thyme
¼ tsp	1 ml	oregano
¼ tsp	1 ml	chili powder
¼ tsp	1 ml	paprika
¼ tsp	1 ml	black pepper
¼ tsp	1 ml	white pepper
¼ tsp	1 ml	cayenne pepper
3 tbsp	45 ml	flour
4 cups	1 L	hot beef broth (see page 42)
3 cups	750 ml	diced potatoes
1 cup	250ml	sour cream
¼ cup	60 ml	tomato paste

Preparation:

Dice the bacon.

Cut deep criss-cross slits in the beef and stuff with the bacon.

In a large kettle or Dutch oven, heat the butter and brown the beef. Add the onion and cook until tender.

Blend the salt, herbs and spices together. Dust the beef with the seasonings. Continue to cook the beef for 5 minutes. Sprinkle with flour and continue to cook for 3 minutes over low heat.

Add the broth and simmer for 1 ¼ hours.

Add the potatoes and continue to simmer for an additional 30 minutes. Remove the roast, stir in the sour cream and tomato paste. Simmer for an additional 5 minutes. Serve at once with Russia salad, root vegetables or stir fried vegetables.

Serves 6

Russian Meatballs

Ingredients:

Sauce:

¼ cup	60 ml	butter
2	2	minced garlic cloves
2	2	diced carrots
1	1	diced onion
2	2	diced celery stalks
3 ¼ lbs	1.5 kg	peeled, seeded and chopped tomatoes
3	3	bay leaves
1 tsp	5 ml	each of thyme leaves, oregano leaves, basil leaves, black pepper
1 tsp	5 ml	salt

Meatballs:

⅔ lb	300 g	lean ground veal
⅔ lb	300 g	lean ground beef
⅔ lb	300 g	lean ground pork
1 cup	250 ml	dry seasoned bread crumbs
1	1	minced onion
3	3	beaten eggs
½ tsp	3 ml	each of salt, white pepper, thyme leaves, paprika
3 tbsp	45 ml	oil
2 cups	500 ml	tomato sauce
2 cups	500 ml	chicken broth (see page 210)
1 cup	250 ml	sour cream

Pasta:

1 tbsp	15 ml	each of sage, rosemary, oregano, thyme, chervil, marjoram or basil (choose one or a combination to total weight)
3	3	eggs
1 tbsp	15 ml	olive oil
2 ½ cups	625 ml	semolina flour
		ice water only if required

Preparation:

Sauce:

In a large kettle, heat the butter and sauté the garlic, carrot, onion and celery until tender. Add the tomatoes and seasonings. Reduce heat and simmer for 3 hours. Strain the sauce and return to pot. Continue to simmer until very thick.

Meatballs:

In a large mixing bowl combine the meats with the bread crumbs, onion, eggs and seasonings. Roll into meatballs. Heat the oil in a large skillet and brown the meatballs. Add the tomato sauce and broth. Simmer for 1 hour.

Stir in the sour cream and simmer for 15 additional minutes. Serve over the noodles.

Pasta:

Beat the eggs with the oil and herbs. Slowly add the flour and knead into a smooth ball (add small amounts of ice water if required).

Knead the dough for 15 minutes and allow to rest for 15 minutes. Roll out the dough. Lightly dust with flour. Fold in three and roll out again. Repeat 6 to 8 times.

Now pass the dough through the pasta machine, setting the rollers gradually down until you reach the desired thickness. The result should be a smooth sheet of dough ready to process as you require.

Pass through a pasta machine, or cut into lingine noodles. Cook pasta in 8 cups (2 L) of boiling salted water until al dente.

Serves 6

Finnish Stuffed Fish

Ingredients:

¼ cup	60 ml	butter
2	2	minced green onions
½ tsp	3 ml	fresh chopped dill
1 tbsp	15 ml	chopped cilantro
½ tsp	3 ml	salt
¼ tsp	1 ml	black pepper
½ cup	125 ml	cream
½ lb	225 g	cooked lobster meat
4 tsp	20 ml	lemon juice
2 cups	500 ml	seasoned bread crumbs
6-6 oz	6-170 g	sole fillets

Sauce:

2 tbsp	30 ml	butter
2 tbsp	30 ml	flour
1 cup	250 ml	chicken broth (see page 210)
¼ cup	60 m	cream
½ cup	125 ml	grated Swiss cheese

Preparation:

In a small sauce pan, melt the butter. Add the onions with the dill, cilantro, salt, pepper, cream, lobster meat and lemon juice. Pour into a mixing bowl and stir in the bread crumbs.

Place the fish on a greased baking sheet. Top with stuffing. Bake uncovered in a preheated 375°F (190°C) oven for 25 minutes.

Sauce:

While fish bakes, heat the butter in a small sauce pan. Add the flour. Reduce the heat and cook for 2 minutes. Stir in the broth and cream and simmer until thick. Blend in the cheese. Place fish on a serving plate. Smother with sauce. Serve.

Serves 6

Fun Food Facts

There is a simple rule to follow in cooking any kind of fish by itself. For each inch (2.5 cm) of thickness, cook the fish for ten minutes (5 minutes per side), whether broiling, grilling, frying, poaching or baking.

Finland

Sacher Torte

Ingredients:

Cake:

3 oz	80 g	bitter-sweet chocolate
2 oz	60 g	semi-sweet chocolate
2 cups	500 ml	pastry flour
¼ tsp	1 ml	salt
½ cup	125 ml	butter
1 ½ cups	375 ml	granulated sugar
6	6	eggs

Frosting:

½ cup	125 ml	apricot preserve
¾ lb	340 g	almond paste*
10 oz	300 g	semi-sweet chocolate
1 ½ tsp	8 ml	oil
1 cup	250 ml	whipping cream

Preparation:

Cake:

In a double boiler melt the chocolate. Sift the flour and salt together, twice.

Whip the egg whites to soft peaks. Cream the butter with sugar until very light.

Add the egg yolks one at a time, beating well after each addition. Fold in the flour and chocolate in thirds. Fold in the egg whites.

Pour into a 9" (22 cm) buttered and floured springform pan. Bake in a preheated 350°F (180°C) oven for 45 minutes or until an inserted toothpick comes out clean. Cool for 10 minutes before transferring to a cooling rack.

Frosting:

Heat the apricot until thin; spread on the cake. Thinly roll the almond paste on a surface lightly dusted with cornstarch. Cover the entire cake then trim to fit.

Heat the chocolate in a double boiler. Stir in the oil and pour over the cake. Refrigerate 1 hour. Whip the cream and serve on the side with the cake.

* Almond paste may be purchased from any cake decorating store or bakery.

 Fun Food Facts

Almond

To blanch an almond, simply pour boiling water over the nuts. Quickly drain and rinse in cold water. Drain again and rub the skins off. To toast almond slices, quickly toss them in a small skillet over medium heat until golden brown. Almonds contain a high degree of oil and therefore need no additional oil when toasting.

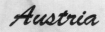 *Austria*

Kartoffelpuffer

Ingredients:

2 tbsp	30 ml	flour
1 tsp	5 ml	salt
¼ tsp	1 ml	baking powder
¼ tsp	1 ml	cracked black pepper
6	6	medium potatoes
2	2	eggs
1	1	minced garlic clove
1 tbsp	15 ml	grated onion
¼ cup	60 ml	butter
½ cup	125 ml	crumbled bacon
1 ½ cups	375 ml	sour cream

Preparation:

Combine the flour, salt, baking powder and pepper together in a mixing bowl.

Pare and grate the potatoes and pat completely dry. Stir into the dry mixture. Beat in the eggs. Add the garlic and onion.

Heat the butter in a skillet and fry small pancakes to golden brown on each side. Serve with bacon and sour cream.

Serves 4

Germany

Austrian Stuffed Chicken

Ingredients:

3 oz	80 g	sliced mushrooms
1	1	fine diced medium onion
1 tbsp	15 ml	safflower oil
2 ½ cups	625 ml	cold, cooked rice
½ cup	125 ml	peas
1 ¼ tsp	6 ml	salt
1 ¼ tsp	6 ml	black pepper
1 ¼ tsp	6 ml	thyme leaves
1 ¼ tsp	6 ml	basil
¼ tsp	1 ml	cinnamon
1	1	egg
5 lbs	2 kg	chicken
2 cups	500 ml	Tomato Sauce

Preparation:

Sauté the mushrooms and onion in a large skillet with the oil until all the liquid has evaporated. Cool to room temperature. Blend into the cooked rice along with the peas, seasonings and egg.

Stuff this mixture into the chicken. Truss the chicken. Place the chicken into a roaster and roast in a 325°F (160°C) oven for 2½ hours. Check for doneness. Remove chicken from oven. Scoop the stuffing into a serving dish. Carve the chicken. Serve with Tomato Sauce on the side.

Tomato Sauce

Ingredients:

¼ cup	60 ml	butter
2	2	minced garlic cloves
2	2	diced carrots
1	1	diced onion
2	2	diced celery stalks
3 ¼ lbs	1.5 kg	peeled, seeded and chopped tomatoes
3	3	bay leaves
1 tsp	5 ml	thyme leaves
1 tsp	5 ml	oregano leaves
1 tsp	5 ml	basil leaves
1 tsp	5 ml	black pepper
1 tsp	5 ml	salt

Preparation:

In a large kettle, heat the butter and sauté the garlic, carrot, onion and celery until tender. Add the tomatoes and seasonings. Reduce heat and simmer for 3 hours.

Strain the sauce and return to the pot. Continue to simmer to desired thickness.

Serves 6

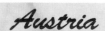

Austria

Scampi Aromatici

Ingredients:

Shrimp:

¼ cup	60 ml	oil
¼ cup	60 ml	flour
1	1	finely diced Spanish onion
2	2	finely diced green bell peppers
3	3	finely diced celery stalks
2 cups	500 ml	peeled, seeded, and chopped tomatoes
2 tsp	10 ml	salt
1 tsp	5 ml	each of oregano leaves, thyme leaves, basil leaves
2 tbsp	30 ml	stone ground prepared Dijon mustard
1 ½ cups	375 ml	chicken broth (see page 210)
1 tbsp	15 ml	brown sugar
1 ½ lbs	675 g	peeled and deveined tiger prawns
¼ cup	60 ml	chopped green onions
3 tbsp	45 ml	chopped parsley

Rice:

2 tbsp	30 ml	butter
⅓ cup	80 ml	finely diced onion
¼ cup	60 ml	finely diced celery
¼ cup	60 ml	finely diced red bell pepper
5 cups	1.25L	chicken broth (see page 210)
2 cups	500 ml	long grain rice
½ tsp	3 ml	each of basil, thyme, oregano, chervil
1 tbsp	15ml	chopped chives
2 tbsp	30 ml	chopped parsley

Preparation:

Shrimp:

Heat the oil in a large pan or Dutch oven. Add the flour. Reduce the heat and cook into a light brown roux (paste). Add the onions, peppers and celery. Sauté until tender, stirring constantly. Add the tomatoes, seasonings, mustard, broth and sugar. Simmer covered for 20 minutes. Add the prawns and continue to simmer uncovered for 10 minutes. Stir in the green onion and parsley. Serve at once over the cooked rice.

Rice:

In a sauce pan heat the butter. Add the vegetables and sauté until tender. Add the chicken broth and rice. Bring to a boil. Reduce to a simmer and cook until rice has absorbed the liquid. Blend in the herbs. Serve.

Serves 4

Italy

Rouladen

Ingredients:

2 ¼ lbs	1 kg	Round steak
4 oz	120 g	ground veal
2 oz	60 g	bacon
1	1	small onion
1	1	carrot
1	1	celery stalk
¼ tsp	1 ml	lemon rind
½ tsp	3 ml	each of salt, basil leaves, pepper, thyme leaves
2 cups	500 ml	fine bread crumbs
1	1	egg
3	3	large dill pickles cut into spears
3 tbsp	45 ml	oil
3 tbsp	45 ml	butter
4 tbsp	60 ml	flour
1 ½ cups	375 ml	beef stock (see page 42)
¾ cup	180 ml	heavy cream
2 tbsp	30 ml	chopped parsley

Dumpling:

1 cup	250 ml	unbleached flour
1 ½ tsp	8 ml	baking powder
½ tsp	3 ml	salt
½ cup	125 ml	buttermilk
4 cups	1 L	beef broth (see page 42)

Preparation:

Preheat the oven to 350°F (180°C).

Pound the steak very thin. In a food processor grind the veal, bacon, onion, carrot, and celery very fine. Transfer to a mixing bowl and add the lemon, seasonings and bread crumbs. Mix thoroughly. Add the egg to bind. Spread the stuffing over the steak. Top with pickles. Roll and tie together.

Heat the oil and butter in a sauce pan. Sear the steak on each side and transfer to a casserole dish. Sprinkle the flour into the skillet. Reduce heat and cook for 2 minutes. Add the beef stock and cream. Simmer for 5 minutes. Pour the sauce over the steak.

Bake in the oven for 2 hours. Remove the steak and untie. Place on a platter and pour sauce over. Sprinkle with parsley for garnish before serving.

Dumpling:

Sift the flour, baking powder and salt together in a mixing bowl. Gradually add the milk until a light soft dough is formed.

Bring the broth to a boil. Drop the dumplings by tablespoons into the broth. Cover and simmer for 15 minutes before serving. Do not uncover during the simmering process.

Serves 6

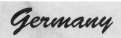

Schwarzwalder Kirschen Torte

Ingredients:

Cake:

2 tbsp	30 ml	cocoa powder
2 cups	500 ml	pastry flour
1 tsp	5 ml	baking powder
¼ tsp	1 ml	salt
4 oz	120 g	semi-sweet chocolate
½ cup	125 ml	butter
1 ½ cups	375 ml	granulated sugar
2	2	eggs
1 cup	250 ml	milk

Filling and Frosting:

2 cups	500 ml	black cherries - pitted, canned
½ cup	125 ml	juice from the cherries
2 tbsp	30 ml	cornstarch
¼ cup	60 ml	Kirsch or cherry brandy
2 cups	500 ml	whipping cream
½ cup	125 ml	confectioners sugar
1 cup	250 ml	chocolate shavings

Preparation:

Cake:

Sift the cocoa, flour, baking powder and salt together three times.

Melt the chocolate in a double boiler.

Cream the butter and sugar until very light. Add the eggs, one at a time, beating after each addition.

Stir in the chocolate. Incorporate the flour and milk in one third additions. Pour batter into 2-8" (20 cm) buttered and floured round cake pans. Bake in a preheated 350°F (180°C) oven for 35-40 minutes. Cool for 10 minutes and transfer to a cooling rack. Turn cake out and cool completely. Fill and frost with the following.

Filling and Frosting:

Heat the cherries in a sauce pan. Mix the cherry juice with the cornstarch. Add to the cherries and boil until mixture thickens. Cool to warm. Sprinkle cakes with Kirsch.

Spread the cherries on the first cake and top with the second. Whip the cream. Fold in the sugar and spread or pipe onto the cake. Garnish with chocolate.

Germany

Schmorbraten

Ingredients:

Stew:

3 tbsp	45 ml	butter
3 tbsp	45 ml	minced onions
2 tsp	10 ml	salt
½ tsp	3 ml	each of garlic powder, onion powder, salt
¼ tsp	1 ml	each of thyme, oregano, chili powder, paprika, black pepper, white pepper, cayenne pepper
2 ¼ lbs	1 kg	cubed beef round
3 tbsp	45 ml	flour
4 cups	1 L	hot beef broth (see page 42)
1 ½ cups	375 ml	diced potatoes
1 cup	250 ml	sour cream
¼ cup	60 ml	tomato paste

Dumpling:

4 cups	1 L	flour
1 tsp	5 ml	salt
2	2	eggs
¼ cup	60 ml	water
2	2	slices of bacon
2 cups	500 ml	beef broth (see page 42)

Preparation:

Stew:

In a large kettle or Dutch oven heat the butter and add the onions. Cook until tender without browning.

Blend the salt, herbs and spices together. Dust the beef with the seasonings and add to the pot. Cook the beef until brown. Sprinkle with flour and continue to cook for 3 minutes over low heat.

Add the broth and simmer for 1 ¼ hours.

Add the potatoes and continue to simmer for an additional 30 minutes. Stir in the sour cream, tomato paste and simmer for 5 minutes longer. Serve at once with dumplings.

Dumpling:

Sift the flour with the salt. Place in a mixing bowl and knead in the eggs. Add the water (just enough to form a stiff paste).

Roll the dough out on a flour dusted surface and allow to dry very hard. Once dry, break into pieces and grate with a coarse vegetable grater.

Fry the bacon in a skillet and strain the meat (use for some other cuisine), reserving 2 tbsp (30 ml) of bacon fat.

Pour the bacon fat into a small sauce pot. Add the broth and bring to a boil. Cook the dumplings for 4-5 minutes. Serve with stew.

Serves 6

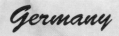

Germany

Smoked Pork Loin with Red Cabbage

Ingredients:

Pork Loin:

2 ¼ lbs	1 kg	Smoked pork loin
1	1	finely diced medium onion
2	2	finely diced medium carrots
2	2	finely diced celery stalks
2	2	peeled, seeded, diced tomatoes
¼ cup	60 ml	melted butter
1 ½ cups	375 ml	chicken broth (see page 210)
2 tbsp	30 ml	bacon fat or garlic flavour oil
2 tbsp	30 ml	flour
½ cup	125 ml	sour cream
½ tsp	3 ml	each of cracked black pepper, caraway seeds

Cabbage:

1	1	shredded, medium head red cabbage
¼ cup	60 ml	butter
1 tbsp	15 ml	granulated sugar
1 tsp	5 ml	salt
⅓ cup	90 ml	water
⅓ cup	90 ml	white wine or Cranberry Herb Vinegar
¼ cup	60 ml	red currant preserves
¼ cup	60 ml	grated apple
½ tsp	3 ml	caraway seeds

Preparation:

Pork Loin:

Place the pork loin in a Dutch oven and arrange the vegetables around it. Pour the butter and chicken broth over the loin and vegetables. Cover and simmer until all but a ½ cup (125 ml) of liquid has evaporated. Remove the meat to a serving platter.

Heat the bacon fat in a sauce pan. Add the flour and cook over medium heat for 4 minutes, stirring continually or until hazelnut in colour. Add the reserved vegetables, broth and sour cream. Simmer until thick. Stir in the pepper and caraway seeds. Pour the sauce over the loin and serve with cabbage.

Cabbage:

Preheat the oven to 325°F (160°C).

In a large kettle or Dutch oven heat the butter, sugar, salt, water and vinegar. Add the cabbage and bring to a boil. Cover and place in the oven. Bake for 2 hours. Stir in the red currant and apples and continue to bake for 15 minutes. Place in a serving bowl or garnish around the pork loin. Sprinkle with caraway seeds. Serve with Kartoffelpuffer (see page 260).

Serves 6

Germany

Basque Rabbit

Ingredients:

2 ¼ lbs	1 kg	boneless rabbit
¼ cup	60 ml	oil
3	3	medium diced onions
3	3	pared, sliced carrots
1 cup	250 ml	chicken broth (see page 210)
3	3	peeled, seeded, chopped large tomatoes
2 cups	500 ml	white wine
1 cup	250 ml	brandy
1 tsp	5 ml	salt
1 tsp	5 ml	black pepper
1 tsp	5 ml	thyme leaves

Rice:

1 ½ cups	375 ml	brown rice
3 cups	750 ml	chicken broth (see page 210)
1	1	Spanish onion
10 oz	285 ml	spinach
3 tbsp	45 ml	butter
1 cup	250 ml	Feta cheese

Preparation:

Wash the rabbit and pat dry.

Heat the oil in a large skillet and brown the rabbit. Add the onions and carrots and sauté until the vegetables are tender. Remove and reserve the rabbit. Add the broth, tomatoes, wine, brandy and seasonings, purée.

Return the rabbit and simmer for 45 minutes. Serve with the rice.

Rice:

Bring rice and chicken stock to a boil. Cover and simmer until rice is tender.

While rice cooks, finely dice the onion. Wash and trim the spinach. Heat the butter in a skillet. Add the onion and sauté until tender. Add the spinach and cook quickly.

Once rice has cooked, drain any excess liquid. Stir in the onion mixture with the cheese.
Serve at once.

Serves 6

 Fun Food Facts

Rice

The staple food for more than 60% of the world's people, rice is obtainable year round. The best way to cook any of the three types of white rice, short, medium or long grain, is in 2 cups (500 ml) of water, 1 tsp (5 ml) salt and 1 cup (250 ml) of rice. Bring to a rapid boil, reduce to a simmer and cook for 15 minutes. Keep the rice covered during the cooking process. Do not stir the rice. Stirring breaks the grains and causes the rice to turn soggy. Serve the rice as soon as possible after cooking. Rice will dry out the longer it sits. White rice has had the outer husk and bran layer removed and the rice is then polished. Use short or medium grains for sticky rice or sushi. Long grain for light and fluffy rice.

 France

Russian Salad

Ingredients:

½ lb	225 g	cooked, diced lobster meat
½ lb	225 g	boneless, cooked, diced chicken meat
½ cup	125 ml	blanched peas
½ cup	125 ml	finely diced, blanched carrots
3 oz	80 g	french cut, blanched green beans
3	3	pared, diced, blanched potatoes
1	1	pared, diced, blanched turnip
1 ½ cups	375 ml	mayonnaise
1 tbsp	15 ml	lemon juice
½ tsp	3 ml	each of salt, black pepper and paprika
6-8	6-8	washed Romaine leaves

Preparation:

Blend the lobster, chicken and vegetables in a mixing bowl.

Blend the mayonnaise with the lemon and seasonings. Mix into the salad. Refrigerate for 30 minutes.

Place the Romaine leaves around a salad bowl. Scoop the salad into the centre of the leaves. Serve.

Serves 6

Russia

Danish Meatballs

Ingredients:

Meatballs:

1 lb	454 g	lean ground pork
1 lb	454 g	ground lamb
½ cup	125 ml	dry fine bread crumbs
2 tbsp	30 ml	finely chopped onion
1 tsp	5 ml	salt
1 tsp	5 ml	black pepper
1 cup	250 ml	chicken broth (see page 210)
¼ cup	60 ml	butter

Potato:

1 lb	454 g	potatoes
2 tbsp	30 ml	butter
4	4	eggs
¼ cup	60 ml	heavy cream
1 cup	250 ml	freshly grated Parmesan cheese
1 cup	250 ml	flour
½ tsp	3 ml	salt
½ tsp	3 ml	chili powder
½ tsp	3 ml	black pepper
½ tsp	3 ml	paprika
½ tsp	3 ml	thyme
2 cups	500 ml	fine bread crumbs
4 cups	1 L	safflower oil

Preparation:

Meatballs:

Combine the pork, lamb, bread crumbs, onion, seasonings and broth together in a mixing bowl. Roll into small balls.

Heat the butter in a skillet and fry the balls until cooked through. Reserve hot.

Potatoes:

Pare and boil the potatoes. Mash and press through a sieve or process in a food processor until smooth. Add the butter, 1 egg yolk, cream and cheese; blend until very smooth.

Shape into an even amount of 2" (5 cm) squares. Cool.

Mix the flour with the seasonings. Beat the remaining eggs. Dust the potatoes with the flour; dip in the eggs and dredge with bread crumbs.

Heat the oil. Deep fry the potatoes until golden brown.

Serve the potatoes and meatballs together.

Serves 6

Mushroom & Steak Pie

Ingredients:

1 ½ lbs	675 g	round steak
½ lb	225 g	small button mushrooms
⅓ cup	80 ml	butter
1	1	diced, large Spanish onion
1 tbsp	15 ml	Worcestershire sauce
1 ½ cups	375 ml	beef broth (see page 42)
½ cup	125 ml	sherry
1 tsp	5 ml	thyme
1 tsp	5 ml	crushed rosemary
1 tsp	5 ml	cracked black pepper
1 tsp	5 ml	salt
3 tbsp	45 ml	flour

Crust:

1 ½ cups	375 ml	sifted all purpose flour
½ tsp	3 ml	salt
½ cup	125 ml	shortening
4-5 tbsp	60-75 ml	water
1 tbsp	15 ml	melted butter

Preparation:

Trim the steak of all fat and cut into 1" (2.5 cm) cubes.

Brush the mushrooms. Heat ½ of the butter in a sauce pan. Add the steak, mushrooms and sliced onions. Sauté until brown. Add the Worcestershire, broth, sherry and seasonings. Reduce heat and simmer for 1¼ hours.

Heat the remaining butter in a skillet. Add the flour and cook for 5 minutes over low heat. Stir into the beef and simmer until thickened. Cool to room temperature.

Crust:

Preheat the oven to 350°F (180°C).

Sift the flour and salt together into a mixing bowl. Cut the shortening into the flour with a pastry cutter or fork until pastry forms walnut size. Add the water and toss. Use only enough water to bind the pastry. Divide pastry in two. Roll out one on a lightly floured surface and fit into a 9" (22 cm) deep pie plate. Fill with the beef mixture.

Roll out the second pie dough and fit on the top. Fold the dough over and crimp the edges to seal. Brush with the melted butter. Bake for 30-35 minutes or until golden brown. Remove from oven cool for 10 minutes. Slice and serve.

Serves 6

Scotland

Scottish Shepherd's Pie

Ingredients:

3 tbsp	45 ml	safflower oil
1 lb	454 g	ground lamb
1	1	minced onion
2	2	minced celery stalks
2	2	pared, minced carrots
3 oz	80 g	sliced mushrooms
1	1	minced garlic clove
¼ cup	60 ml	flour
½ cup	125 ml	veal broth (see page 42)
2 tbsp	30 ml	tomato paste
1 tsp	5 ml	Worcestershire sauce
½ tsp	3 ml	thyme leaves
½ tsp	3 ml	chervil
½ tsp	3 ml	salt
½ tsp	3 ml	paprika
½ tsp	3 ml	pepper
2 cups	500 ml	creamed corn
4 cups	1 L	hot mashed potatoes
2 cups	500 ml	grated sharp Cheddar

Preparation:

In a large skillet heat the oil, fry the ground lamb. Add the vegetables and sauté until tender. Sprinkle with flour and continue to cook for 2 minutes. Add the broth, tomato paste, Worcestershire and seasonings. Simmer until thick.

Spoon into a large casserole dish. Cover mixture with the creamed corn. Spread mashed potatoes over the corn. Sprinkle cheese over top.

Bake in a preheated 400°F (200°C) oven for 15 minutes or until cheese is golden brown.

Serves 6

 ## Fun Food Facts

Cheese

When choosing the cheese you wish to purchase, keep in mind some of the following:

All cheese should be kept between 36°F and 40°F. Keeping cheese is not advisable if you must freeze it. If you must, keep it tightly wrapped in ½ lb (225 g) sizes. Keep it no longer than 90 days and allow it to thaw under refrigeration. Never freeze baked cheesecakes. They tend to crumble.

Store the soft cream type cheeses for no more than 14 days. Be sure they are tightly covered. Hard cheeses keep for 60-90 days tightly wrapped in the refrigerator. If mould appears, cut if off. The cheese is still good. However, that would not be true if the mould had penetrated the entire block. If this happens, discard the entire block. Of course, the blue type of cheeses are mould ripened which is the reason for their great flavour. Use mozzarella as soon as possible. The older it gets, the softer and when cooked tends to clear.

Locally made cheese will cost much less than the imports of similar kind. Processed cheese usually cost less than the mild; mild less than medium; medium less than old or sharp.

Cheese cooked too fast or at high temperatures will be stringy and possibly tough. It should be noted that one cup of grated cheese is about 4 ounces.

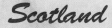 *Scotland*

Scottish Flan with Shortbread

Ingredients:

Flan:

1 cup	250 ml	granulated sugar
¼ cup	60 ml	water
3	3	eggs
3	3	egg yolks
1 tbsp	15 ml	lemon peel grated
2 cups	500 ml	milk
½ cup	125 ml	Drambuie liqueur

Shortbread:

1 cup	250 ml	butter
¾ cup	180 ml	granulated sugar
2 ¼ cups	560 ml	flour
½ cup	125 ml	cornstarch

Preparation:

Flan:

Preheat oven to 350°F (180°C).

Heat ⅔ cup (170 ml) of sugar with the water over medium heat until it turns a golden caramel colour. Pour into a 6 cup (1.5 L) flan dish, swirl to completely coat the sides.

Beat the eggs, egg yolks, remaining sugar, lemon peel, milk and liqueur. Pour into the flan dish and cover with a lid or foil wrap. Set the flan dish into a large sauce pot and fill two thirds up the outside of the flan.

Bake in the oven for 30 minutes or until an inserted knife comes out clean. Uncover, place a serving dish over the flan and invert. Serve the flan with the sauce and shortbread.

Shortbread:

Cream the butter with the sugar until very light.

Sift the flour and cornstarch together. Fold into the creamed mixture. Roll out the dough and form into desired shapes. Bake in a preheated 225°F (105°C) oven for 35 minutes. Sprinkle with granulated sugar if desired.

Serves 6

 Fun Food Facts

Flowers

Today, many cooks have realized the advantages of using edible flowers, not only to enhance their final plates but also as a flavour enhancing herb.

You may use any of the following:

Butterblossom summer squash - has a mild flavour of the squash from which it is picked.

Calendula, pot marigold - slight mild pepper flavour. Enhances soups and salads.

Carnation - mild flavour. It is usually available year round, and comes in a great variety of colors that will complement any dish.

Dianthus - has a mild clove flavour. Available in pink, rose, red and white.

Polish Apple Bars

Ingredients:

4 cups	1 L	sifted all purpose flour
1 tsp	5 ml	baking powder
1 ¼ cups	310 ml	confectioners sugar
1 ⅔ cups	420 ml	butter
6	6	egg yolks
2 tbsp	30 ml	yogurt
6	6	very large apples, cored, pared, sliced
¼ cup	60 ml	apple juice
½ tsp	3 ml	ground cinnamon
¼ tsp	1 ml	ground allspice, nutmeg
⅛ tsp	pinch	cloves
1 cup	250 ml	granulated sugar
3 tbsp	45 ml	cornstarch
3 tbsp	45 ml	lemon juice
¼ cup	60 ml	dry fine bread crumbs

Preparation:

Sift together the flour, baking powder and confectioners sugar (reserve 2 tbsp (30 ml) of the confectioners sugar). Cut in the butter. Add the egg yolks and yogurt. Mix until a coarse walnut size mix has been formed. Divide into 2 and press into small balls. Refrigerate one ball and freeze the second.

Preheat the oven to 375°F (190°C).

Place the apples into a sauce pan. Add the apple juice and spices. Cover and simmer for 10 minutes. Add the sugar and continue to cook for an additional 5 minutes. Blend the cornstarch with the lemon juice and add to the apples. Simmer for 3 more minutes.

Grease a large casserole dish. Roll out the refrigerated dough ball on a floured surface and place into the casserole dish. Pour in the apple sauce. Sprinkle with bread crumbs. Grate the frozen dough, sprinkle over the bread crumbs.

Bake for 1 hour or until golden brown. Cool to room temperature. Sprinkle with the reserved confectioners sugar. Slice and serve warm with apple cinnamon ice cream.

 Fun Food Facts

Apples

Since Johnny Appleseed planted those first few seeds, apples have been falling onto heads of people like Sir Isaac Newton ever since. But it takes more than gravity to cook a good apple. It takes the knowledge of what a good cooking apple is. Try using any of the following. They are all excellent for baking, sauces, pies, or just good eating. Baldwin, Empire, Red and Golden Delicious, Granny Smiths, Ida Reds, Lodi, Macintosh, Mutsu, Russets, as well as many others. Choose fresh, unbruised, firm fruit for the best results. Whenever possible don't pare the apples. The skin contains the major share of its nutritional value.

Poland

Bavarian Apple Torte

Ingredients:

Base:

½ cup	125 ml	soft butter
⅓ cup	80 ml	granulated sugar
¼ tsp	1 ml	vanilla
1 cup	250 ml	all purpose flour
¼ cup	60 ml	raspberry jam

Filling:

2	2	(250 g) pkg cream cheese at room temperature
½ cup	125 ml	granulated sugar
1 tsp	5 ml	vanilla
2	2	eggs

Topping:

¾ cup	175 ml	granulated sugar
1 tsp	5 ml	cinnamon
8 cups	2 L	apple slices
1 cup	250 ml	sliced almonds

Preparation:

Base:

Cream the butter, sugar and vanilla. Add the flour and mix well. Press into the bottom of a 10" (23 cm) springform pan. Spread the crust with jam.

Filling:

Beat the cream cheese, sugar and vanilla until smooth. Add the eggs, one at a time, beating well after each addition. Pour evenly over jam.

Topping:

Combine sugar and cinnamon and toss with sliced apples. Spoon over the cream cheese layer. Sprinkle with almonds. Bake in a preheated oven at 350°F (180°C) for 75 minutes or until golden. Chill 8 hours.

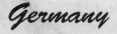

Germany

English Tea Time Torte

Ingredients:

5	5	eggs-separated
¾ cup	180 ml	granulated sugar
½ cup	125 ml	ground almonds
¼ cup	60 ml	butter
2 ½ cups	625 ml	confectioners sugar
10 oz	300 g	melted, unsweetened chocolate
1 tsp	5 ml	almond extract
2 tbsp	30 ml	melted butter
¼ cup	60 ml	toasted almonds

Preparation:

Preheat the oven to 350°F (180°C).

Lightly grease two 8" (18 cm) round cake pans; dust with flour.

Beat the egg yolks with the sugar until thick and creamy.

Beat the egg whites until soft peaks form. Fold into the egg yolks along with the ground almonds. Pour equal amounts of batter into the cake pans. Bake for 30 minutes or until firm. Cool completely before turning out.

Frosting:

Cream the butter with a ½ cup (125 ml) of confectioners sugar, fold in 4 tbsp (60 ml) of the melted chocolate. Spread between the cakes and stack together.

Blend the remaining chocolate with 2 cups (500 ml) of confectioners sugar, extract and melted butter. Beat until very light and fluffy, adding just enough water to make the frosting spreadable. Frost the cake and garnish with the whole almonds.

 Fun Food Facts

Eggs

Eggs for breakfast, lunch and dinner, eggs have come into their rightful culinary position and have cracked their way to the top of delightful cuisine. Many who have regimented the egg to a place where it only comes out as breakfast or perhaps during baking, have thought of it in a very limited way. Egg-citing new culinary treats created from imaginative cooks, are making the humble egg more egg-ceptional than any other food item.

Eggs are being offered to guests in more and more egg-travagant ways, showing the guest the classic and novelle possibilities of what was held in ignominy. No longer there, eggs have risen to new heights that even the most perfect of souffles could not imagine.

Eggs are not complicated to prepare. They take but minutes to offer your guest a egg-perience of a life time. Known as natures most perfect food, eggs are essential in every area of cuisine. Unless otherwise stated in a recipe, large eggs are what is required. When using eggs in baking be sure to bring them to room temperature. The yolks will cream easier and the white will beat up finer. Eggs usually require little cooking, extending the cooking will give a poor appearance and toughen the egg.

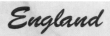

England

Cornish Pasty & Salad

Ingredients:

1 ½ tsp	8 ml	salt
4 cups	1 L	flour
¾ cup	180 ml	butter
1 cup	250 ml	water
1 lb	454 g	shredded rump steak
1	1	minced small onion
1	1	pared, grated small turnip
3	3	pared and sliced thinly, large potatoes
1 tsp	5 ml	each of cracked black pepper, thyme leaves, Spanish paprika, salt
2	2	egg whites

Salad:

½ head	½ head	bibb lettuce
½ head	½ head	chopped chicory
1 oz	30 g	sliced black truffles
2	2	egg yolks
⅓ cup	80 ml	olive oil
2	2	anchovy fillets
½ tsp	3 ml	Dijon mustard
3 tbsp	45 ml	vinegar
2 tbsp	30 ml	lemon juice
3 tbsp	45 ml	black caviar
12	12	yellow and orange nasturtium flowers or pansies

Preparation:

Preheat the oven to 350°F (180°C).

Mix ½ tsp (3 ml) of the salt with the flour. Cut in the butter and blend. Add 1 cup of water and knead into a stiff dough.

Roll the dough out on a lightly flour dusted surface to ⅛" (3 mm) thick. Cut into 6" (15 cm) rounds.

Mix the beef, remaining salt, onion, turnip, potatoes, and seasoning together. Place equal amounts of the beef mixture on one half of the pastry round and fold the other half over, pinch the edges to seal.

Place the pastries on a baking sheet. Brush with the egg whites and bake for 1 ¼ hours.

Salad:

Blend the two lettuces. Sprinkle with the sliced truffles.

Place the egg yolks into a blender. On high speed slowly incorporate the oil into the eggs forming a thick mayonnaise. Blend in the anchovy, mustard, vinegar, and lemon.

Pour this dressing over the lettuce and toss. Plate lettuce on well chilled plates. Sprinkle with caviar and garnish with flowers.

Serves 6

England

Paella

Ingredients:

½ lb	225 g	clams
½ lb	225 g	mussels
2 ¼ lbs	1 kg	chicken pieces
1 cup	250 ml	seasoned flour
½ cup	125 ml	oil
1	1	onion diced
1	1	diced green bell pepper
3	3	diced celery stalks
2	2	minced garlic cloves
½ tsp	3 ml	saffron
1 tsp	5 ml	thyme
1 tsp	5 ml	oregano
1 tsp	5 ml	basil
1 tsp	5 ml	cracked black pepper
6 cups	1.5 L	chicken broth (see page 210)
2 cups	500 ml	white wine
2 cups	500 ml	crushed tomatoes
3 cups	750 ml	long grain rice
1 lb	454 g	crab legs & claws
1 lb	454 g	peeled and deveined shrimp
½ lb	225 g	diced ham
2 cups	500 ml	peas

Preparation:

Preheat the oven to 375°F (190°C).

Clean and debeard the clams and mussels.

Dust the chicken with the seasoned flour. Heat the oil in a large kettle or Dutch oven and brown the chicken. Add the onion, green pepper, celery and garlic. Sauté until the vegetables are tender, remove the chicken from the pot and drain excess oil.

Add the seasonings and cook for 1 minute. Add the chicken broth, wine and tomatoes. Bring to a boil.

Place the rice into a very large casserole dish. Top with the chicken, mussels, clams, crab, shrimp ham and peas.

Pour the stock over the chicken and seafood. Bake in the oven for 30 minutes or until rice is tender. Do not stir.

Remove from oven. Cover and allow to sit for 10 minutes before serving.

Serves 8

Classic English Trifle

Ingredients:

Cake:

¾ cup	180 ml	butter
1 ½ cups	375 ml	granulated sugar
8	8	eggs
2 ¼ cups	560 ml	flour
4 tsp	20 ml	baking powder
1 cup	250 ml	milk
½ cup	125 ml	cream sherry
¼ tsp	1 ml	salt
1 tsp	5 ml	grated orange peel

Custard:

4	4	eggs
¼ cup	60 ml	sugar
⅛ tsp	pinch	salt
2 cups	500 ml	scalded milk
½ tsp	3 ml	vanilla extract

Topping:

1 cup	250 ml	cream sherry
2 cups	500 ml	raspberry preserves
2 cups	500 ml	whipping cream
½ cup	125 ml	confectioners sugar
1 tsp	5 ml	vanilla extract
4 cups	1 L	fresh strawberries
½ cup	125 ml	toasted sliced almonds

Preparation:

Cake:

Cream the butter and sugar until very light. Beat in the eggs one at a time, incorporating well. Mix the milk with the sherry and orange peel.

Sift together the flour, salt and baking powder.

Incorporate the flour and liquid into the eggs in thirds. Pour into 2-9" (22 cm) greased and floured round cake pans. Bake in a preheated 350°F (180°C) oven for 25-30 minutes. Cool to room temperature and slice the cakes in two.

Custard:

Beat the eggs with the sugar and salt. Place on top of a double boiler and gradually beat in the scalded milk. Cook for 8-10 minutes until thick. Beat in the vanilla. Cool to room temperature.

Assembly:

Sprinkle the cakes with the sherry. Spread each half with raspberry preserves and cut into large cubes.

Whip the cream. Fold in the confectioners sugar and the vanilla.

In a 8 cup (2 L) bowl alternate layers of cake, custard, strawberries (reserve 8 whole berries for the top) and whipping cream. Garnish with the almonds and whole berries.

Chill until ready to serve.

England

Lapin Forestiere

Ingredients:

4 tbsp	60 ml	safflower oil
1 ½ lbs	675 g	rabbit, cut into quarters
8	8	slices of bacon
20	20	button mushrooms
20	20	pearl onions
3	3	diced celery stalks
3	3	diced carrots
4 tbsp	60 ml	flour
1 cup	250 ml	peeled, seeded, chopped tomatoes
2 cups	500 ml	red wine
1 cup	250 ml	beef stock (see page 42)
2 tsp	10 ml	Worcestershire sauce
1 tbsp	15 ml	soy sauce
½ tsp	3 ml	Dijon mustard
¼ tsp	1 ml	salt
¼ tsp	1 ml	cracked black pepper
2 tbsp	30 ml	butter
8 oz	225 g	chanterelles

Preparation:

Heat the oil in a large kettle. Add the rabbit and brown. Dice the bacon and add to the rabbit along with the vegetables. Sauté for 3 minutes. Sprinkle with flour and cook for 3 minutes. Add the remaining ingredients, except the butter and chanterelles. Cover and simmer gently for 1½ hours.

Heat the butter in a skillet and sauté the chanterelles. Place the rabbit over rice or noodles. Sprinkle with chanterelles.

Serves 6

 Fun Food Facts

Rabbit

Although not readily accepted in North America, rabbit is a welcomed dish in the rest of the world. The meat tends to be white like chicken, more intense in flavour, yet less fatty. Four ounces of stewed rabbit meat contains 245 calories, 33.2 grams of protein, 0 carbohydrates, 11.5 milligrams of fat, 46 milligrams of sodium and 0 grams of fibre. Rabbit can be a great substitute for those considering alternate cuisines.

France

Le Waterzoie

Ingredients:

1-5 lbs	1-2 kg	whole chicken
1	1	lemon
10 cups	2.5 L	cold chicken stock (see page 210)
1	1	onion, stuck with a clove
2	2	diced celery stalks
2	2	diced carrots
1	1	bouquet garni*
2 cups	500 ml	white wine
3 cups	750 ml	pared and diced potatoes

Preparation:

Rub the chicken with the lemon. Place in a large kettle and cover with chicken stock.

Add the onion, celery, carrot and bouquet garni. Cover and bring to a simmer for 2½-4 hours. Skim the stock to remove any impurities that raise to the top. Discard bouquet garni.

Remove the chicken and reserve hot. Add the wine and potatoes. Simmer for an additional 30 minutes (or until potatoes are cooked).

Carve the chicken and place into large serving bowls. Cover with stock and vegetables. Serve.

Serves 6

 Fun Food Facts

Wine

When cooking with red or white wine, use the same wine that you intend to serve during the meal.

ie. When making a sauce with burgundy, serve the same burgundy with the dinner.

 Fun Food Facts

* A bouquet garni is a bundle of herbs tied in a cheese cloth (j-cloth works great). It will consist of your choice of all or several of the following: Parsley, bay leaf, thyme, marjoram, sage, basil and cloves.

Belgium

Italian Seafood Salad

Ingredients:

2	2	garlic cloves, pounded into a paste
2	2	egg yolks
½ tsp	3 ml	salt
pinch	pinch	pepper
½ tsp	3 ml	Dijon mustard
1 cup	250 ml	olive oil
4 tsp	20 ml	wine vinegar
16	16	cherry tomatoes
1	1	julienne sliced red bell pepper
1	1	julienne sliced yellow bell pepper
1	1	julienne sliced green bell pepper
1	1	sliced Spanish onion
1 cup	250 ml	diced cooked lobster
1 cup	250 ml	cooked sea scallops
1 cup	250 ml	cooked large shrimp

Preparation:

In a blender or food processor cream the garlic, egg yolks, salt, pepper and mustard.

With the machine running, add the oil in a slow thin stream. Add the vinegar and blend.

In a large mixing bowl combine the remaining ingredients. Pour the sauce over and toss to coat. Serve chilled.

Serves 6

Fun Food Facts

Olive Oil

Made from ripe black olives, olive oil is available in three types. Virgin or extra virgin are light and smooth in flavour and usually golden yellow in color. First quality and Second quality are slightly darker with a hint of green and a little harsher in flavour. Other olive oils are infused with differing flavours; fresh herbs, back pepper, garlic, chili pepper, cinnamon and citrus fruits, all enhance dishes that require subtle flavouring.

Italy

Vandermint Torte

Ingredients:

Cake:

¾ cup	180 ml	butter
1 ⅞ cups	470 ml	brown sugar
3	3	well beaten eggs
½ cup	125 ml	boiling water
¼ cup	60 ml	Vandermint liqueur
3 oz	80 g	bitter-sweet chocolate
2 ¼ cups	560 ml	pastry flour
1 ½ tsp	8 ml	baking soda
¾ tsp	4 ml	baking powder
¾ tsp	4 ml	salt
¾ cup	180 ml	buttermilk

Preparation:

Cake:

Cream the butter with the sugar until very light and fluffy. Add the eggs, beating well.

Pour the water and liqueur over the chocolate in a sauce pan. Heat over medium heat to a thick syrup. Cool. Add to egg mixture.

Sift the flour, soda, powder and salt together three times. Incorporate the flour and buttermilk into creamed mixture in thirds. Pour batter into 2-9" (22 cm) greased and floured cake pans.

Bake in a preheated 350°F (180°C) oven for 25-30 minutes. Cool for 10 minutes before transferring cakes to cooling rack.

Frost with Vandermint Coffee Frosting.

Vandermint Coffee Frosting

Ingredients:

⅓ cup	80 ml	light cream
1 cup	250 ml	granulated sugar
1 oz	30 g	bitter-sweet chocolate
1 tbsp	15 ml	Vandermint liqueur
½ tsp	3 ml	instant coffee
1 tbsp	15 ml	hot water
2 tbsp	30 ml	butter

Preparation:

In a double boiler cook the cream, sugar, chocolate and the coffee, which has been dissolved in the hot water. Add the butter and cook for 6 minutes. Beat until frosting reaches a spreadable consistency.

* Vandermint liqueur is a Dutch liqueur with a coffee mint flavouring.

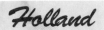

Holland

Minestrone Milanese

Ingredients:

1 cup	250 ml	navy beans
3 tbsp	45 ml	butter
2	2	minced garlic cloves
½ cup	125 ml	sliced onion
½ cup	125 ml	diced celery
½ cup	125 ml	diced green bell pepper
½ cup	125 ml	mushrooms
½ cup	125 ml	diced zucchini
3	3	pared, diced, medium potatoes
2 cups	500 ml	peeled, seeded, diced tomatoes
5 cups	1.25 L	chicken broth (see page 210)
2 cups	500 ml	cooked, diced chicken
2 tsp	10 ml	Worcestershire sauce
1 tsp	5 ml	each of basil leaves, salt
½ tsp	3 ml	each of thyme leaves, oregano leaves
2 cups	500 ml	cooked penne noodles
1 cup	250 ml	freshly grated Parmesan cheese

Preparation:

Soak the beans overnight or for 8 hours. Simmer the beans until soft in 8 cups (2 L) of water. Drain and reserve

Heat the butter in a large kettle or pan. Add the garlic, onion, celery, bell peppers, mushrooms and zucchini. Sauté until tender.

Add the potatoes and tomatoes and sauté for 5 minutes.

Pour in the chicken broth along with the diced chicken, beans, Worcestershire sauce, basil, thyme, oregano and salt. Simmer gently for 15-20 minutes (or until potatoes are cooked, yet firm).

Stir in the noodles and cheese. Cook for 2 minutes longer. Serve.

Serves 8

 Fun Food Facts

Minestrone

There are as many recipes for minestrone as there are cooks. The only real rule for minestrone is that the soup must contain, rice, beans or pasta, tomatoes and a variety of vegetables.

Italy

Polish Style Crêpes

Ingredients:

Crepes:

1 cup	250 ml	flour
¼ tsp	1 ml	salt
¼ tsp	1 ml	each of pepper, nutmeg
½ tsp	3 ml	Worcestershire sauce
2 tbsp	30 ml	safflower oil
¼ cup	310 ml	milk
¼ cup	60 ml	soda water
2	2	eggs
¼ cup	60 ml	butter

Filling:

3 tbsp	45 ml	butter
½ lb	225 g	Mushrooms
2	2	chopped green onions
2 cups	500 ml	cooked diced chicken
1 cup	250 ml	Ricotta cheese
½ tsp	3 ml	basil leaves
2	2	eggs
¼ cup	60 ml	milk
1 ½ cups	375 ml	fine dry seasoned bread crumbs

Sauce:

4 tbsp	60 ml	butter
4 tbsp	60 ml	flour
2 cups	500 ml	milk
½ tsp	3 ml	salt
½ tsp	3 ml	white pepper
pinch	pinch	nutmeg

Preparation:

Crêpes:

Sift the flour, salt, pepper and nutmeg together. Blend in the Worcestershire, oil, milk, and soda water. Beat 2 eggs and add to the liquid. Blend into the dry ingredients. Beat until a smooth thin batter is formed.

To cook the crêpes, spread about 3 tbsp (45 ml) of batter in a lightly buttered hot skillet. Cook about 1½ minutes. Turn the crêpes and cook 1 minute over medium heat

Filling:

Heat the butter in a large skillet. Sauté the mushrooms until all the liquid has evaporated. Transfer to a mixing bowl and add the green onion, chicken, cheese and basil leaves. Place 2 tbsp (30 ml) of filling on each crepe. Fold over the ends and roll. Blend the eggs with the milk. Dip each crepe into the egg mixture and roll in the bread crumbs.

Heat a small amount of butter in a skillet and fry each crepe until golden brown. Repeat the process until all crepes have been cooked. Reserve warm in a greased casserole dish.

Sauce:

Melt the butter in a sauce pan. Add flour and stir into a paste (roux). Cook for 2 minutes over low heat.

Add the milk and stir. Simmer until thickened. Add the seasonings and simmer for an additional 2 minutes.

Pour sauce over crepe casserole. Bake in a preheated 350°F (180°F) oven for 15 minutes.

Serves 6

Poland

Vienna Shrimp

Ingredients:

1 ½ lbs	750 g	tiger prawns
1 cup	250 ml	white wine dry
1 tbsp	15 ml	butter
1 tbsp	15 ml	flour
½ cup	125 ml	light cream
2 tbsp	30 ml	lemon juice
½ tsp	3 ml	salt
¼ tsp	1 ml	white pepper
¼ cup	60 ml	tomato purée
1 tsp	5 ml	grated lemon rind

Rice:

3 cups	750 ml	orange juice
1 ¼ cups	310 ml	long grain rice
1 ½ tbsp	20 ml	butter
2 tbsp	30 ml	granulated sugar
2 tbsp	30 ml	orange peel zest
½ cup	125 ml	unsalted broken cashew nuts

Preparation:

Shell and devein the prawns. Place into a sauce pan and pour the wine over. Simmer gently over low heat for 6-8 minutes, until prawns are tender but not rubbery. Remove to a serving platter and reserve hot.

Heat the butter in a skillet. Add the flour and cook for 2 minutes over low heat. Whip in the wine. Add the cream and simmer for 5 minutes. Stir in the lemon juice, seasonings, tomato purée and lemon rind. Simmer for an additional 3 minutes. Pour over prawns. Serve at once with rice.

Rice:

Bring orange juice to a boil. Add rice. Cover and simmer until the liquid has been absorbed.

Stir in the butter, sugar, orange peel and nuts. Serve.

Serves 4

Fun Food Facts

Tomato

Tomato is a fruit not a vegetable. It was first discovered in South America and for some time considered a toxic member of nightshade. The tomato was received in Europe by Spanish royalty where its flavour eventually spread throughout the continent. Known as a love apple, tomatoes found their way into most cuisines. Today, tomatoes are heavily relied upon in appetizers, soups, salads, entrees, condiments and preserves to bring that just right flavour.

Tomato purée is cooked tomato which has been reduced to a thick sauce. Tomato paste has had the cooking process extended and thus most of the moisture is evaporated. Use small amounts of paste to give a tomato flavour to your dishes.

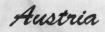

Austria

A Taste of Italy Crêpes

Ingredients:

6 oz	170 g	fine ground prosciutto
6 oz	170 g	cooked mild Italian sausage meat chopped
4 tbsp	60 ml	unsalted butter
3	3	eggs
½ cup	125 ml	bread crumbs
¼ cup	60 ml	freshly grated Romano cheese
12	12	Basic crêpes
1 cup	250 ml	Ricotta cheese
1 tbsp	15 ml	olive oil
1	1	small diced onion
1	1	minced garlic clove
2 cups	500 ml	peeled, seeded and diced tomatoes
2 tsp	10 ml	fresh chopped basil leaves
1 tbsp	15 ml	fresh chopped parsley
½ cup	125 ml	grated Provolone

Preparation:

Blend the meats with 3 tbsp (45 ml) of butter, eggs, bread crumbs and Romano cheese. Mix thoroughly. Chill 1 hour.

Place the filling evenly over each crêpe. Divide the Ricotta over the crêpes and roll together. Place in a greased casserole dish.

Heat the oil and remaining butter in a sauce pan. Cook the onion with the garlic until tender. Add the tomatoes and herbs. Reduce heat to a simmer. Cook for 15 minutes. Pour sauce over crêpes. Sprinkle with Provolone and bake in a preheated 350°F (180°C) oven for 35 minutes.

Serve with Italian Seafood Salad.

Serves 6

Basic Crêpe:

Ingredients:

1 cup	250 ml	flour
¼ tsp	1 ml	salt
¼ tsp	1 ml	each of pepper, nutmeg
½ tsp	3 ml	Worcestershire sauce
2 tbsp	30 ml	safflower oil
1 cup	250 ml	milk
¼ cup	60 ml	soda water
2	2	eggs
¼ cup	60 ml	butter

Preparation:

Sift the flour, salt, pepper and nutmeg together. Blend in the Worcestershire, oil, milk and soda water. Beat the eggs and add to the liquid. Blend into the dry ingredients. Beat until a smooth thin batter is formed.

To cook the crêpes, spread about 3 tbsp (45 ml) of batter in a lightly buttered hot skillet. Cook about 1½ minutes. Turn the crêpe and cook for 1 minute over medium heat.

Wiener Schnitzel à la Oscar

Ingredients:

1 ½ lbs	675 g	veal shoulder
2	2	eggs
¼ cup	60 ml	milk
½ cup	125 ml	flour
1 cup	250 ml	seasoned, fine bread crumbs
¼ cup	60 ml	safflower oil
1 ½ cups	375 ml	crab meat
18	18	blanched asparagus spears
¾ cup	180 ml	béarnaise sauce

Béarnaise sauce:

3 tbsp	45 ml	white wine
1 tbsp	15 ml	dried tarragon leaves
1 tsp	5 ml	lemon juice
½ cup	125 ml	butter
3	3	egg yolks
1 tsp	5 ml	fresh chopped tarragon

Preparation:

Cut the veal shoulder into 6-4 oz (6-120 g) pieces. Flatten and tenderize each piece into a cutlet with a meat mallet.

Blend the eggs into the milk. Dust each cutlet with flour; dip into the egg wash and dredge with bread crumbs.

Heat the oil in a large skillet. Fry each cutlet to golden brown on each side. Place on a baking sheet.

Divide the crab meat over each cutlet. Top with 3 asparagus spears and 2 tbsp (30 ml) of béarnaise sauce. Place under the oven broiler for 1½ minutes or until golden brown. Serve.

Béarnaise sauce:

Combine the wine, tarragon and lemon juice in small sauce pan. Over high heat reduce to 2 tbsp (30 ml), then strain.

In another small sauce pan, melt the butter and heat to almost boiling.

In a blender or food processor, process egg yolks until blended.

With machine running, add the butter in a slow thin stream. With the machine on slow, add reduced wine mixture. Process just until blended, place in a serving bowl. Stir in the fresh tarragon.

Serves 6

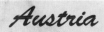

Austria

Prinzregenten Torte

Ingredients:

Cake:

1 ¾ cups	430 ml	granulated sugar
⅓ cup	80 ml	hot water
3 cups	750 ml	pastry flour
1 tbsp	15 ml	baking powder
½ tsp	3 ml	salt
¾ cup	180 ml	butter
3	3	eggs
1 tsp	5 ml	vanilla
⅔ cup	160 ml	milk

Filling:

1 cup	250 ml	granulated sugar
¼ cup	60 ml	cornstarch
2	2	eggs
1 ½ cups	375 ml	milk
1 tsp	5 ml	vanilla
3 oz	80 g	semi-sweet chocolate

Frosting:

10 oz	300 g	semi-sweet chocolate
1 ½ tsp	8 ml	oil

Preparation:

Cake:

Place ½ cup (125 ml) of sugar in a heavy sauce pan. Over medium heat cook the sugar, stirring constantly until it browns. Remove from heat and add the water. Allow to cool.

Sift the flour, baking powder and salt together.

Cream the butter and remaining sugar together until very light. Beat in the eggs, 1 at a time.

Mix the cooled syrup and add the vanilla and milk.

Alternate the flour and liquid into the creamed mixture in thirds.

Cut 8-8" (20 cm) rounds from wax paper and place on pastry sheets. Divide the batter evenly over the rounds to 1½ " (35 mm) from the edges. Bake 7-8 minutes in a preheated 350°F (180°C) oven. Remove wax paper. Fill and stack each layer after cooling.

Filling:

In a sauce pan or a double boiler, blend the sugar with the cornstarch and eggs. Whip in the milk and vanilla. Heat over medium heat. Stir in the chocolate. Cook until sauce is very thick. Cool and spread over the cakes.

Frosting:

Melt the chocolate in a double boiler. Stir in the oil. Pour over cake while hot.

Austria

Spicy Irish Stew

Ingredients:

3 tbsp	45 ml	butter
3 tbsp	45 ml	minced onions
2 tsp	10 ml	salt
½ tsp	3 ml	garlic powder
½ tsp	3 ml	onion powder
¼ tsp	1 ml	thyme
¼ tsp	1 ml	oregano
¼ tsp	1 ml	chili powder
¼ tsp	1 ml	paprika
¼ tsp	1 ml	black pepper
¼ tsp	1 ml	white pepper
¼ tsp	1 ml	cayenne pepper
2 ¼ lbs	1 kg	cubed beef round
3 tbsp	45 ml	flour
4 cups	1 L	hot beef broth (see page 42)
1 ½ cups	375 ml	diced potatoes
1 cup	250 ml	sour cream
¼ cup	60 ml	tomato paste

Dumplings:

1 cup	250 ml	unbleached flour
1 ½ tsp	8 ml	baking powder
½ tsp	3 ml	salt
½ cup	125 ml	buttermilk

Preparation:

In a large kettle or Dutch oven heat the butter. Add the onions and cook until tender, without browning.

Blend the salt, herbs and spices together. Dust the beef with the seasonings and add to the pot. Cook the beef until brown. Sprinkle with flour and continue to cook for 3 minutes over low heat.

Add the broth and simmer for 1½ hours.

Add the potatoes and continue to simmer for an additional 30 minutes. Stir in the sour cream and tomato paste. Simmer for 5 minutes longer. Serve at once with dumplings.

Dumplings:

Sift the flour, baking powder and salt together in a mixing bowl. Gradually add the milk until a light soft dough is formed.

Drop into the stew in small spoonfuls. Cover and simmer for 15 minutes before serving. Do not uncover during the simmering process.

Serves 6

Ireland

Pêches Melba

Ingredients:

Sauce:

1 ½ lbs	675 g	fresh raspberries
¼ cup	60 ml	granulated sugar
1 tbsp	15 ml	lemon juice
2 tsp	10 ml	cornstarch

Ice Cream:

4 cups	1 L	cream - medium
1	1	vanilla bean
5	5	egg yolks
¾ cup	180 ml	granulated sugar

Peaches:

4 cups	1 L	water
1 ½ cups	375 ml	granulated sugar
1 tbsp	15 ml	vanilla extract
6	6	large peaches, stoned, peeled and halved

Preparation:

Sauce:

Purée the raspberries in a food processor. Strain through a sieve (to remove seeds) into a sauce pan. Whisk in the sugar. Heat to a boil; reduce to simmering.

Blend the lemon and cornstarch. Add to the sauce and simmer until thick.

Ice Cream:

Scald the cream with the vanilla bean in a double boiler. Beat the egg yolks with the sugar. Slowly beat into the cream and cook, stirring constantly, until thick. (Do not over cook or eggs will curdle.) Discard vanilla bean. Remove from heat. Cool. Chill and freeze in an ice cream maker according to directions.

Peaches:

Heat the water in a sauce pan. Add the sugar and vanilla. Bring to a boil; reduce to half its volume. Reduce the heat and poach the peaches for 5 minutes. Cool. Chill.

Place a peach in a fluted dish, top with ice cream, top with a second peach. Smother with sauce and serve at once.

Serves 6

 Fun Food Facts

Peaches

This is a classic recreation by the worlds greatest chef, Auguste Escoffier. He adored an opera singer, Nellie Melba, for whom he named this and other creations.

Originally from China, the Peach Tree now yields fruit the world over where the climate is just right to support the fuzzy fruit. There are two main types of peaches; freestone and cling-stone. Freestone peaches have a softer meat and will separate more easily from it's skin and pit. Cling-stone have a firmer meat and separate with some difficulty. However, they tend to be sweeter. Either offer great eating and will serve well in poaching, preserving and baking.

Norwegian Curried Pork

Ingredients:

3 tbsp	45 ml	butter
3 tbsp	45 ml	minced onion
2 tsp	10 ml	salt
½ tsp	3 ml	garlic powder
½ tsp	3 ml	onion powder
1 tbsp	15 ml	curry powder
2 ¼ lbs	1 kg	cubed pork
3 tbsp	45 ml	flour
4 cups	1 L	hot beef broth (see page 42)
1 ½ cups	375 ml	raw rice
1 cup	250 ml	sour cream
¼ cup	60 ml	tomato paste
4	4	hard boiled eggs chopped
3	3	diced apples
¼ cup	60 ml	chopped gerkins
1 cup	250 ml	mango chutney

Preparation:

In a large kettle or Dutch oven, heat the butter. Add the onions and cook until tender, without browning.

Blend the salt and spices together. Dust the pork with the seasonings and add to the pot. Cook the pork until brown. Sprinkle with flour and continue to cook for 3 minutes over low heat.

Add the broth and simmer for 1¼ hours.

Add the rice and continue to simmer for an additional 30 minutes. Stir in the sour cream and tomato paste. Simmer for 5 minutes longer. Serve at once garnished with the eggs, apples, gerkins and chutney.

Serves 6

 Fun Food Facts

Rice

You may use brown rice which is rice that has only its outer husk removed. This rice takes longer to cook, up to 30 minutes, so be patient, the wait is worth it.

 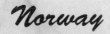

Asia

"If there is anything we are serious about, it is neither religion nor learning, but about food," said Chinese scholar Lin Yutang, and so the people learned about food. Of the noble cuisines of the world Oriental would rank as the first, for it is through their love for food and respect for what ingredients go into the finished dish that demands perfection.

The essence of Oriental cuisines is within the heart of the person preparing the dish. No dish is considered to difficult or time consuming, for it is served as an expression of the cook. It is a reflection of their personality. Food combining, now popular in the West, was actually first thought of by Confucius. The correct ingredients, prepared in the proper manner, served with the right sauce was the only thing to be served. Otherwise there was no sense in eating. Be frugal, not wasteful, also is the thinking of the Oriental cook; thus anything edible is meant to be ate. No food is considered inferior and all is meant to be served in its best possible manner for it is meant to nourish the spirit and soul as well the body.

Wok cookery became the standard of Oriental cooking due to a lack of wood. Food had to be prepared quickly to conserve the fire. It remains as the principal method of Oriental cookery and provides food that tends to be fresh and more nourishing than that of Western cuisine.

The Orientals introduced to the West sensible dining as well. Food was served so that one enjoyed the experience and not seen ripping and tearing it with a knife and fork. Thus, the chopsticks were introduced. Orientals willingly shared their culinary prowess with all visitors. Soon certain spices, noodles, and technique all travelled back with the visitor Westward bound. The West introduced oranges, other spices, nuts, onions, mustards, tomatoes and even sugar to the Orient. Today the exchange continues, many countries embrace Chinese, Thai, Indonesian and Japanese cuisine warmly, while the Orient looks to the west to train their cooks in French, Spanish, German and North American styles of cookery.

You can enjoy our travelling experience with Sushi and Sashimi, Cha Gió, Com Chien, Kal Bi Chicken, Pork & Chicken Adobo or Baki Goreng, or any other of the excellent dishes we've selected for you.

Philippines Fish Stew

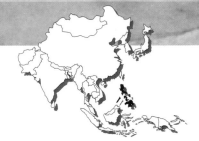

Ingredients:

3 tbsp	45 ml	butter
1	1	sliced red bell pepper
1	1	sliced green bell pepper
1	1	sliced small onion
1 tbsp	15 ml	chopped fresh parsley
1	1	chopped leek
3	3	minced garlic cloves
2 cups	500 ml	peeled, seeded, chopped tomatoes
6 cups	1.5 L	fish broth
¼ cup	60 ml	raw rice
¼ lb	120 g	peeled and deveined shrimp
½ lb	225 g	sliced red snapper
¼ lb	120 g	sliced calamari
¼ lb	120 g	clams, in shell
¼ lb	120 g	crab claws
1	1	bouquet garni
		salt and pepper if desired

Preparation:

In a large Dutch oven or kettle, heat the butter. Add the vegetables and sauté until tender. Add the parsley, leek, garlic, tomatoes and broth. Bring to a boil and add the rice. Reduce heat and simmer for 20 minutes.

Add the fish, seafood, and bouquet garni. Cover and simmer for 15 minutes.

Discard the bouquet garni. Serve the stew with fresh bread.

Serves 6

 Fun Food Facts

Bouquet-garni

A bouquet-garni is a bundle of fresh or dry herbs tied together and placed within a simmer stock to enhance the flavour thereof. Many bouquet-garni's vary depending on what the final intent of the stock is to be used for. The general use of a bouquet-garni should consist of: 2 sprigs of fresh thyme, 2 sprigs of marjoram, 6 peppercorns, 1 bay leaf, 6 sprigs of parsley and 1 leek, tied together in a cheesecloth (a j-cloth also works well).

Shrimp Dumplings

Ingredients:

1 cup	250 ml	ice water
1 tbsp	15 ml	oil
1 tsp	5 ml	salt
2 ¼ cups	560 ml	flour
1 cup	250 ml	chopped shrimp
¼ cup	60 ml	lean ground beef
1 cup	250 ml	minced water chestnuts
1 tbsp	15 ml	minced ginger
¼ cup	60 ml	minced green onion
¼ cup	60 ml	minced lemon grass
1	1	egg
1 tsp	5 ml	cracked black pepper
¼ cup	60 ml	soy sauce
2 tsp	10 ml	Worcestershire sauce
1	1	sliced lemon

Preparation:

In a mixing bowl blend the water, oil, ¼ tsp (1 ml) of salt and flour into a smooth dough. Divide the dough into 1¼" (31 mm) balls. Roll to paper thin on a flour dusted surface.

Blend the shrimp, beef, water chestnuts, ginger, onion, lemon grass, egg, remaining salt and the pepper. Mix thoroughly. Spoon 1 tbsp (15 ml) of filling onto each dough patty. Roll up like a crepe and seal. Place in a steamer and steam for 30 minutes.

Mix the soy sauce with the Worcestershire sauce. Serve along side the dumplings. Garnished with the lemon slices.

Serves 4

Fun Food Facts

Soy Sauce, Soy Bean

Soy beans are the most nutritious of the bean family. Extremely high in protein soy beans are an excellent substitute for meats. Bean cakes or tofu is the product of fermented soy beans, usually found in three varieties soft, semi-firm and firm. Soy bean tofu contains 82 calories, 9 grams of protein, 2.7 grams of carbohydrates, 4.8 grams of fat, 0 milligrams of cholesterol, 8 milligrams of sodium, and 0.1 grams of fibre. Soy sauce is a dark strong heavily salted condiment which is made through a brewing process of fermented soy beans, salt and water.

Philippines

Chinese Pork Tenderloin

Ingredients:

1 ½ lbs	675 g	pork tenderloin
⅓ cup	80 ml	safflower oil
1 tsp	5 ml	peeled, minced ginger root
2	2	minced garlic cloves
¼ cup	60 ml	light soy sauce
⅓ cup	80 ml	honey liquid
2 tbsp	30 ml	sherry
4 drops	4 drops	red food colouring (optional)

Preparation:

Trim and slice the pork into ½" (19 mm) pieces.

Blend 2 tbsp (30 ml) of oil with the remaining ingredients. Pour over the pork and marinate refrigerated for 4-6 hours.

Heat the remaining oil in a wok. Drain the pork and reserve the marinate. Fry the pork thoroughly. Drain any excess oil. Add the marinate and continue to fry until all the liquid has evaporated.

Serve with rice.

Serves 4

China

Lamb Curry

Ingredients:

3 tbsp	45 ml	oil
1 ½ lbs	680 g	boneless cubes, lamb
1	1	diced large onion
3	3	diced apples
2 tsp	10 ml	flour
2 tsp	10 ml	ground coriander*
1 tsp	5 ml	ground cumin*
½ tsp	3 ml	turmeric*
½ tsp	3 ml	ground cinnamon*
1 tbsp	15 ml	chili powder
2 cups	500 ml	chicken broth (see page 210)
2 tbsp	30 ml	lime juice
½ cup	125 ml	coconut milk
2	2	minced garlic cloves
2 tbsp	30 ml	minced ginger
⅓ cup	80 ml	seedless raisins
¼ cup	60 ml	mango chutney
¼ cup	60 ml	almonds
4 cups	1 L	cooked basamati rice

Preparation:

In a large kettle heat the oil and brown the lamb. Add the onion and apples and cook for 3 minutes.

Stir in the flour and the seasonings. Reduce heat and simmer for 3 minutes. Add the broth, lime juice and coconut milk. Simmer for 45 minutes. Add the garlic and ginger and continue to simmer for 15 minutes longer.

Stir in the raisins, chutney and almonds. Simmer for 5 minutes.

Place the rice on serving plates. Smother with stew, serve with additional chutney if required.

Serves 6

* Substitute 4 tsp (20 ml) of Garama Masala.

Fun Food Facts

Garama Masala

Garama means hot, masala powder, mixture of spices, thus Garama masala is a hot spicy mixture. Although there are many variations of Garama Masala we offer this one as a very good general purpose powder.

Ingredients:

1 tbsp	15 ml	ground coriander, cumin
2 tsp	10 ml	ground ginger, turmeric
½ tsp	3 ml	each of cayenne pepper, black pepper
1 ½ tsp	8 ml	ground cardamon
¼ tsp	1 ml	each of ground cloves, allspice, ground bay leaves, ground nutmeg,
½ tsp	3 ml	ground cinnamon

Preparation:

Combine the spices in a spice grinder, blend well.

India

Samosa

Ingredients:

Pastry:

3 ½ cups	875 ml	unbleached flour
1 tsp	5 ml	salt
½ cup	125 ml	oil
½ cup	125 ml	water

Filling:

3	3	medium potatoes
1 lb	454 g	ground lamb
2 tbsp	30 ml	red pepper oil
1	1	finely diced onion
¾ cup	180 ml	peas
1 tbsp	15 ml	minced ginger
2	2	finely chopped serrano chilies
¼ cup	60 ml	finely chopped cilantro
3 tbsp	45 ml	water
4 tsp	20 ml	salt
1 tsp	5 ml	cumin
1 tsp	5 ml	garam masala
¼ tsp	1 ml	cayenne pepper
¼ tsp	1 ml	black pepper
¼ tsp	1 ml	white pepper
3 tbsp	45 ml	lime juice
1	1	beaten egg

Preparation:

Sift the flour and salt together. Add the oil. Mix forming a coarse meal. Add the water and knead into a smooth, stiff ball. Reserve covered for 45 minutes.

Boil the potatoes until tender. Allow to cool to room temperature. Peel, and cut into a coarse dice.

Heat the pepper oil in a large sauce pan. Add the lamb and brown. Add the potatoes and onions and cook for 3 minutes. Add the peas, ginger, chilies, cilantro, water, seasonings and lime juice. Bring to a boil. Reduce heat and simmer until all moisture has evaporated. Cool completely.

Divide the dough in 20 equal pieces. Roll each piece into 6" (21 cm) round. Place equal amounts of filling on each round; fold in half and seal the edges.

Place on a lightly greased baking sheet. Brush with the eggs and bake for 30-35 minutes or until golden brown.

Serves 4

India

Beef Noodle Soup

Ingredients:

¾ lb	340 g	flank steak
2 tbsp	30 ml	peanut oil
4	4	minced garlic cloves
2	2	sliced celery stalks
1	1	sliced red sweet bell pepper
1	1	diced small onion
2	2	diced green onions
6 cups	1.5 L	beef broth (see page 42)
2 tbsp	30 ml	soy sauce
1 tsp	5 ml	Worcestershire sauce
¾ lb	340 g	vermicelli rice noodles
1 cup	250 ml	bean sprouts
2 tbsp	30 ml	chopped cilantro
2 tsp	10 ml	crushed red chilies

Preparation:

Trim the steak of all excess fat and thinly slice.

Heat the oil in a sauce pan and brown the beef. Add the garlic and other vegetables and fry for 2 minutes.

Pour the broth, soy sauce and Worcestershire over and bring to a boil. Reduce the heat. Add the noddles and bean sprouts. Simmer for 3 minutes.

Ladle into serving bowls and garnish with cilantro and chilies. Serve at once.

Serves 6

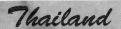

Thailand

Tandoori Chicken

Ingredients:

2 ¼ lbs	1 kg	chicken
½ cup	125 ml	tandoori powder
½ cup	125 ml	plain yogurt
1 tsp	5 ml	salt
1 tbsp	15 ml	mustard oil
2	2	large Spanish onions
1	1	sweet green bell pepper
1	1	sweet red bell pepper
2 tbsp	30 ml	red pepper oil
2	2	limes

Preparation:

Cut the chicken into serving pieces and remove the skin. Make several deep incision in each piece. Place on a baking sheet.

Mix the tandoori powder, yogurt, salt and mustard oil together.

Mix the paste over the chicken and refrigerate over night.

Preheat the oven to 350°F (180°C).

Cover the chicken with foil wrap and bake for 45 minutes. Turn the oven on broil and broil for 10 minutes.

Thin slice the onions, and peppers. Heat the pepper oil in a large skillet and sauté the onion and peppers until tender.

Place the chicken on a serving platter. Smother with the onions and peppers. Juice the limes and pour over the chicken. Serve.

Serves 6

 Fun Food Facts

Tandoori Masala

Tandoori is the name of a highly seasoned curry powder, which is what masala simply means (powder). Tandoori will contain a blend of coriander, fenugreek, salt, cinnamon, cumin, peppers, onion powder, ginger, cloves, garlic, bay, nutmeg and celery. It is most noticably used in Tandoori chicken but the marinade works well with lamb, pork, veal. It may be a little too strong for most fish.

India

Ceylon Beef

Ingredients:

3 tbsp	45 ml	safflower oil
2 lbs	908 g	shoulder beef, cut in thin strips
1 cup	250 ml	sliced onions
1 cup	250 ml	sliced mushrooms
2	2	minced garlic cloves
2 tbsp	30 ml	minced ginger
3 tbsp	45 ml	flour
½ tsp	3 ml	salt
2 tsp	10 ml	ground coriander
1 tsp	5 ml	ground cumin
½ tsp	3 ml	turmeric
½ tsp	3 ml	ground cinnamon
2 cups	500 ml	seeded, peeled, diced tomatoes
1 cup	250 ml	coconut milk
¼ cup	60 ml	sherry
½ cup	125 ml	toasted sliced almonds
2 cups	500 ml	snow peas

Preparation:

Heat the oil in a large skillet or sauce pan. Add the beef and sauté to brown.

Add the onions, mushrooms, garlic and ginger, continue cooking until vegetables are tender. Sprinkle with flour. Reduce heat and cook for an additional 2 minutes.

Add the salt, seasonings, tomatoes, coconut milk and sherry. Bring to a boil. Reduce heat and simmer for 15-20 minutes. Add the almonds and peas, continue cooking for an additional 3 minutes. Serve with rice.

Serves 6

Sweet Potato & Pineapple Kebabs

Ingredients:

2	2	large pare boiled cubed sweet potatoes
1	1	pared cubed pineapple
3	3	large cubed apples
2 tbsp	30 ml	lemon juice
½ cup	125 ml	melted butter or ghee
1 tsp	5 ml	ground cinnamon
¼ tsp	2 ml	ground cloves, nutmeg

Preparation:

Skewer the potatoes, pinapples and apples. Soak in the lemon juice for 15 minutes. Brush the skewers with the melted butter and sprinkle lightly with the spices. Broil for 5 minutes per side over medium heat and serve at once.

Mulligatawny Soup

Ingredients:

3 tbsp	45 ml	butter
1	1	finely diced large onion
2	2	finely diced large carrots
2	2	finely diced celery stalks
3 tbsp	45 ml	flour
3 cups	750 ml	chicken stock (see page 210)
½ cup	125 ml	whipping cream
½ cup	125 ml	coconut milk
2 cups	500 ml	cooked diced chicken
1 tsp	5 ml	curry powder
1 ½ cups	375 ml	cooked rice
⅓ cup	80 ml	toasted sliced almond

Preparation:

Heat the butter in a large sauce pan. Add the vegetables and sauté until tender. Stir in the flour and cook 2 minutes over low heat. Add the chicken stock, cream, coconut milk, chicken and curry powder. Bring to a boil. Reduce heat and simmer for 20 minutes.

Stir in the rice and simmer for 5 minutes. Garnishing with the almonds. Serve.

Serves 4

India

Philippines Rice Bake

Ingredients:

2 ¼ lbs	1 kg	chicken pieces
1 cup	250 ml	seasoned flour
½ cup	125 ml	oil
1	1	diced onion
1	1	diced green bell pepper
3	3	diced celery stalks
2	2	minced garlic cloves
1 tbsp	15 ml	minced ginger
1 tsp	5 ml	thyme
1 tsp	5 ml	oregano
1 tsp	5 ml	basil
1 tsp	5 ml	cracked black pepper
1 tsp	5 ml	paprika
6 cups	1.5 L	chicken broth (see page 210)
2 cups	500 ml	coconut milk
2 cups	500 ml	crushed tomatoes
3 cups	750 ml	long grain rice
6	6	pared, sliced potatoes
1 lb	454 g	spicy sausage
½ lb	225 g	diced ham
2 cups	500 ml	peas
½ cup	125 ml	green stuffed olives
3	3	quartered, hard boiled eggs

Preparation:

Preheat the oven to 375°F (190°C).

Dust the chicken with the seasoned flour. Heat the oil in a large kettle or Dutch oven and brown the chicken. Add the onion, green pepper, celery, garlic and ginger. Sauté until the vegetables (except potatoes) are tender. Remove the chicken from the pot and drain excess oil.

Add the seasonings and cook for 1 minute. Add the chicken broth, coconut milk and tomatoes. Bring to a boil.

Place the rice into a very large casserole dish. Top with the potatoes, chicken, sausage, ham and peas.

Pour the stock over the chicken and meats. Bake in the oven, uncovered, for 30 minutes or until rice is tender. Do not stir.

Remove from oven and cover and allow to sit for 10 minutes, garnish with the olives and eggs before serving, if desired.

Serves 6

Philippines

Indonesian Fried Rice

Ingredients:

8 oz	225 g	ground pork
4 oz	120 g	lean ground beef
½ tsp	3 ml	cracked black pepper
2 tbsp	30 ml	finely chopped cilantro
4	4	minced garlic cloves
½ tsp	3 ml	cinnamon
2	2	minced green onions
¼ tsp	1 ml	crushed red chilies flakes
1 tbsp	15 ml	fish sauce*
1	1	stalk, minced lemon grass
2	2	eggs
½ cup	125 ml	flour
2 tbsp	30 ml	safflower oil

Rice:

2	2	beaten eggs
3 tbsp	45 ml	garlic flavoured oil
1	1	thinly sliced shallot
1	1	minced garlic clove
1 tbsp	15 ml	minced ginger
4	4	red chilies
¼ lb	120 g	diced, boneless chicken
¼ lb	120 g	peeled, deveined small shrimp
3 cups	750 ml	cooked rice
¼ cup	60 ml	oyster sauce

Preparation:

In a small mixing bowl combine the pork, beef, pepper, cilantro, garlic, cinnamon, green onion, red chilies, fish sauce, lemon grass and eggs. Roll into small meatballs. Dust in the flour. Heat the safflower oil in a large skillet or wok. Fry the meatballs for 5 minutes. Cool. Thinly slice.

Rice:

Heat 1 tbsp of oil in a skillet and fry the eggs. Cool to room temperature and chop.

Heat the remaining oil in a wok or large skillet, fry the shallot, garlic, ginger and red chilies for 30 seconds.

Add the meatballs, chicken and shrimp and fry 4 minutes. Add the rice and continue to fry 3 minutes longer. Add the chopped eggs and oyster sauce. Mix and serve.

* Available at Japanese and Oriental food stores.

Serves 4

Philippines Pork Stew

Ingredients:

1 ½ lbs	675 g	pork loin
3 tbsp	45 ml	safflower oil
2	2	sliced Spanish onions
2 tsp	10 ml	paprika
¼ cup	60 ml	sherry
20	20	button mushrooms
¼ lb	120 g	sliced oyster mushrooms - fresh or rehydrated
2	2	crushed garlic cloves
1 tbsp	15 ml	minced ginger
1 tbsp	15 ml	Worcestershire sauce
1 tsp	5 ml	basil
¼ cup	60 ml	wine vinegar
¼ cup	60 ml	flour
4	4	cubed, pared large potatoes
2 cups	500 ml	beef stock (see page 42)
1 cup	250 ml	crushed tomatoes
1 cup	250 ml	peas
¼ cup	60 ml	bread crumbs
1	1	sliced sweet red bell pepper
1	1	sliced sweet green bell pepper

Preparation:

Dice the pork loin into ¾" (19 mm) cubes.

Heat the oil in a large Dutch oven, add the onion and paprika sauté until tender. Add the pork and continue to sauté until the pork has browned. Add the sherry, mushrooms, garlic, ginger, Worcestershire, basil and vinegar. Simmer until most of the liquid has evaporated. Sprinkle with flour and cook 3 minutes.

Add the potatoes, stock and tomatoes. Cover and simmer until sauce has thickened and potatoes are tender. Sprinkle with peas and bread crumbs. Top with bell peppers and continue to cook for 10 minutes. Serve with a garden salad.

Serves 4

 Fun Food Facts

Aprita

Aprita is the Filipino word which describes a dish which contains meat, tomatoes and vegetables, in essence a Filipino stew. Aprita has it's origins with Spain as it was the Spanish who brought European cuisines to the Philippine island. This can be seen in much of the cuisine there, even the Filipino names for the dishes resemble those of their Spanish cousins.

Pork & Chicken Adobo

Ingredients:

2 ¼ lbs	1 kg	boneless chicken
1 lb	454 g	pork loin
¾ cup	180 ml	cider vinegar
1 tbsp	15 ml	cracked black pepper
1 tsp	5 ml	salt
10	10	whole, garlic cloves
½ cup	125 ml	water
1 tbsp	15 ml	oil
4	4	chicken livers
3 tbsp	45 ml	soy sauce

Preparation:

Cut the chicken into serving pieces. Trim the pork of excess fat and cut into ¾" (19 mm) cubes.

In a sauce pan combine the chicken, pork, vinegar, pepper, salt and garlic. Marinate for 2 hours. Remove the chicken and bring to a boil. Reduce heat and simmer for 30 minutes. Add the chicken and simmer until the mixture is nearly dry. Add the water and continue to simmer for an additional 20-30 minutes.

Remove the garlic, heat the oil in a skillet and fry the garlic until brown, return to the stew.

Pound the chicken livers into a paste and add to the stew along with the soy sauce. Simmer until thick. Serve with rice.

Serves 6

Philippines

Indonesian Fried Noodles

Ingredients:

8 oz	225 g	ground pork
4 oz	120 g	lean ground beef
½ tsp	3 ml	cracked black pepper
2 tbsp	30 ml	finely chopped cilantro
4	4	minced garlic cloves
¼ tsp	1 ml	ground cinnamon
2	2	minced green onions
1	1	stalk, minced lemon grass
4	4	eggs
½ cup	125 ml	flour
3 tbsp	45 ml	safflower oil
¼ cup	60 ml	red pepper oil
¼ lb	120 g	peeled, deveined shrimp
¼ lb	120 g	boneless, skinless chicken
1	1	thinly sliced medium onion
¼ head	¼ head	shredded cabbage
1 cup	250 ml	bean sprouts
3 tbsp	45 ml	soy sauce
1 tbsp	15 ml	red chili paste
2 tbsp	30 ml	fish sauce*
1 lb	454 g	cooked, hot vermicelli noodles

Red Chili Paste:

7	7	dried red chilies
2 tsp	10 ml	Laos powder* (see page 354)

½ tsp	3 ml	cloves
½ tsp	3 ml	cinnamon
½ tsp	3 ml	nutmeg
½ tsp	3 ml	salt
1	1	stalk lemon grass, chopped
1 ½ tbsp	28 ml	fish sauce*
6	6	fried minced garlic cloves

Preparation:

Sauce:

In a small mixing bowl combine the pork, beef, pepper, cilantro, garlic, cinnamon, green onion, lemon grass and two eggs. Roll into small meatballs. Dust in the flour. Heat the safflower oil in a large skillet or wok and fry the meatballs for 5 minutes.

Beat the remaining eggs, heat 1 tbsp (15 ml) of red pepper oil in a skillet and fry the eggs, (do not fold the omelette over). Remove from heat, cool and slice.

Heat the remaining red pepper oil in a large wok, fry the shrimp and chicken until cooked thoroughly.

Add the vegetables, meatballs, fried eggs, soy sauce, red chili paste, fish sauce and cook for an additional 3 minutes. Plate the noodles and smother with stir fry.

Red Chili Paste:

In food processor combine the chilies, Laos powder, and spices. Add the remaining ingredients and process into a smooth paste.

* Available at Japanese and Oriental food stores.

Serves 4

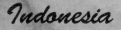

Indonesia

Indonesia Crab Cakes

Ingredients:

1 cup	250 ml	flour
1	1	beaten large egg
¼ cup	60 ml	water
½ cup	125 ml	bean sprouts
1	1	stalk, diced lemon grass
3	3	diced green onions
1	1	minced garlic clove
½ tsp	3 ml	salt
½ cup	125 ml	cooked crab meat
1 tbsp	15 ml	lime juice
¼ tsp	1 ml	crushed red chilies
1 cup	250 ml	oil

Sauce:

1 ¼ cups	310 ml	granulated sugar
1 ½ cups	375 ml	dark soy sauce
2	2	minced garlic cloves
¼ tsp	1 ml	Chinese five spice
¼ tsp	1 ml	Laos powder
1	1	bay leaf
¼ cup	60 ml	water

Preparation:

Beat the flour with the egg and water. Add the bean sprouts, lemon grass, onions, garlic, salt and crab. Beat in the lemon juice and chilies.

Heat the oil in a large skillet. Drop spoonfuls of batter into the oil and fry to golden brown on each side. Serve at once with sauce.

Sauce:

Caramelize the sugar in a heavy sauce pan. Add the remaining ingredients and bring to a boil. Reduce heat and simmer for 10 minutes. Serve as a dip for the crab cakes.

Serves 4

 Fun Food Facts

Laos Powder

Laos is the Indonesia term for a root better known in Oriental markets as "galangal". It is also called kha, ka in Thai and rieng in Vietnamese. Galangal is a root plant similar in odour, appearance and flavour to ginger but is somewhat more mild and less spicy than its cousin. Galangal is sold in fresh root (difficult to find outside Asia), dry slices (rehydrated for 20 minutes in warm water before using) and in a dried ground powder form. Sold in Indonesian stores as Laos powder, it is well worth the effort and trip to visit such a market.

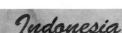

Cashew Chicken

Ingredients:

Red Chili Paste:

7	7	dried red chilies
2 tsp	10 ml	Laos powder* (see page 354)
½ tsp	3 ml	each of cloves, cinnamon, nutmeg, salt
1	1	stalk lemon grass, chopped
1 ½ tbsp	28 ml	fish sauce*
6	6	fried minced garlic cloves

Chicken:

1 ½ lbs	680 g	chicken
2 tbsp	30 ml	oil
8	8	green onions, sliced 1" (2.5 cm) long
2	2	minced garlic cloves
2 tsp	10 ml	minced ginger
2 tbsp	30 ml	soy sauce
1 tbsp	15 ml	fish sauce*
¼ cup	60 ml	water
2 tsp	10 ml	cornstarch
1 tbsp	15 ml	lime juice
¾ lb	340 g	cold, cooked, rice vermicelli
½ cup	125 ml	roasted cashews

Preparation:

Paste:

In food processor combine the chilies, Laos powder, and spices. Add the remaining ingredients and process into a smooth paste.

Chicken:

Remove the skin and bones from the chicken, cut into cubes.

Heat the oil in a wok or large skillet. Add the paste and fry for 30 seconds. Add the chicken and fry for 3 minutes. Add the onions, garlic and ginger. Continue to fry for 3 minutes.

Add the soy sauce, fish sauce and water. Reduce the heat and simmer for 2 minutes. Mix the cornstarch with the lime juice and pour over the chicken. Simmer until thick.

Place the vermicelli on a large serving platter. Cover with chicken and sprinkle with cashews. Serve at once.

* Available at Japanese and Oriental food stores.

Serves 4

Teriyaki Salmon

Ingredients:

⅓ cup	80 ml	brown sugar
1 tsp	5 ml	ground ginger
1 cup	250 ml	beef broth (see page 42)
⅓ cup	80 ml	soy sauce
2 tbsp	30 ml	cornstarch
¼ cup	60 ml	white wine
4-6 oz	4-170 g	salmon steaks, 1" (2.5 cm) thick

Preparation:

Dissolve the sugar and ginger in the broth and soy sauce in a sauce pan. Bring to a boil. Blend the cornstarch in the wine. Add to the broth and simmer until thickened. Cool.

Place salmon in a shallow tray. Cover with the sauce and marinate 1 hour, refrigerated.

Grill the salmon steaks on a charbroiler over medium coals or in the oven for 10 minutes, turning once. Brush with sauce several times during grilling.

Serves 4

China

Red Curry Shrimp

Ingredients:

Paste:

1 tbsp	15 ml	cayenne pepper
½ tsp	3 ml	caraway seeds
2 tsp	10 ml	ground coriander
1 tbsp	15 ml	Laos powder* (see page 354)
1 tsp	5 ml	salt
1 tsp	5 ml	black pepper
1 tsp	5 ml	lime zest
2 tbsp	30 ml	minced cilantro
4	4	minced shallots
4 tsp	20 ml	minced garlic
¼ cup	60 ml	red pepper olive oil

Shrimp:

1 ½ lbs	680 g	large shrimp
3 tbsp	45 ml	coconut butter
1 ½ cups	375 ml	thick coconut milk
2	2	minced serrano chilies
2	2	minced garlic cloves
3 tbsp	45 ml	fish sauce*
1 tsp	5 ml	brown sugar
2 tbsp	30 ml	lime juice

Preparation:

Paste:

Grind the cayenne, caraway, coriander, laos powder, salt and pepper fine.

Place the powder into a food processor. Add the remaining ingredients and purèe into a smooth paste. Use as required. Reserve the remainder in an air tight container refrigerated. Paste will keep up to 2 weeks.

Shrimp:

Peel and devein the shrimp.

Heat the coconut butter in a wok. Add 2 tbsp (30 ml) of the curry paste. Stir, cooking for 3 minutes. Add the coconut milk and bring to boil. Add the remaining ingredients and return to a boil.

Add the shrimp and simmer for 7-8 minutes.

Serve with rice.

* Available at Japanese and Oriental food stores.

Serves 4

Koi Gung

Ingredients:

2 ¼ lbs	1 kg	shrimp
6	6	lemons
6	6	limes
2 tbsp	30 ml	grated ginger
3	3	minced garlic cloves
2	2	minced serrano peppers
4	4	thinly sliced scallions
2 tbsp	30 ml	coarse salt
1 tbsp	15 ml	cracked black pepper
1 tsp	5 ml	oil
3	3	beaten eggs
1 cup	250 ml	cooked ground pork
1	1	stalk, minced lemon grass
1	1	head lettuce
1	1	bunch cilantro
1	1	peeled, sliced cucumber

Sauce:

1 ½ tbsp	23 ml	granulated sugar
1 tsp	5 ml	tamarind concentrate*
4 tbsp	60 ml	water
2 tbsp	30 ml	fish sauce*
1 tbsp	15 ml	soy sauce

1 tbsp	15 ml	mung beans, roasted, pounded into powder
1 tsp	5 ml	coconut oil
3 ½ tbsp	53 ml	thick coconut milk

Preparation:

Peel and devein the shrimp.

Cut the lemons and limes in half and juice the fruit. In a large stainless or glass bowl combine the juices, ginger, garlic, peppers, scallions, salt and pepper. Add the shrimp and marinate for 2 hours, refrigerated. Drain the shrimp and reserve the marinate.

Heat the oil in a frying pan and fry the eggs. Cool and cut into thin strips.

Toss the pork, lemon grass, eggs and shrimp together in a mixing bowl. Tear the leaves from the lettuce and arrange on a serving platter. Garnish with cucumber slices and cilantro leaves. Pour the sauce over and serve.

Sauce:

Combine all the sauce ingredients together in a sauce pan with ½ cup (125 ml) of the reserved marinate. Heat for 3 minutes and pour over the shrimp.

* available in Oriental food stores.

363

Asian Barbecued Ribs

Ingredients:

Sauce:

½ cup	125 ml	Hoisin sauce
3 tbsp	45 ml	orange juice
3 tbsp	45 ml	sherry
1 tbsp	15 ml	peeled, minced fresh ginger
1	1	minced garlic clove
½ tsp	3 ml	Chinese five spice
2 tbsp	30 ml	soy sauce
2 tbsp	30 ml	red wine vinegar
1 tbsp	15 ml	Dijon mustard
1 tbsp	15 ml	chili paste*

Ribs:

2 ¼ lbs	1 kg	baby back pork ribs
1 tbsp	15 ml	salt
1 tsp	5 ml	Chinese five spice
1 tsp	5 ml	pepper

Preparation:

Sauce:

Combine all the ingredients together in a mixing bowl, cover and refrigerate.

Ribs:

Cut the ribs into 5 bone sections. Combine the seasonings and sprinkle over ribs. Roast in preheated 350°F (180°C) oven for 1 ½ hours.

Grill ribs for 15 minutes over medium coals, brushing frequently with sauce. Brush 1 final time before serving.

Serves 4

 Fun Food Facts

Mustard

Burning must, that is what the word mustard means, it is derived from the Latin words "mustum ardens." Mustard has been used for trade and spice since before the Egyptians world rule. It's seed was used as an illustration of success by Jesus in Matthew 13.

It is believed that mustards first use in various cuisines was to mask spoiling food. However it wasn't long before people found that it was a pleasant condiment on most meats regardless of their stability. Every Royal house in Europe had a person who was comissioned as "mustarderian" the official mustard maker.

Dijon France is said to be the home of mustard, supposed to have been first developed into a fine condiment there. Dijon along with Norwich England rule the world for their production of the highest quality mustard. The world over has heard "Pardon me, do you have any Grey Poupon" which is of course the finest Dijon mustard known for more than three centuries. Mr. Grey developed a secret mustard recipe. Mr. Poupon gave the financial backing to market it, thus Grey Poupon was born, the year 1777.

* Available at Asian stores or in the Oriental food section of any supermarket.

Oriental Scallops

Ingredients:

½ cup	125 ml	soy sauce ·
¼ cup	60 ml	oyster sauce
¼ cup	60 ml	sherry
1 tbsp	15 ml	Worcestershire sauce
1 lb	454 g	large sea scallops
¼ cup	60 ml	flour
3 tbsp	45 ml	safflower oil
2	2	crushed garlic cloves
1 tbsp	15 ml	finely julienne cut ginger root
2	2	dried red chili peppers

Preparation:

In a mixing bowl combine the soy sauce, oyster sauce, sherry and Worcestershire sauce.

Wash the scallops and pat dry. Dust with the flour.

In a wok or large skillet heat the oil and sauté the garlic, ginger and red chilies for 30 seconds. Add the scallops and cook for 2 minutes. Pour in the sauce. Reduce heat and cook until most of the liquid has evaporated.

Serve at once.

Serves 4

China

Sweet 'N' Sour Chicken

Ingredients:

2 ¼ lbs	1 kg	chicken cut into 8 pieces
3 tbsp	45 ml	olive oil
1 tsp	5 ml	Chinese five spice
1 ½ cups	375 ml	pineapple chunks
½ cup	125 ml	water
⅓ cup	80 ml	vinegar
¼ cup	60 ml	packed brown sugar
1 tbsp	15 ml	soy sauce
2 tbsp	30 ml	cornstarch
1 cup	250 ml	pineapple juice
¾ cup	180 ml	thinly sliced green or red bell pepper
½ cup	125 ml	thinly sliced onion

Preparation:

Place the chicken in a shallow baking pan. Brush with oil and sprinkle with Chinese five spice. Bake in a preheated 350°F (180°C) oven for 45 minutes.

In a small sauce pan combine the pineapple chunks, water, vinegar, and sugar. Stir until sugar is dissolved. Add the soy sauce and bring mixture to a boil.

Combine the cornstarch with the pineapple juice and add to the sauce. Simmer until sauce is thick. Stir in the vegetables and pour over the chicken.

Continue to cook the chicken for 10 minutes longer. Serve with Apple Rice with Dates and Nuts.

Serves 4

Apple Rice with Dates and Nuts

Ingredients:

1 ½ cups	375 ml	long grain rice
4 cups	1 L	apple juice
¾ cup	180 ml	chopped pitted dates
½ cup	125 ml	toasted sliced almonds

Preparation:

Bring the rice to a boil in the apple juice. Cover and reduce heat to a simmer. Simmer until liquid has been absorbed.

Stir in the dates and almonds. Serve at once.

Serves 4

 Fun Food Facts

Chinese Five Spice

A blend of star anise, cinnamon, fennel, cloves and ginger. The most common of the spices used in oriental cookery. You may make your own by combining 2 tsp (10 ml) each of fennel, cloves, and ginger along with 1 tbsp (15 ml) each of star anise and cinnamon, grind into a fine powder.

 China

369

Thai Crab Stuffed Shrimp

Ingredients:

12	12	tiger shrimp
4 tbsp	60 ml	butter
1 ¾ cups	440 ml	flour
1 ½ cups	375 ml	milk
2 ½ cups	625 ml	cooked crab meat
½ tsp	3 ml	each of garlic granulas, ground ginger
2	2	eggs
2 cups	500 ml	fine dry bread crumbs
4 cups	1 L	peanut oil

Sauce:

1 ½ cups	375 ml	golden seedless raisins
¼ cup	60 ml	white wine vinegar
1 tbsp	15 ml	crushed red chili flakes
5	5	minced garlic cloves
1 tsp	5 ml	salt
1 cup	250 ml	crushed tomatoes
1 cup	250 ml	plum preserves
1 cup	250 ml	pineapple juice
¼ cup	60 ml	brown sugar

Preparation:

Peel and devein the shrimp. Slice three quarters down the centre. Flatten with a meat mallet. Place on a baking sheet.

Heat the butter in a sauce pan and add 4 tbsp (60 ml) of flour. Reduce heat and cook for 2 minutes. Add 1 cup (250 ml) of milk. Cook, stirring until a very thick sauce is formed. Cool to room temperature.

Stir in the crab meat. Place 2 tbsp (30 ml) of filling on each shrimp. Chill for 2 hours.

Blend the seasoning with the remaining flour. Beat the eggs in the remaining milk. Dust the shrimp with the seasoned flour; dip in the egg milk and dredge in the bread crumbs.

Heat the oil to 360°F (180°C). Fry the shrimp until golden brown. Plate the shrimp and serve with the sauce.

Sauce:

In a food processor purée the raisins, vinegar, chili flakes, garlic, salt and tomatoes. Add the preserves, pineapple juice and sugar. Blend thoroughly.

Serves 4

China

Lamb with Chinese Mushrooms

Ingredients:

1 ½ lbs	675 g	boneless lamb
8	8	dried Chinese black mushrooms
1 ½ tsp	8 ml	cornstarch
4 tsp	20 ml	light soy sauce
1	1	egg white
¼ cup	60 ml	safflower oil
1	1	minced garlic clove
2 tsp	10 ml	granulated sugar
3 tbsp	45 ml	oyster sauce
2 tbsp	30 ml	rice wine

Preparation:

Cut the lamb into thin slices.

Soak the mushrooms in warm water for 1 hour.

Blend the cornstarch with soy sauce and egg white. Pour over the lamb and marinate refrigerated for 1 hour.

Drain the mushrooms and slice into thin strips.

Heat the oil in a wok. Stir fry the mushrooms and garlic. Add the lamb and fry 2 minutes. Add the sugar, oyster sauce, and wine. Continue to fry until most of the liquid has evaporated.

Serve with steamed rice.

Serves 6

China

Indonesian Spiced Beef

Ingredients:

2 ¼ lbs	1 kg	beef flank steak
2 cups	500 ml	water
½ cup	125 ml	red pepper olive oil
1	1	large Spanish onion
8	8	sliced garlic cloves
3 tbsp	45 ml	Chile Paste
½ tsp	3 ml	salt
1 cup	250 ml	chopped tomatoes

Chili Paste:

1 tbsp	15 ml	cayenne pepper
½ tsp	3 ml	caraway seeds
2 tsp	10 ml	ground coriander
1 tbsp	15 ml	Laos powder*
1 tsp	5 ml	salt
1 tsp	5 ml	black pepper
1 tsp	5 ml	lime zest
2 tbsp	30 ml	minced cilantro
4	4	minced shallots
4 tsp	20 ml	minced garlic
¼ cup	60 ml	red pepper olive oil

Preparation:

Beef:

Trim the beef of all excess fat. Heat the water in a large kettle or Dutch oven. Add the beef and bring to a boil. Reduce heat and simmer for 30 minutes. Cool to room temperature and thinly slice. Be sure the beef is absolutely dry after slicing.

Heat ½ the oil in a wok. Add the beef and fry until brown and crisp. Remove the beef and reserve warm.

Add the remaining oil to the wok and fry the onion and garlic for 3 minutes. Add the chili paste, salt and tomatoes. Cook for 3 minutes. Add the beef and continue to cook for an additional 3 minutes.

Paste:

Grind the cayenne, caraway, coriander, Laos powder, salt and pepper fine.

Place the powder into a food processor. Add the remaining ingredients and purée into a smooth paste. Use as required. Reserve the remainder, refrigerated, in an air tight container. Paste will keep up to 2 weeks.

* Available at Japanese and Oriental food stores. (see page 354)

Serves 4

War Won Ton Soup

Ingredients:

¼ lb	120 g	peeled, deveined, small shrimp
¼ lb	120 g	lean ground pork
3	3	chopped green onions
2 tbsp	30 ml	soy sauce
1	1	crushed garlic clove
¼ tsp	1 ml	Chinese five spice blend
½ tsp	3 ml	salt
¼ lb	120 g	won ton wrappers
6 cups	1.5 L	chicken broth (see page 210)
3	3	chopped chives
1	1	sliced, medium onion
1 cup	250 ml	broccoli florets
1 cup	250 ml	button mushrooms
½ cup	125 ml	pared, sliced, carrots
¼ lb	120 g	peeled, deveined, large shrimp

Preparation:

In a food processor, place the small shrimp, pork, green onions, soy sauce, garlic, spice and salt. Process for 1 minute on slow.

Place a small amount of the mixture on a won ton wrapper. Brush the wrapper with water and fold over into a triangle. Pull the three corners together and press to seal. Repeat until all mixture is used.

Place the broth into a large pot and bring to a boil. Add the won tons and cook for 6 minutes.

Add the remaining ingredients and cook for an additional 6 minutes.

Serve at once.

Serves 6

Deep Fried Won Tons

Make the won tons as described in the recipe. Fry in 4 cups (1 L) of safflower or peanut oil which has been heat to 375°F (190°C) until golden brown. Serve with a plum sauce, available in the Oriental section of your grocer or make ours.

Plum Sauce

Ingredients:

1 cup	250 ml	plum preserves
¼ cup	60 ml	white wine vinegar
1 tsp	5 ml	red pepper chili flakes
1 tsp	5 ml	cornstarch

Preparation:

Whip all the ingredients together in a sauce pan, bring to a boil, reduce the heat and simmer for 3 minutes. Use as required.

Japanese Tuna Vegetable Soup

Ingredients:

6 cups	1.5 L	chicken broth (see page 210)
18	18	pearl onions
1	1	julienne sliced leek
1	1	diced turnip
2 cups	500 ml	bamboo shoots
1 cup	250 ml	diced firm tofu
2 oz	60 g	grated dried tuna*

Preparation:

Place the stock in a large kettle. Add the onions, leek and turnip and bring to a boil. Boil until the turnip is tender. Add the bamboo, tofu and tuna. Simmer for 5 minutes. Serve very hot.

Serves 6

* Dried tuna is available in Oriental food markets.

Japan

Thai Satay

Ingredients:

1 lb	454 g	boneless chicken breasts
3	3	minced garlic cloves
1 tbsp	15 ml	minced ginger
½ tsp	3 ml	crushed red chilies
1 tbsp	15 ml	brown sugar
3 tbsp	45 ml	lime juice
1 tbsp	15 ml	soy sauce
1 tbsp	15 ml	fish sauce*
½ tsp	3 ml	tamarind pulp*
2 tbsp	30 ml	water
1 tbsp	15 ml	oil

Sauce:

1 tbsp	15 ml	red pepper oil
1	1	minced medium onion
1 tsp	5 ml	crushed red chilies
2 tbsp	30 ml	fish sauce*
1 cup	250 ml	thick coconut milk
2	2	stalks diced lemon grass
2 tbsp	30 ml	soy sauce
¼ tsp	1 ml	salt
4 tsp	20 ml	lime juice
½ cup	125 ml	chunky style peanut butter

Preparation:

Cut the chicken into thin strips 2" (5 cm) long. Skewer on water soaked bamboo skewers and place into a square baking pan.

In a mixing bowl blend the garlic with the remaining ingredients. Pour over the skewered chicken. Marinate for 1½ hours.

Grill the skewered chicken over medium heat for 6 minutes

Sauce:

Heat the oil in a sauce pan. Add the onion and sauté until tender. Add the chilies, fish sauce, coconut milk, lemon grass, soy sauce and salt. Reduce heat and simmer for 5 minutes. Stir in the lime juice and chunky style peanut butter. Simmer for 5 minutes longer. Serve along side the Satay.

* Available at Japanese and Oriental food stores.

Serves 6

Lemon Grass Chicken

Ingredients:

1 ½ lbs	680 g	chicken thighs
3	3	stalks minced lemon grass
2 tbsp	30 ml	soy sauce
2 tbsp	30 ml	sherry
2 tsp	10 ml	Worcestershire sauce
2 tbsp	30 ml	chicken broth (see page 210)
¼ tsp	1 ml	salt
1 tsp	5 ml	sugar
¼ tsp	1 ml	cracked black pepper
1 tsp	5 ml	crushed red chilies
¼ cup	60 ml	safflower or peanut oil
2 tsp	10 ml	minced ginger
2	2	minced garlic cloves
1	1	medium diced green bell pepper
1	1	medium diced onion
½ tsp	3 ml	cornstarch
1 tbsp	15 ml	water

Preparation:

Remove the bones from the chicken and cut into strips. Place into a mixing bowl.

Blend together the lemon grass, 1 tbsp (15 ml) soy sauce, 1 tbsp (15 ml) sherry and 1 tsp (5 ml) Worcestershire sauce. Pour over the chicken and marinate for 4 hours, refrigerated.

Combine the remaining soy sauce, sherry, Worcestershire sauce with the chicken broth, salt, sugar, pepper and chilies.

Heat the oil in a wok, add the ginger, garlic and cook for 15 seconds. Add the bell pepper and onion. Fry for 2 minutes.

Add the chicken with the marinate and fry for 3 minutes. Add the sauce and continue to fry for 2 minutes.

Combine the cornstarch with the water and add to the chicken. Simmer until sauce is thick. Serve at once with rice or noodles.

Serves 4

 Fun Food Facts

Lemon Grass

A plant of south east Asia, lemon grass is an essential ingredient in Thai, Indonesian and Vietnamese cookery. Lemon grass resembles a short woody stem, as it is very fibrous, it should be minced before cookery. It can be used whole if discarded before serving your menu item. If lemon grass is unavailable substitute lemon zest. Lemon grass is very high in vitamin A and C, it is recommended for digestive problems as well.

Yakitori

Ingredients:

⅓ cup	80 ml	brown sugar
1 tbsp	15 ml	minced ginger
1 cup	250 ml	beef broth (see page 42)
⅓ cup	80 ml	soy sauce
2 tbsp	30 ml	cornstarch
¼ cup	60 ml	sherry
2 tbsp	30 ml	oil
4-6 oz	4-175 g	boneless, skinless chicken breasts

Preparation:

In a sauce pan, dissolve the sugar and ginger in the broth and soy sauce. Bring to a boil.

Mix the cornstarch with the sherry and add to the sauce. Reduce heat and simmer until sauce thickens. Cool.

Dice the chicken into large cubes and skewer onto water soaked bamboo skewers. Brush the oil over the chicken skewers. Grill over medium coals for 5 minutes per side. Brush frequently with sauce while cooking. Brush 1 final time and serve.

Serves 4

Japan

Stir Fried Vegetables

Ingredients:

6	6	rehydrated Chinese black mushrooms
¾ cup	180 ml	water
4 tsp	20 ml	dark soy sauce
1 ½ tsp	8 ml	sesame oil
1 tbsp	15 ml	granulated sugar
4	4	celery stalks
1	1	sweet red bell pepper
¼ head	¼ head	Chinese cabbage
2 oz	60 g	spinach leaves
1	1	small head bok choy
3	3	green onions
4 tsp	20 ml	peanut oil
5 drops	5 drops	red pepper oil
2	2	minced garlic cloves
1 tbsp	15 ml	minced ginger
2 tbsp	30 ml	light soy sauce
1 tbsp	15 ml	sherry
1 tbsp	15 ml	lime juice
1 ½ tsp	8 ml	cornstarch

Preparation:

Remove the stems from the mushrooms and slice. Mix half the water, dark soy sauce, sesame oil and sugar in a small sauce pan. Add the mushrooms and simmer until most of the liquid has evaporated.

Coarsely chop the vegetables.

Heat the peanut and red pepper oils. Fry the garlic and ginger, add the vegetables and fry for 4 minutes. Blend the remaining water with light soy sauce, sherry, lime juice and cornstarch. Add to the vegetables and simmer for 1 minute.

Serves 6

 Fun Food Facts

Sherry

This fortified wine is used in various forms of cuisine. In most ethnic groups sherry has seemingly gained favour as an excellent flavouring. Sherry is a blended wine which has been aged for no less than seven years. Originally made in Andalusia, Spain, good quality sherry type wines are being produced in various other regions. Types of sherry include: Fino; pale and dry, Oloroso; honeyed and dark, Amontillado; aged longer thus heavier in flavour without harshness, Amoroso; very light in colour (brandy like), confection in taste is used in desserts, Brown sherry, sometimes called "cream" sherry is dark in colour, smooth in taste, aged longer than others. The most famous of the sherries is "Harvey's Bristol Cream". Exporting sherry of Jerez, Spain, Harvey's of Bristol England have become the standard of excellence the world over for the fine wine. The name Bristol Cream came by a chance remark of an aristocratic lady who also had a sample of sherry called "Bristol milk", her remark "if that is the milk then this surely must be the cream". The name stuck and today is the mark of the most superior of all sherries.

Vietnam

Vietnamese Spring Rolls

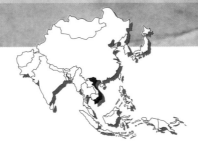

Ingredients:

2 oz	60 g	cellophane noodles*
½ lb	225 g	shrimp meat
1 tbsp	15 ml	fish sauce*
¼ tsp	1 ml	crushed red chilies
2	2	green onions
1	1	pared, shredded, small carrot
1 cup	250 ml	shredded cabbage
¼ cup	60 ml	finely diced, shiitake mushrooms
1 tbsp	15 ml	brown sugar
1 tbsp	15 ml	soy sauce
2 cups	500 ml	water
8	8	sheets large round rice paper*
4 cups	1 L	safflower or peanut oil

Sauce:

1 tbsp	15 ml	red pepper oil
1	1	medium onion minced
1 tsp	5 ml	crushed red chilies
2 tbsp	30 ml	fish sauce*
½ cup	125 ml	crushed tomatoes
½ cup	125 ml	chicken broth (see page 210)
¼ cup	60 ml	sherry
2 tbsp	30 ml	soy sauce
¼ tsp	1 ml	salt
4 tsp	20 ml	lime juice
½ cup	125 ml	chunky style peanut butter

Preparation:

Cut the noodles into small pieces and place into a mixing bowl. Add the shrimp meat, fish sauce, red chilies, green onions, carrot, cabbage and mushrooms; mix thoroughly.

Place the sugar, soy sauce and water in large mixing bowl. Dip 1 sheet of rice paper into the water and cut into four. Place 2 tbsp (30 ml) of mixture into the centre of each triangle. Fold the corners in and roll together. Set aside and repeat the process until all the filling mixture has been used. Heat the oil to 360°F (180°C). Fry the rolls until golden brown. Serve with the sauce on the side.

Sauce:

Heat the oil in a sauce pan. Add the onion and sauté until tender. Add the chilies, fish sauce, tomatoes, chicken broth, sherry, soy sauce and salt. Reduce heat and simmer for 5 minutes. Stir in the lime juice and chunky style peanut butter. Simmer for 5 minutes longer.

* Available at Japanese or Oriental food stores.

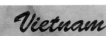

Vietnam

Sweet & Sour Ribs

Ingredients:

4 lbs	1.75 kg	spare ribs
⅓ cup	80 ml	soy sauce
1 cup	250 ml	brown sugar
¾ cup	180 ml	vinegar
½ cup	125 ml	sherry
2 tbsp	30 ml	oyster sauce
1	1	thinly sliced green or red bell pepper
1 tbsp	15 ml	chopped candied ginger
¾ cup	180 ml	pineapple chunks
2 tsp	10 ml	cornstarch
2 tbsp	30 ml	water

Preparation:

Cut the ribs into 2" (5 cm) size pieces. Place on a baking sheet. Bake in a preheated 325°F (160°C) oven for 1½ hours or until crisp.

Blend the soy sauce, sugar, vinegar, sherry, oyster sauce, green pepper in a sauce pan. Bring to a boil. Add the ginger and pineapple chunks.

Blend the cornstarch with the water and add to the sauce. Remove from the heat as soon as the sauce thickens. Pour over the ribs and serve.

Serves 4

China

Com Chien

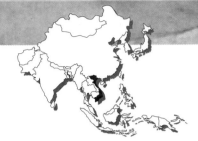

Ingredients:

3 tbsp	45 ml	oil
½ lb	125 g	shredded pork
½ lb	125 g	small shrimp
3	3	minced garlic cloves
1	1	Spanish onion
1	1	finely diced celery stalk
2	2	stalks lemon grass, finely chopped
¼ cup	60 ml	finely chopped shiitake mushrooms
1 tsp	5 ml	salt
¼ tsp	1 ml	cracked black pepper
¼ tsp	1 ml	crushed red chilies
3 cups	750 ml	cooked long grain rice
1 tbsp	15 ml	soy sauce
1 tbsp	15 ml	fish sauce*
1 cup	250 ml	peas
2	2	beaten eggs

Preparation:

In a wok heat the oil, add the pork and cook through. Add the shrimp, garlic, onion, celery, lemon grass and mushrooms. Fry for 5 minutes.

Stir in the salt, pepper, chilies and rice. Fry for an additional 5 minutes. Stir in the soy sauce, fish sauce, peas and eggs. Continue to fry until eggs are cooked through.

* Available at Japanese and Oriental food stores.

Serves 4

 Fun Food Facts

Fish Sauce

Called nam pla in Thai and nouc mam in Vietmanese, fish sauce is light in colour similar to soy sauce. Fish sauce is a blend of water, salt and anchovy extracts, made by salting the fillets and allowing them to ferment. The liquid that flows from the fermenting process is gathered and used in making the sauce. As it is very strong in flavour and aroma a small amount per dish will suffice.

Vietnam

393

Tempura

Ingredients:

1	1	egg
1 cup	250 ml	ice cold water
2 tbsp	30 ml	white wine
2 cups	500 ml	flour
4 cups	1 L	oil
1 lb	454 g	peeled, deveined, large shrimp
1	1	sliced, large Spanish onion
2	2	sliced, pared large carrots
1	1	sliced zucchini
1 cup	250 ml	broccoli florets

Sauce:

1 tbsp	15 ml	dashino-moto*
1 cup	250 ml	water
1 tbsp	15 ml	brown sugar
2 tbsp	30 ml	sake (rice wine)
¼ cup	60 ml	soy sauce
1 tbsp	15 ml	fresh grated ginger

Preparation:

Beat the egg. Add the water. Blend in the wine and add 1 cup (250 ml) of the flour. Keep the batter light by not over beating.

Heat the oil to 350°F (180°C).

Dust the shrimp and vegetables in the remaining flour; dip into the batter and fry in the oil until lightly brown in colour.

Sauce:

Boil the dashino-moto in the water for 3 minutes. Add the remaining ingredients. Remove from heat and serve along side the fried shrimp and vegetables.

Serves 4

 Fun Food Facts

Dashino-moto

Dashino-moto is Japanese for soup base, usually it refers to soup base of bonito, which is a member of the tuna family caught extensively in the Atlantic ocean. Dashino-moto usually contains MSG and salt as well as other flavour enhancers. Use in soups and sauces.

* Dashino-moto is availiable at Oriental Food stores.

Chinese Short Soup

Ingredients:

⅓ lb	150 g	peeled and deveined shrimp
⅓ lb	150 g	minced pork
3	3	scallions
1	1	minced garlic clove
½ tsp	3 ml	minced ginger root
1 tbsp	15 ml	sherry
1 tbsp	15 ml	soy sauce
½ tsp	3 ml	Worcestershire sauce
36	36	won ton wrappers
8 cups	2 L	chicken broth (see page 210)

Preparation:

Mince the shrimp and blend with the pork.

Mince the scallions and blend into the meats with the garlic, ginger, sherry, soy and Worcestershire.

Divide the mixture evenly among the won ton wrappers. Moisten the edges of the wrappers and fold in two to seal. Then pinch together the three edges.

Heat the chicken broth to a boil in a large kettle. Drop the won tons into the broth and cook for 10 minutes. Serve 6 won tons per person along with the broth.

Serves 6

China

Grilled Kal Bi Chicken

Ingredients:

6-6 oz	6-170 g	boneless, skinless chicken breasts
⅓ cup	80 ml	soy sauce
3 tbsp	45 ml	sesame oil
3 tbsp	45 ml	sherry
½ cup	125 ml	minced scallions
2	2	minced garlic cloves
2 tsp	10 ml	minced fresh ginger
3 tbsp	45 ml	brown sugar

Preparation:

Flatten the chicken breasts and place them in a large shallow pan.

Combine the remaining ingredients together to form a marinate. Pour the marinate over chicken and marinate, refrigerated, for 3 hours. Drain the chicken and reserve marinate.

Grill over medium heat for 7-8 minutes per side. Baste frequently with marinate.

Serves 6

China

Sushi

Ebi Prawns

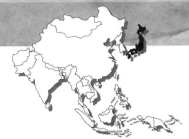

Ingredients:

1 lb	454 g	large prawns
4 cups	1 L	water
1 cup	250 ml	white wine
1	1	lemon
1	1	small onion
1	1	celery stalk
1 tsp	5 ml	salt
½ tsp	3 ml	peppercorns
1 ½ cups	375 ml	sushi rice

Rice:

1 cup	250 ml	water
¾ cup	180 ml	medium grain rice
1 ½ tbsp	23 ml	vinegar
1 ½ tbsp	23 ml	lemon juice
2 tbsp	30 ml	granulated sugar
½ tsp	3 ml	salt

Preparation:

Skewer the prawns with bamboo skewers along the underside of the prawn.

In a large pot, bring to a boil the water, wine, lemon, onion, celery and seasonings.

Place the skewered shrimp into the boiling liquid. Remove the shrimp once they float. Drop them into ice cold water. Once cooled, remove the skewer and peel away the shell, leaving the tail tip.

Butterfly the shrimp by cutting along the middle from the underside. Do not cut through.

Rice:

Bring the water to a boil and add the rice. Reduce heat. Cover and cook until rice absorbs the liquid.

In a small sauce pan, combine the vinegar, lemon juice, sugar and salt. Bring to a boil. Reduce heat and simmer until sugar is dissolved, pour into rice. Let stand until liquid is absorbed by the rice. Cool.

Place small amounts of rice in the shrimp cut and wrap the shrimp around it.

Serve at once.

Serves 4

 Fun Food Facts

Sushi rice

Sushi rice is a medium grain rice, highly polished with corn syrup and corn starch. There are many varieties of sushi rice on the market, one of the finest is Kokuho Rose, a high quality rice milled in California. Kokuho means treasure, with our recipes and this rice, these menu items will be ones your guests will treasure.

Japan

Sushi

California Roll Sushi

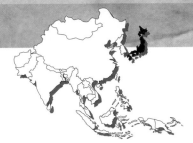

Ingredients:

Rice:

1 cup	250 ml	water
¾ cup	180 ml	medium grain rice
1 ½ tbsp	23 ml	vinegar
1 ½ tbsp	23 ml	lemon juice
2 tbsp	30 ml	granulated sugar
½ tsp	3 ml	salt

Sushi:

1	1	sheet of nori*, cut in half
1 cup	250 ml	sushi rice
1 tsp	5 ml	Dijon mustard
1	1	finely sliced, small cucumber
1	1	avocado, sliced fine
1 cup	250 ml	cooked crab meat

Preparation:

Rice:

Bring the water to a boil and add the rice. Reduce the heat, cover and cook until rice absorbs the liquid.

In a small sauce pan, combine the vinegar, lemon juice, sugar and salt. Bring to a boil. Reduce heat and simmer until sugar is dissolved. Pour into the rice. Let stand until liquid is absorbed by the rice. Cool.

Sushi:

Lay the nori flat, spread with a thin layer of rice.

Turn over and spread with mustard.

Layer with cucumber, avocado and crab meat. Roll in jelly roll fashion.

Wrap with a piece of plastic wrap. Roll tightly. Remove wrap and cut into 8 slices. Serve.

* Nori is a toasted, dried seaweed product available in most Asian food stores and the gourmet section of some supermarkets.

Serves 4

Fun Food Facts

Avocados

Avocados are natures answer to butter. Rich and creamy avocados are delightful in salads, soups and sauces. They blend well with most international cuisines as they are cultivated in the Americas, Middle East and Africa. Avocados are a good source of vitamins such as A,B,C,D,E and are high in calcium. One average size avocado contains 306 calories, 3.6 grams of protien, 12 grams of carbohydrates, 30 grams of fat, 0 milligrams of cholesterol, 21 milligrams of sodium, 3.7 grams of fibre.

Sushi

Cream Cheese Smoked Salmon Sushi

Ingredients:

1 cup	250 ml	water
¾ cup	180 ml	short grain rice
1 ½ tbsp	23 ml	vinegar
1 ½ tbsp	23 ml	lemon juice
2 tbsp	30 ml	granulated sugar
½ tsp	3 ml	salt
1	1	piece nori* 7" x 8" (18 x 20 cm)
2 oz	60 g	smoked salmon
4 oz	120 g	cream cheese
1	1	julienne cut spring onion

Preparation:

Bring the water to a boil and add the rice. Reduce heat. Cover and cook until rice absorbs the liquid.

In a small sauce pan, combine the vinegar, lemon juice, sugar and salt. Bring to a boil. Reduce heat and simmer until sugar is dissolved. Pour into rice. Let stand until liquid is absorbed by the rice. Cool.

Place a piece of nori on a slightly dampened tea towel. Top with rice and pack down firmly. Place a generous portion of salmon along a short end. Beside it, place a strip of cream cheese and onion.

Roll in jelly roll fashion. Using a very sharp knife, cut into 1" (2.5 cm) slices.
Serve.

Yields 8 Slices

* Nori is a toasted, dried seaweed product available in most Asian food stores and the gourmet section of some supermarkets.

Japan

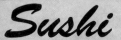

Sushi

Temaki Grilled Salmon Sushi

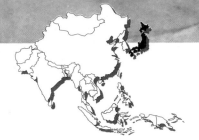

Ingredients:

8 oz	225 g	salmon fillet
1	1	sheet nori*
1 cup	225 g	sushi rice
1	1	pared, julienne cut carrot
1	1	small, julienne cut cucumber
1 oz	28 g	alfalfa sprouts

Rice:

1 cup	250 ml	water
¾ cup	180 ml	medium grain rice
1 ½ tbsp	23 ml	vinegar
1 ½ tbsp	23 ml	lemon juice
2 tbsp	30 ml	granulated sugar
½ tsp	3 ml	salt

Preparation:

Grill or broil the salmon, skin side down. Once cooked, cut the fish into julienne strips.

Cut the nori into 8 pieces. Place small amounts of the salmon and the remaining ingredients on the nori and wrap in a conical shape.

Rice:

Bring the water to a boil and add the rice. Reduce heat. Cover and cook until rice absorbs the liquid.

In a small sauce pan, combine the vinegar, lemon juice, sugar and salt. Bring to a boil. Reduce heat and simmer until sugar is dissolved. Pour into rice. Let stand until liquid is absorbed by the rice. Cool.

Serve.

* Nori is a toasted, dried seaweed product available in most Asian food stores and the gourmet section of some supermarkets.

Serves 4

 Fun Food Facts

Salmon

Salmon is the worlds most popular fish. Salmon is sold fresh to markets in various species caught both in the Atlantic and Pacific oceans. The most popular species are the Atlantic, Chinook, Coho, Sockeye, Chum and Pinks. Salmon is most likely the oldest known gourmet fish, salmon bones were once discovered in the residence of a cave man. On the west coast of the Americas the native people thought so highly of the salmon that it was elevated to godhood. Salmon caught in the north Atlantic is prized by the people of Great Britain and the Scandinavians. Escoffier (the King of Chefs) knew the value of cooking salmon as simply as possible and recommended that it be served on it's own, simply cooked with butter. Some smoked salmon types are: Danish smoked; a cold smoked salmon from Denmark. Indian Cured or Cold smoked; salmon that has been smoked for up to two weeks, smoked principally by the West Coast American indians and often sold in small cedar boxes to retain the smoked flavour. Kippered salmon; salmon that has been soaked in brine and has either been cold or hot smoked. Types vary depending on the country, cold smoked in Great Britain or hot smoked in the Americas. Lox; a brined soaked mildly cured Atlantic or Pacific salmon, popularized by the Russian Jewish community it is now a favourite of all nationalities especially when served with a bagel and cream cheese. Nova Scotia or Nova salmon; Atlantic cold smoked salmon popular along the east coast of America especially, in the ethnic sections of New York.

Japan

Sashimi

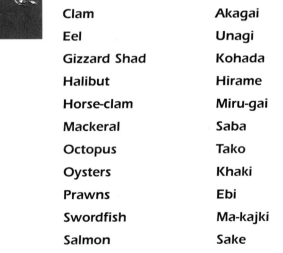

Simply stated, sashimi is raw fish, sliced very thin. The fish varies from season to season but the rule is absolutely fresh. Sashimi is served with wasabi (Japanese green horseradish). This is difficult to find outside of Japan, but a dry powder form is available in oriental shops. Japanese gari (pickled ginger) is also served with sashimi and usually eaten between portions to clear the palate for the next portion.

Some types of sashimi are:

English:	Japanese:
Abalone	Awabi
Bonita	Katsuo
Clam	Akagai
Eel	Unagi
Gizzard Shad	Kohada
Halibut	Hirame
Horse-clam	Miru-gai
Mackeral	Saba
Octopus	Tako
Oysters	Khaki
Prawns	Ebi
Swordfish	Ma-kajki
Salmon	Sake
Scallops	Hotate-gai
Sea Bream	Tai
Sea Eel	Anago
Squid	Ika
Tuna	Maguro
Yellowtail	Hamachi

South Pacific

Nowhere else in the world does one experience the flavours of a country as they do with the Islands of the South Pacific. Each is an island completely depended on what nature provides them with. What grows, what flies, what swims, all play an intricate part in the cuisine of the nation.

As many of the islands were settled by European explorers, the European influence is prevalent throughout. In recent years however, the Asian influence has spread throughout the islands, as has the African influence.

Due to the great quantity of wonderful fruit which is natural in the islands, but exotic elsewhere, one can readily see how the fruit makes the dishes as exciting as the islands themselves. You may choose exhilarating dishes like Veal Cutlets with Kiwi Mandarin Salsa or Blackberry Cream Peppered Veal Chops with Pineapple Mango Carrots, or exotic Pacific fish and seafood like Australian Mahi Mahi, which is dolphin fish (not the dolphin mammal). All your selections will give you the impression of sitting on white sandy beaches, or wading into turquoise seas, or sipping Mai Tai's with that special someone (also something you may do without actually being there). You know dinner is going to be just right.

Crab au Gratin

Ingredients:

4 tbsp	60 ml	butter
2	2	finely diced celery stalks
1	1	finely diced, medium onion
4 tbsp	60 ml	flour
¾ cup	180 ml	heavy cream
¾ cup	180 ml	chicken broth (see page 210)
2 ½ cups	625 ml	cooked crab meat
½ tsp	3 ml	each of oregano leaves, thyme leaves, basil leaves, cayenne pepper, black pepper, onion powder, garlic powder, salt, paprika
½ cup	125 ml	fine dry bread crumbs
1 ¾ cups	410 ml	grated Cheddar cheese

Sauce:

3 tbsp	45 ml	butter
3 tbsp	45 ml	flour
½ cup	125 ml	chicken stock (see page 210)
½ cup	125 ml	heavy cream
½ cup	125 ml	champagne
1 cup	250 ml	rehydrated sundried tomatoes, chopped
1	1	bunch, chopped arugula

Preparation:

Heat the butter in a sauce pan, sauté the celery and onions until tender. Add the flour. Reduce heat and cook for 2 minutes. Add the cream and broth. Cook over low heat stirring until a very thick sauce is formed.

Stir in the crab meat, herbs and spices. Spoon into a casserole dish. Sprinkle with bread crumbs and cheese. Bake In a preheated 350°F (180°C) oven for 30 minutes.

Sauce:

Melt the butter in a saucepan. Add the flour and stir into a paste (roux) cooking over low heat.

Add chicken stock, cream and champagne. Simmer for 10 minutes over medium heat. Stir in the tomatoes and arugula. Simmer for 5 additional minutes.

Plate the crab casserole. Cover with sauce. Serve with rice or noodles.

Serves 4

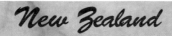

New Zealand

Shark Stew

Ingredients:

1 ½ lbs	675 g	coarsely diced boneless shark
3 cups	750 ml	fish stock
2 tsp	10 ml	salt
1 tsp	5 ml	each of thyme and oregano leaves
3 tbsp	45 ml	butter
20	20	pearl onions
2	2	julienned carrots
2	2	julienned celery stalks
1	1	minced garlic clove
20	20	button mushrooms
3 tbsp	45 ml	flour
1 ½ cups	375 ml	tomato purée

Preparation:

In a Dutch oven, place the shark, stock, salt, thyme and oregano. Cover and simmer for 15 minutes.

In a sauce pan heat the butter. Add the onions, carrots, celery, garlic and mushrooms. Sauté for 5 minutes. Sprinkle with flour and cook for 3 minutes without browning. Pour over the shark and blend. Add the tomato purée and simmer for 5 minutes.

Serve with rice.

Serves 6

Hawaii

Coconut Orange Roughy

Ingredients:

1 ½ lbs	675 g	orange roughy fillets
1 tsp	5 ml	each of salt, paprika, black pepper
10 tbsp	120 ml	butter
1	1	diced Spanish onion
1	1	minced garlic clove
3 tbsp	45 ml	flour
¾ cup	180 ml	blanched, grated almonds
1 tsp	5 ml	crushed red chilies
½ tsp	3 ml	thyme leaves
1	1	bay leaf
¼ cup	60 ml	lemon juice
¼ cup	60 ml	honey
2 cups	500 ml	coconut milk
1 cup	250 ml	grated fresh coconut
¼ cup	60 ml	toasted coconut

Preparation:

Sprinkle the orange roughy with salt, paprika and pepper.

Heat 6 tbsp (90 ml) of butter in a large skillet and fry the onion and garlic until translucent. Sprinkle with flour and cook for 2 minutes. Add the grated almonds, chilies, thyme, bay leaf, lemon juice, honey, coconut milk and fresh coconut.

Cover, reduce heat and simmer for 30 minutes.

Heat the remaining butter in a skillet and sauté the fish for 4 minutes per side. Plate the fish, smother with sauce and serve with a rice pilaff. Garnish with the toasted coconut.

Serves 6

Court Bouillon

Ingredients:

16 cups	4 L	water
1 tbsp	15 ml	green peppercorns
1 tbsp	15 ml	salt
1	1	sliced onion
2	2	chopped carrots
1	1	chopped celery stalk
1	1	lemon cut in half
1 cup	250 ml	white wine
1	1	bouquet garni*

Preparation:

Combine all the ingredients. Bring to a boil. Boil 30 minutes.

Strain through a cheesecloth. Reserve the liquid and discard bouquet.

Use the broth for cooking fish and shellfish.

Yields 16 cups (4 L)

 Fun Food Facts

* A bouquet garni is a cheesecloth with parsley, peppercorns, chervil, thyme, rosemary or other herbs and spices tied within.

 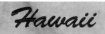

Blackberry Cream Veal Chops
with Pineapple Mango Carrots

Ingredients:

3 cups	750 ml	fresh blackberries
¼ cup	60 ml	heavy cream
6-6 oz	6-180 g	veal chops
¼ cup	60 ml	crushed black peppercorns
¼ cup	60 ml	butter

Carrots:

1 lb	454 g	pared, julienne cut carrots
1 cup	250 ml	crushed pineapple, drain and reserve juice
1 cup	250 ml	mango pulp
¼ cup	60 ml	granulated sugar
1 ½ tbsp	24 ml	cornstarch

Preparation:

Process 2 ½ cups (625 ml) of the blackberries in a food processor until smooth. Using a sieve, strain the blackberries into a saucepan to remove the seeds. Heat to a boil. Reduce the heat and simmer until liquid yields ½ cup (125 ml). Whip in the cream.

While blackberry juice simmers, pat the peppercorns into the veal chops.

Heat the butter in a large skillet and sauté the veal chops to the desired doneness.

Plate the chops. Pour the sauce over the chops and garnish with the remaining blackberries. Serve.

Carrots:

Steam the carrots for 12-15 minutes. Transfer to a serving dish.

Purée the pineapple with the mango in a food processor. Press through the sieve into a small saucepan. Stir in the sugar.

Blend the cornstarch into ¼ cup (60 ml) of reserved pineapple juice. Add to fruit. Cook over low heat until sauce thickens.

Pour the sauce over the carrots and serve at once.

Serves 6

Australia

White Chocolate Strawberry Kiwi Cream

Ingredients:

1 cup	250 ml	whipping cream
¼ cup	60 ml	lemon juice
1 tsp	5 ml	grated lemon zest
6 oz	180 g	grated white chocolate
3 tbsp	45 ml	sugar
2 cups	500 ml	sliced strawberries
3	3	pared, thinly sliced, kiwi

Strawberries:

25	25	fresh large strawberries
4 oz	120 g	grated, white chocolate
1 tbsp	15 ml	melted butter

Preparation:

In a saucepan heat ¼ cup (60 ml) of the whipping cream, lemon juice and zest. Reduce heat and add the chocolate. Stir until very smooth. Pour into a small mixing bowl and refrigerate until cool. Do not allow to set.

Beat the remaining whipping cream with the sugar. Fold the chocolate into the whipped cream. Spoon the sliced fruit into 6 parfait glasses. Cover with the cream. Refrigerate for 4 hours before serving.

Strawberries:

Wash and dry the berries. In a double boiler melt the chocolate and stir in the butter. Dip the strawberries in the chocolate. Place on a sheet of wax paper, allow to harden before removing to a platter. Do not refrigerate.

Garnish the parfait glasses with 1 chocolate dipped strawberry. Serve the remaining strawberries along side.

Serves 6

Fun Food Facts

Strawberries

Due to the expansion of growers, strawberries are now available globally. In Japan some strawberries grow as big as baseballs, unfortunately they are all consumed in that country. Thanks to differing seasons strawberries are now available year round. Strawberries are excellent fresh but lose water (they have more than 90%) quickly when cooked and therefore break down and lose shape. Excellent in jam and jellies, fresh fruit salads, pies, cakes, tortes and cold soups. Strawberries are excellent as a snack. 1 pound (454 g) contains 136 calories, 2.8 grams of protein, 31.9 grams of carbohydrates, 1.7 grams of fat, 0 milligrams of cholesterol, 5 milligrams of sodium, and 2.4 grams of fibre.

Australia

Australian Swordfish

Ingredients:

3 tbsp	45 ml	butter
1 lb	454 g	diced Swordfish
1 cup	250 ml	fresh figs diced (or ½ cup (125 ml) diced dry figs)
1	1	finely diced red bell pepper
3 tbsp	45 ml	flour
2 cups	500 ml	chicken broth (see page 210)
1 cup	250 ml	banana slices
1 ½ cups	375 ml	Béarnaise Sauce

Preparation:

Heat the butter in a large skillet. Sauté the Swordfish, figs and pepper until tender. Sprinkle with flour and continue to sauté for 2 minutes. Add the broth and simmer until thickened. Stir in the banana slices.

Spoon into four 4" (10 cm) ramekins. Top with Béarnaise Sauce.

Place in a preheated 500°F (250°C) oven for 5-6 minutes or until golden brown. Serve at once with rice.

Béarnaise Sauce

Ingredients:

3 tbsp	45 ml	white wine
1 tbsp	15 ml	dried tarragon leaves
1 tsp	5 ml	lemon juice
½ cup	125 ml	butter
3	3	egg yolks
1 tsp	5 ml	fresh chopped tarragon

Preparation:

Combine the wine, tarragon and lemon juice in a small sauce pan. Over high heat reduce to 2 tbsp (30 ml). Strain.

In another small sauce pan, melt the butter and heat to almost boiling.

In a blender or food processor, process the egg yolks until blended. With the machine running, add the butter in a slow thin stream. With the machine on slow, add the reduced wine mixture. Process just until blended. Place in a serving bowl. Stir in the fresh tarragon.

Vanilla Seafood

Ingredients:

3 tbsp	45 ml	olive oil
1 lb	454 g	sliced lobster tail meat
1 lb	454 g	large peeled & deveined shrimp
1	1	sliced red onion
1	1	sliced yellow bell pepper
1	1	sliced green bell pepper
3 oz	80 g	sliced mushrooms
1 cup	250 ml	chopped tomatoes
¼ cup	60 ml	white wine
2 tsp	10 ml	vanilla extract
½ tsp	3 ml	paprika
½ tsp	3 ml	cayenne pepper
½ tsp	3 ml	thyme
½ tsp	3 ml	basil
½ tsp	3 ml	cracked black pepper
½ tsp	3 ml	salt
3 cups	750 ml	hot cooked rice, or noodles

Preparation:

Preheat the oven to 400°F (200°C).

Heat the oil in a large skillet or wok. Sauté the lobster, shrimp and vegetables, until the lobster is cooked. Add the tomatoes, wine, vanilla and seasonings. Reduce heat and simmer for 6 minutes.

Place the rice into a 9" x 13" casserole dish, smother with seafood mixture, bake in the oven for 15 minutes. Serve at once.

Serves 6

 Fun Food Facts

Vanilla

Along with the cacao bean, bell peppers, chilies, peanuts, potatoes, tomatoes, avocado, pineapple, various beans, gourds and squashes, vanilla originally was a discovery of Spanish explorers who brought all these back to Europe. It was however, already a widely used substance of the Latin American native people. The vanilla (pod) bean comes from the vanilla plant which is a member of the orchid family. Using a vanilla bean in food may give a stronger flavour than extract and should be used whenever possible. Pure extract should be the choice over an artificial flavouring which obtains its flavouring through oil and cloves. To make vanilla sugar, place two large beans in a glass jar, cover with two cups (500 ml) of granulated sugar. Cover and keep in a dark place for 2 weeks before using.

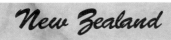 *New Zealand*

Beefsteak Tomato Tart

Ingredients:

1 ½ cups	375 ml	sifted all purpose flour
½ tsp	3 ml	salt
½ cup	125 ml	shortening
4-5 tbsp	60-75 ml	water
½ cup	125 ml	freshly grated Romano cheese
4	4	eggs
2 cups	500 ml	Ricotta cheese
2	2	minced garlic cloves
2 tbsp	30 ml	fresh chopped basil
8	8	sliced, large tomatoes
2 tbsp	30 ml	garlic flavoured oil
1 tbsp	15 ml	fresh chopped thyme
1 tsp	5 ml	coarse ground salt
1 tsp	5 ml	cracked black pepper

Preparation:

Preheat the oven to 375°F (190°C).

Sift the flour and salt together into a mixing bowl. Cut the shortening into the flour with a pastry cutter or fork until pastry forms walnut size. Add the water, only enough to bind the pastry, toss. Divide pastry in two. Roll out and fit into 2-9" (22 cm) pie dishes.

Sprinkle each crust with Romano cheese.

Blend the eggs, Ricotta, garlic and basil together until smooth. Pour into pie shells. Arrange the tomatoes on top of the Ricotta mixture. Brush with the oil. Sprinkle with the thyme, salt and pepper.

Bake for 20-25 minutes. Cool to room temperature. Serve with Salad Aida.

Yields 2 Pies

Salad Aida

Ingredients:

1 head	1 head	curly endive lettuce
8	8	julienne cut marinated artichokes
4	4	tomatoes cut in wedges
1	1	julienne cut green bell pepper
1	1	julienne cut red bell pepper
3	3	chopped hard boiled eggs
½ cup	125 ml	extra virgin olive oil
3 tbsp	45 ml	red wine vinegar
1 tsp	5 ml	each of basil, tarragon
¼ tsp	1 ml	salt
¼ tsp	1 ml	cracked black pepper

Preparation:

Wash, trim and cut the lettuce. Place in a salad serving bowl. Arrange the artichoke, tomatoes, peppers and eggs around the lettuce.

Blend the oil, vinegar and seasoning. Pour over the salad and serve.

Serves 6

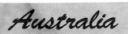

Australia

Peach Clafouti
with Lemon Creme Anglaise

Ingredients:

2 cups	500 ml	peaches, sliced
5 tbsp	75 ml	granulated sugar
2 cups	500 ml	evaporated milk
3	3	eggs
¼ cup	60 ml	flour
½ tsp	3 ml	almond extract
½ tsp	3 ml	vanilla extract

Sauce:

¾ cup	180 ml	granulated sugar
6	6	egg yolks
2 cups	500 ml	scalded milk
1 tsp	5 ml	lemon extract
1 tsp	5 ml	grated lemon zest

Preparation:

Preheat the oven to 350°F (180°C).

Sprinkle 2 tbsp (30 ml) of sugar over the peaches. Grease an 8" (20 cm) round baking pan. Line with the peaches.

In a food processor combine the remaining sugar, milk, eggs, flour and extracts until smooth. Pour over the peaches and bake for 45 minutes or until an inserted toothpick comes out clean. Serve warm with the sauce.

Sauce:

In the top of a double boiler whisk the sugar with the egg yolks until light and pale. Place over simmering water. Slowly whip in the milk. Cook until sauce thickens, stirring constantly.

Remove from the heat, stir in the extract and zest.

Serves 6

 Fun Food Facts

Milk

Milk, natures most complete food. All of what is good for man (and some that is not) derives from milk. Evaporated milk is milk which has 50% of its water removed. When using a recipe that calls for 1 cup (250 ml) of milk and you find yourselves without, you may use a ½ cup (125 ml) of evaporated milk along with ½ cup (125 ml) of water. Other types of milk are whole fresh milk with 4% butter fat or higher. Homogenized milk is the same as whole milk but it is cooked which allows the butter fat to remain within the milk and not separate. 2% milk, is milk which has had 2% of the butter fat removed. Skim milk, is milk that has had most of the butter fat removed, therefore less calories, 90 as compared to 150 for whole milk. Buttermilk the liquid of butter making, sweet cream buttermilk is very high in caloric value 1 cup (250 ml) contains 464 calories. Condensed milk, milk which has had 60% of its water removed and sugar added. Dry milk solids which has had 95% of the moisture removed.

Australia

Hawaiian Cheesecake

Ingredients:

Crust:

1 cup	250 ml	flaked coconut
1 cup	250 ml	ground roasted filberts
⅓ cup	90 ml	granulated sugar
¼ cup	60 ml	melted butter

Filling:

1 ½ lbs	750 ml	cream cheese
1 cup	250 ml	granulated sugar
¼ cup	60 ml	coconut creme nectar
1 cup	250 ml	heavy cream
1 ½ cups	750 ml	crushed pineapple - well drained
3	3	eggs
¼ cup	60 ml	coconut rum
2 tsp	10 ml	rum extract
1 cup	250 ml	shredded, toasted coconut

Sauce:

1 cup	250 ml	crushed pineapple, drain and reserve juice
1 cup	250 ml	mango pulp
¼ cup	60 ml	granulated sugar
1 tbsp	15 ml	cornstarch

Preparation:

Crust:

Combine the ingredients. Press onto the bottom of a 9" (22 cm) springform pan. Refrigerate for 10 minutes. Bake 7 minutes in a preheated 350°F (180°C) oven.

Filling:

Cream the cheese with the sugar until smooth. Blend in the coconut creme, cream and pineapple. Beat in the eggs, one at a time. Incorporate coconut rum and rum extract. Pour into shell.

Bake in a preheated 350°F (160°C) oven for 90 minutes. Turn oven off. Prop the door open and rest cake for 30 minutes. Sprinkle with the coconut. Transfer to a cooling rack. Cool to room temperature.

Refrigerate 8 hours or overnight before serving. Slice and serve with the sauce.

Sauce:

Purée the pineapple with the mango in a food processor. Press through the sieve into a small saucepan. Stir in the sugar.

Blend the cornstarch into ¼ cup (60 ml) of reserved pineapple juice. Add to the fruit. Cook over low heat until sauce thickens.

Hawaii

Hawaiian Spicy Tiger Prawns

Ingredients:

3 tbsp	45 ml	safflower oil
3	3	finely diced onions
2	2	finely diced green bell peppers
3	3	finely diced celery stalks
1 cup	250 ml	pineapple chunks
2 cups	500	peeled, seeded and chopped tomatoes
2 tsp	10 ml	salt
2 tsp	10 ml	paprika
1 tsp	5 ml	garlic powder
1 tsp	5 ml	onion powder
1 tsp	5 ml	cayenne pepper
1 tsp	5 ml	basil leaves
½ tsp	3 ml	white pepper
½ tsp	3 ml	black pepper
½ tsp	3 ml	oregano leaves
½ tsp	3 ml	thyme leaves
2 tsp	10 ml	Worcestershire sauce
¼ tsp	1 ml	Tabasco™ sauce
6	6	diced green onions
1	1	bunch, chopped parsley
2 ½ lbs	1 kg	tiger prawns or very large shrimp
1 quantity	1 quantity	court bouillon (see page 416)
3 cups	750 ml	cooked rice

Preparation:

Heat the oil in a large sauce pan. Sauté the onion, green pepper and celery until tender. Add the pineapple, tomatoes and seasoning, Worcestershire sauce, and Tabasco™ sauce. Simmer gently until the desired thickness has been achieved (about 4 hours).

Add the green onion and parsley. Simmer for 15 minutes longer.

During the last half hour of simmering of the sauce, bring the court bullion to a boil. Peel and devein the tiger prawns. Add to the court bouillon, simmer gently until cooked, approximately 12 minutes.

Plate the rice. Smother with sauce and top with prawns.

Serve at once.

Serves 6

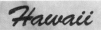

Hawaii

Veal Cutlets

with Kiwi Mandarin Salsa

Ingredients:

Salsa:

4	4	peeled and diced kiwi
2	2	mandarin oranges, segments
½ cup	125 ml	jicama, peeled and diced
¼ cup	60 ml	chopped argrula
½ cup	125 ml	finely diced red bell pepper
1 tbsp	15 ml	lime juice
1	1	minced jalapeño pepper

Veal Cutlets:

6-4 oz	6-120 g	veal cutlets
1	1	egg
¼ cup	60 ml	milk
½ cup	125 ml	flour
1 cup	250 ml	seasoned bread crumbs
3 tbsp	45 ml	safflower oil

Preparation:

Salsa:

In a large mixing bowl blend the kiwi, mandarins, jicama, argrula, bell pepper, lime juice and jalapeño. Chill for 30 minutes.

Veal Cutlets

Pound the cutlets thin with a meat mallet. Mix the egg with the milk. Dust the cutlets with flour; dip into the egg wash and dredge in the bread crumbs.

Heat the oil in a large skillet. Fry the cutlets until golden brown on both sides. Plate the cutlets. Top with the salsa. Serve at once.

Serves 6

Fun Food Facts

Kiwi

Often thought as the fruit of New Zealand, the kiwi is actually a fruit of the Orient known as the Chinese gooseberry. It first began to be grown in New Zealand in 1906. Lacking a name it was given the name of the small furry flightless national bird of New Zealand. The kiwi fruit was once believed to be a cross between a strawberry and a watermelon because of its green flesh and many seeds, a most unlikely story indeed for there is no record of its actual origin. Use kiwi extensively in appetizers, soups, salads, entrees and desserts. One kiwi is about 2"x 3" (5 cm x 7.5 cm) and contains 55 calories, .9 grams of protein, 13.5 grams of carbohydrates, 0.4 grams of fat, 0 milligrams of cholesterol, 4 milligrams of sodium, 1.0 grams of fibre.

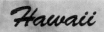

Spring Lamb Stew

Ingredients:

1 lb	454 g	boneless spring lamb
3 tbsp	45 ml	butter
20	20	peeled pearl onions
20	20	brushed button mushrooms
1 ½ cups	375 ml	Parisian cut carrots
2 tbsp	30 ml	flour
2 cups	500 ml	Parisian cut potatoes
2	2	bay leaves
¼ cup	60 ml	sherry
1 ¾ cups	410 ml	beef or veal broth (see page 42)
2 tsp	10 ml	chopped basil

Rice:

2 tbsp	30 ml	butter
⅓ cup	80 ml	finely diced onion
¼ cup	60 ml	finely diced celery
¼ cup	60 ml	finely diced red bell pepper
5 cups	1.25 L	chicken broth (see page 210)
2 cups	500 ml	long grain rice
½ tsp	3 ml	basil
½ tsp	3 ml	thyme
½ tsp	3 ml	oregano
½ tsp	3 ml	chervil
1 tbsp	15 ml	chopped chives
2 tbsp	30 ml	chopped parsley

Preparation:

Dice the lamb into ½" (19 mm) cubes.

Heat the butter in a large sauce pan. Add the lamb and brown. Add the onions, mushrooms, carrots and cook until tender. Stir in the flour. Reduce the heat and cook for 5 minutes.

Add the potatoes, bay leaves, sherry, broth and basil. Simmer for 1 ¼ hours. Serve with rice.

Rice:

In a saucepan, heat the butter. Add the vegetables and sauté until tender. Add the chicken broth and rice. Bring to a boil. Reduce to a simmer. Cook until rice has absorbed the liquid.

Blend in the herbs. Serve.

Serves 6

Tuna Steaks

with Pineapple Melon Salsa

Ingredients:

1 cup	250 ml	pineapple chunks
1 cup	250 ml	honeydew melon balls
½ cup	125 ml	peeled, diced jicama
¼ cup	60 ml	chopped arugula
½ cup	125 ml	finely diced red bell pepper
1 tbsp	15 ml	lime juice
1	1	minced jalapeño pepper
3 tbsp	45 ml	garlic oil
6-4 oz	6-120 g	tuna steaks 1" (2.5 cm) thick

Preparation:

In a large mixing bowl blend the pineapple, melon, jicama, arugula, bell pepper, lime juice and jalapeño. Chill for 30 minutes.

Brush the tuna with the garlic oil. Grill over medium coals for 5 minutes per side. Serve with the salsa on the side.

Serves 6

Fun Food Facts

Tuna can be served like most beef steaks; rare, medium or well done. It's your call.

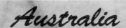

Pineapple Zucchini Cake

Ingredients:

4	4	eggs
1 cup	250 ml	granulated sugar
1 cup	250 ml	vegetable oil
2 cups	500 ml	all purpose flour
1 ½ tsp	7 ml	baking powder
1 tsp	5 ml	salt
2 tsp	10 ml	cinnamon
2 cups	500 ml	grated zucchini
1 ½ cups	375 ml	pared, finely diced pineapple
1 cup	250 ml	raisins
1 cup	250 ml	slivered almonds

Preparation:

In a large bowl, beat the eggs until very light and frothy. Add the sugar gradually, beating until very light. Gradually whip in the oil.

Sift together the flour with baking powder, salt and cinnamon. Slowly add to the egg mixture.
Stir in the zucchini, pineapple, raisins and nuts.

Pour into a greased 9" (22 cm) springform pan. Bake in a preheated 350°F (180°C) oven for 60 to 70 minutes or until an inserted toothpick comes out clean.

Cool in the pan 10-15 minutes before removing. Turn cake out and cool completely. Frost with Cream Cheese Frosting.

Serves 4

Cream Cheese Frosting

Ingredients:

9 oz	255 g	cream cheese - softened
¾ cup	180 ml	butter - softened
1 ½ tsp	8 ml	vanilla extract
4 cups	1 L	sifted icing sugar (confectioners)

Preparation:

Beat the cream cheese, butter and vanilla until very smooth and fluffy. Gradually beat in the icing sugar until spreading consistency.

Hawaii

Baron of Roast Veal

Ingredients:

¼ cup	60 ml	flour
2 tbsp	30 ml	dry mustard
1 tsp	5 ml	basil
½ tsp	3 ml	each of thyme leaves, chervil, salt
5 lbs	2.2 kg	baron of veal
2 tbsp	30 ml	Worcestershire sauce
1	1	chopped onion
2	2	chopped carrots
2	2	chopped celery stalks
1	1	bay leaf
1 cup	250 ml	red wine
1 cup	250 ml	beef broth or water (see page 42)

Preparation:

Preheat the oven to 325°F (160°C).

Mix the flour, mustard and seasonings together. Rub into the roast. Place roast into a roasting pan. Pour the Worcestershire over the roast.

Surround the roast with the vegetables and bay leaf. Pour in the red wine and water.

Bake to desired doneness. Baste often.

Use the pan juices to make gravy.

Serves 8

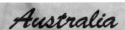

Australia

Phyllo Pears
in Butterscotch Cream Sauce

Ingredients:

Pears:

4	4	sheets phyllo pastry
¼ cup	60 ml	melted butter
6	6	medium pears
⅓ cup	80 ml	slivered almonds
¼ cup	60 ml	granulated sugar
½ tsp	3 ml	cinnamon
¼ tsp	1 ml	allspice

Sauce:

3 oz	80 g	butterscotch chips
¾ cup	180 ml	confectioners sugar
¼ cup	60 ml	boiling water
1 cup	250 ml	whipping cream
1	1	egg white
1 tsp	5 ml	vanilla extract

Pare and core the pears from the blossom end, do not remove stems. Fill the core cavity with almonds. Place into the pastry lined ramekin.

Mix the remaining butter with the sugar and spices. Pour over the pears. Bake for 25 minutes or until pastry is golden brown. Serve hot with the sauce.

Sauce:

In a double boiler melt the butterscotch. Stir in the sugar and water. Remove from the heat and cool.

Whip the cream and fold into the butterscotch. Whip the egg white and fold into the mixture along with vanilla.

Serves 6

Preparation:

Pears:

Preheat the oven to 375°F (190°C).

Lightly grease 6 ramekin dishes.

Brush 1 sheet of pastry with melted butter and lay on a flat surface. Brush a second sheet with butter and lay on top of the first. Repeat the process until all pastry is used. Cut the pastry into 6 equal pieces. Line the ramekins with the pastry.

Australia

Down Under Barbecued Dinner

Ingredients:

Chops:

6-6 oz	6-170 g	veal chops
1 tbsp	15 ml	chili powder
½ tsp	3 ml	each of oregano leaves, thyme leaves, basil leaves, onion powder, garlic powder, salt, white pepper, black pepper
¼ tsp	1 ml	cayenne pepper
½ cup	125 ml	butter
4	4	minced garlic cloves
½ cup	125 ml	fresh chopped cilantro
1 tsp	5 ml	Dijon mustard
1 tsp	5 ml	lemon zest
2 tbsp	30 ml	olive oil

Vegetables:

1	1	eggplant
1	1	large zucchini
1	1	red bell pepper
1	1	yellow bell pepper
2	2	large pared carrots
1	1	Spanish onion
¾ cup	180 ml	olive oil
¼ cup	60 ml	lemon juice
1 tbsp	15 ml	grated onion
1	1	minced garlic clove
½ tsp	3 ml	salt

¼ tsp	1 ml	each of basil, thyme, oregano, paprika, black pepper
1 tbsp	15 ml	sherry
1 tsp	5 ml	Worcestershire sauce

Preparation:

Chops:

Trim the chops of excess fat.

Combine the seasonings and sprinkle on the chops. Cover the veal chops and refrigerate for 1 hour.

Combine the butter with the garlic, cilantro, mustard and lemon. Spread on a sheet of wax paper and roll in a cigar shape. Freeze for 1 hour.

Brush the chops with the oil. Grill for 7 minutes over medium heat.

Slice the butter in thick rounds. Place one round on each serving of 2 veal chops. Serve at once with vegetables.

Vegetables:

Trim the vegetables and cut into large slices. Place in a mixing bowl.

Combine the remaining ingredients and pour over the vegetables. Marinate for 1 hour.

Grill the vegetables over medium coals for 10 minutes. Brush several times with the marinate. Brush one final time and serve.

Serves 6

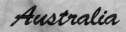

Australia

Melbourne Barby Shrimp

Ingredients:

3 tbsp	45 ml	butter
3 tbsp	45 ml	red pepper oil
1	1	minced medium onion
1	1	minced garlic clove
⅔ cup	170 ml	tomato catsup
⅔ cup	170 ml	liquid honey
¼ cup	60 ml	cider vinegar
1 tbsp	15 ml	Worcestershire sauce
½ tsp	3 ml	each of thyme leaves, oregano leaves, basil leaves, paprika, black pepper, chili powder, salt
½ tsp	3 ml	liquid smoke
1 ½ lbs	680 g	peeled, deveined, large shrimp

Preparation:

Heat the butter with 2 tbsp (30 ml) of oil in a saucepan. Add the onion and garlic and sauté until tender.

Add the catsup, honey, vinegar, Worcestershire, seasonings and liquid smoke flavouring. Simmer until sauce is thick and glossy. Cool.

Brush the shrimp with the remaining oil. Grill over medium coals 3 minutes per side. Brush frequently with sauce. Brush 1 final time before serving.

Serves 4

Australia

Fresh Kiwi Sorbet

with Warm Kiwi Banana Lime Salsa

Ingredients:

¾ cup	180 ml	granulated sugar
¾ cup	180 ml	water
3 tbsp	45 ml	lemon juice
3 tbsp	45 ml	lime juice
2 ½ cups	625 ml	puréed kiwi

Sauce:

1 ½ cups	325 ml	water
⅓ cup	80 ml	sugar
1 tsp	5 ml	rum extract
¼ cup	60 ml	lime juice
4	4	pared, quartered kiwi
4	4	sliced, small bananas

Preparation:

In a saucepan heat the sugar and water. Stirring constantly, bring to a boil. Remove from heat and cool to room temperature. Combine the syrup, lemon and lime. Chill to very cold. Stir in the kiwi. Pour into a ice cream maker and freeze according to the manufactures directions.

Sauce:

In a saucepan, heat the water and sugar. Bring to a boil. Reduce heat and simmer to half its volume. Add the extract and lime juice.

Add the kiwi and simmer for 3 minutes. Add the bananas and simmer for 1 minute. Serve hot over the sorbet.

Serves 4

 Fun Food Facts

Rum

Known by sailors as grog, rumbuillion has been a principal flavouring in cookery since the 1640's and the discovery of sugar. Distilled chiefly throughout the Caribbean, each island has a slightly different recipe. Thus each finished product varies through the addition or extraction of the main ingredient, sugar, specifically molasses made from sugar. Rum is aged for up to 10 years in oak barrels. This aging process along with the addition of caramel, gives rum its golden colour. One ounce of rum has approximately 65 calories.

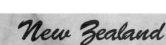 *New Zealand*

Africa

Refined cuisine is usually not what one thinks of when the continent of Africa is mentioned. Yet, Africans have been refining various cuisine since the days of the pharaohs. As people have discovered the secrets locked therein, Africa becomes more and more attractive for intense exciting flavours. What would a steak au poivre be without green peppercorns from the isle of Madagascar, or secret spices from the Moroccan coast.

Many have considered Africa as the dark continent, but I believe that the foods available there are beyond compare. Fine cuisine isn't how fancy something is prepared but rather how well the item is prepared and served. Africans know how to prepare great food. Their cuisine is responsible for flavouring other cuisines such as Cajun\Creole, Caribbean, and is truly the essence of Mediterranean foods.

You may not be able to go on a safari in Africa but from the kitchen you can travel to Egypt and sample a delicious Egyptian Cassoulet or venture to the coast and have Moroccan Grilled Kebobs. Try Khoshaf with Cream Cheese Pound Cake for a sweet tooth craving.

They say that Africa is the home of true barbeque and that is certainly shown to be especially true when you sample dishes like Honey Garlic Yogurt Lamb Chops with Barbequed Turtle Beans and finish with a dessert of White Chocolate Coconut Pecan Torte. Wherever you travel, know that if the dish is hot and spicy, Africa either created its basic ingredients or would love to enjoy it with you.

Egyptian Cassoulet

Ingredients:

¼ lb	120 g	pinto beans
¼ lb	120 g	large lima beans
¼ lb	120 g	black beans
1 ½ lbs	675 g	diced lamb
¾ lb	345 g	smoked sausage
¼ cup	60 ml	olive oil
4 cups	1 L	beef broth (see page 42)
3 tbsp	45 ml	brown sugar
2 tsp	10 ml	Worcestershire sauce
½ tsp	3 ml	dry mustard
½ tsp	3 ml	salt
¼ tsp	1 ml	cracked black pepper
1	1	onion sliced rings
1 cup	250 ml	tomato sauce

Preparation:

Soak the beans in water for 8 hours or overnight. Cook in a large kettle of boiling water until half tender.

In a large skillet brown the lamb and sausage in the oil. Cover with 2 cups (500 ml) of broth and simmer until tender.

Transfer to a casserole dish. Drain the beans and mix with the meats. Add the remaining broth and other ingredients. Blend thoroughly.

Bake in a preheated 350°F (180°C) oven for 1½ hours. Remove from the oven and serve.

Serves 6

Africa

African Lamb Chops

Ingredients:

Lamb:

1 ½ lbs	680 g	lamb chops
½ cup	125 ml	olive oil
2 tbsp	30 ml	cumin powder
1 tbsp	15 ml	ground coriander
1	1	onion grated
4	4	garlic cloves minced
½ tsp	3 ml	cayenne pepper
½ tsp	3 ml	black pepper
1 tsp	5 ml	salt

Rice:

1 cup	250 ml	long grain rice
3 ½ cups	875 ml	coconut milk
¾ cup	180 ml	flaked coconut
¼ cup	60 ml	granulated sugar

Preparation:

Lamb:

Trim the chops of any excess fat. Place into a large baking pan.

In a mixing bowl blend the oil with the remaining ingredients. Pour over the lamb and marinate refrigerated for 3 hours. Grill over medium heat to desired doneness. Serve with the rice.

Rice:

Bring rice and milk to a boil. Stir in the coconut and sugar. Cover and simmer until the liquid has been absorbed.

Serves 6

Fun Food Facts

Cumin

One of the essential ingredients in African, Mexican and Asian cuisine, cumin is actually a member of the carrot family. It is used in many curries along with coriander, cardamon, allspice, mustard, cayenne and other spices. Cumin is an essential ingredient in seasoned salt and is often found in certain chili powder blends.

457

Moroccan Grilled Kebobs

Ingredients:

Kebobs:

2 ¼ lbs	1 kg	boneless chicken
1	1	red bell pepper
1	1	yellow bell pepper
1	1	green bell pepper
20	20	large mushrooms
2	2	onions
1	1	zucchini
1 cup	250 ml	plain yogurt
1 tbsp	15 ml	paprika
½ tsp	3 ml	ground cinnamon
½ tsp	3 ml	ground cumin
¼ tsp	1 ml	cayenne pepper
1 tsp	5 ml	cracked black pepper
4	4	minced garlic cloves
3 tbsp	45 ml	grated onion

Cous cous:

1 ½ cups	375 ml	cous cous
4 cups	1 L	apple juice
¾ cup	180 ml	chopped pitted dates
½ cup	125ml	toasted sliced almonds

Preparation:

Kebobs:

Wash the chicken and cut into large cubes.

Dice the vegetables into large cubes. Skewer on water soaked bamboo skewers alternating with the chicken. Place into a large baking pan.

Blend the yogurt and spices with the garlic and grated onion, pour over the kebobs and marinate for 2½ hours. Grill for 5 minutes per side over medium heat. Serve with cous cous.

Cous cous:

Bring the apple juice to a boil then add the cous cous. Cover, reduce heat, simmer until liquid has been absorbed.

Stir in the dates and almonds. Serve at once.

Serves 6

Honey Garlic Yogurt Lamb Chops

with Barbequed Turtle Beans

Ingredients:

Lamb:

8-3 oz	8-90 g	frenched lamb chops
2	2	minced garlic cloves
3 tbsp	45 ml	liquid honey
¼ cup	60 ml	plain yogurt
1 tsp	5 ml	cracked black pepper

Beans:

1 lb	454 g	turtle beans (black beans)
3 tbsp	45 ml	grated ginger
¾ cup	180 ml	molasses
3 tbsp	45 ml	brown sugar
1	1	fine diced onion
3 tbsp	45 ml	vinegar
½ cup	125 ml	stewed tomatoes
2 tbsp	30 ml	olive oil
4 oz	120 g	diced bacon
4 tsp	20 ml	red chile flakes
½ cup	125 ml	chicken broth (see page 210)

Preparation:

Lamb:

Trim the chops of any excess fat and place in a shallow pan.

Combine the garlic, honey, yogurt and pepper together. Pour over the chops and marinate for 8 hours.

Grill the chops over medium coals for 3 minutes per side, brushing with marinate as chops cook. Serve.

Beans:

Place the beans into a saucepan. Add enough water to cover. Bring to a boil and reduce to a simmer. Cook for 1 hour. Drain the beans. Rinse the beans and add water again to cover.

Add the ginger, molasses, sugar, onion, vinegar, tomatoes and oil. Bring to a boil and reduce to a simmer.

Fry the bacon and drain the fat, add the bacon to the beans along with the pepper flakes and chicken stock. Simmer until very thick.

Serves 4

White Chocolate Coconut Pecan Torte

Ingredients:

Torte:

4 oz	120 g	melted white chocolate, cooled to room temperature
3 cups	750 ml	pastry flour
1 tsp	5 ml	baking powder
1 tsp	5 ml	salt
1 cup	250 ml	butter
1 cup	250 ml	packed brown sugar
1 cup	250 ml	granulated sugar
3	3	large eggs
1 ½ tsp	8 ml	vanilla extract
1 cup	250 ml	buttermilk

Filling:

1 cup	250 ml	heavy cream
1 cup	250 ml	granulated sugar
½ cup	125 ml	butter
3	3	large egg yolks
1 tsp	5 ml	almond extract
1 cup	250 ml	roasted pecan pieces
1 ½ cups	375 ml	toasted coconut

Toppings:

⅓ cup	80 ml	butter
3 tbsp	45 ml	heavy cream
1 tsp	5 ml	vanilla extract

2 oz	60 g	melted white chocolate, cooled to room temperature
2 cups	500 ml	confectioners sugar

Preparation:

Torte:

Preheat the oven to 350°F (180°C). Butter and flour three 9" (22 cm) cake pans.

Sift the flour, baking powder and salt together. Cream the butter and sugar until very light. Add the eggs, one at a time, beating well after each addition. Blend in the vanilla and chocolate. Fold in the flour and buttermilk in alternating thirds.

Divide the batter over each of the three pans. Bake for 25-30 minutes. Cool to room temperature and turn out.

Filling:

Combine the cream, sugar and butter in a saucepan. Heat over medium heat until sugar is dissolved. Blend a ½ cup (125 ml) of the heated cream with the egg yolks. Cook for 10 minutes or until thick. Stir in the pecans and coconut. Spread 2 layers of cake with ¾ of the filling and stack the 3 cakes together.

Topping:

Beat the butter, cream, vanilla and chocolate together. Fold in the sugar beating until very smooth.

Spread the balance of filling on top of the cake. Spread the topping over the cake.

Lamb with Feta Brown Rice

Ingredients:

Lamb:

1 ½ lbs	680 g	lamb racks
⅓ cup	80 ml	fine dry bread crumbs
1 tbsp	15 ml	thyme leaves, dry
2 tsp	10 ml	ground cumin
2 tsp	10 ml	garlic powder
¼ cup	60 ml	Dijon mustard
3 tbsp	45 ml	garlic oil

Rice:

1 ½ cups	375 ml	brown rice
3 cups	750 ml	chicken broth (see page 210)
1	1	Spanish onion
10 oz	280 ml	spinach
3 tbsp	45 ml	butter
1 cup	250 ml	Feta cheese

Preparation:

Lamb:

Preheat the oven to 400°F (200°C).

Trim the lamb racks and cut all fat and meat along the bone.

In a mixing bowl combine the bread crumbs, thyme, cumin and garlic.

Spread the mustard along the lamb racks. Cover the lamb with the bread crumbs. Place on a baking sheet and drizzle with oil.

Roast in the oven for 30 minutes. Remove and slice between the bones. Serve with rice.

Rice:

Bring the rice and chicken stock to a boil. Cover and simmer until rice is tender.

While rice cooks, fine dice the onion. Wash and trim the spinach. Heat the butter in a skillet. Add the onion and sauté until tender. Add the spinach and cook quickly.

Once rice has cooked, drain any excess liquid. Stir in the onion mixture with the cheese. Serve at once.

Serves 4

 Fun Food Facts

Feta Cheese

Feta is a soft crumbly white sharp tasting cheese made from goats milk. It is very popular in Mediterranean countries. It tends to be salty so use a little less salt in your recipe.

Extra Spicy Roast Chicken

Ingredients:

Chicken:

¼ cup	60 ml	hot pepper sauce
5	5	scotch bonnet peppers
10	10	finely diced serrano chilies
2 tbsp	30 ml	chopped rosemary
2 tbsp	30 ml	chopped parsley
2 tbsp	30 ml	chopped basil
3	3	chopped green onions
1 tsp	5 ml	salt
1 tsp	5 ml	cracked black pepper
¼ cup	60 ml	lime juice
¼ cup	60 ml	prepared mustard
3 tbsp	45 ml	orange juice
1 tbsp	15 ml	vinegar
2 ¼ lbs	1 kg	chicken leg quarters

Cous cous:

2 tbsp	30 ml	butter
⅓ cup	80 ml	finely diced onion
¼ cup	60 ml	finely diced celery
¼ cup	60 ml	finely diced red bell pepper
4 cups	1 L	chicken broth (see page 210)
2 cups	500 ml	cous cous

½ tsp	3 ml	basil
½ tsp	3 ml	thyme
½ tsp	3 ml	oregano
½ tsp	3 ml	chervil
1 tbsp	15 ml	chopped chives
2 tbsp	30 ml	chopped parsley

Preparation:

Chicken:

Preheat the oven to 350°F (180°C).

In a saucepan blend together the hot pepper sauce, peppers, chilies, herbs, green onions, salt, pepper, lime juice, mustard, orange juice and vinegar. Simmer over low heat until very thick.

Place the chicken in a roasting pan and spread with the paste.

Roast in the oven for 1 hour. Serve with cous cous.

Cous cous:

In a sauce pan heat the butter. Add the vegetables and sauté until tender. Add the chicken broth and cous cous. Bring to a boil reduce to a simmer. Cook until cous cous has absorbed the liquid.

Blend in the herbs. Serve.

Serves 6

Ginger Glazed Garlic Turkey

Ingredients:

Turkey:

2 ¼ lbs	1 kg	turkey thighs
12	12	minced garlic cloves
1 tsp	5 ml	salt
2 tsp	10 ml	cracked black pepper
2 tbsp	30 ml	olive oil
½ cup	125 ml	brown sugar
3 tbsp	45 ml	grated ginger
1 cup	250 ml	apple juice

Rice:

8	8	slices of bacon
1	1	minced garlic clove
1	1	finely diced small onion
2 cups	500 ml	peeled, seeded and chopped tomatoes
2 cups	500 ml	long grain rice
4 cups	1 L	chicken stock (see page 210)
2 cups	500 ml	tomato juice
1 tsp	5 ml	chervil
½ tsp	3 ml	salt
¼ tsp	1 ml	pepper

Preparation:

Turkey:

Preheat the oven to 350°F (180°C).

Lay the turkey thighs on a baking sheet. Cut 6 slits in the turkey. Stuff each slit with a garlic clove. Sprinkle with salt and pepper. Drizzle the oil over the turkey.

Roast in the oven for 1½ hours or cook thoroughly.

While turkey roasts, blend the sugar, ginger and apple juice in a sauce pan, reduce to half it's volume. Brush the turkey with the glaze 5 times during the last half hour of roasting.

Remove from the oven. Carve and serve with rice.

Rice:

Finely dice the bacon and sauté along with the garlic and onion. Add the tomatoes. Cook gently until most of the moisture has evaporated.

Stir in the rice. Add the chicken stock, tomato juice and seasonings. Cover and simmer until the rice is tender and liquid has been absorbed. Serve.

Serves 6

Fish in Banana Boat

Ingredients:

Boat:

2 ½ cups	625 ml	flour
1 ½ cups	375 ml	sugar
1 ½ tsp	8 ml	baking powder
1 tsp	5 ml	baking soda
½ cup	125 ml	butter
1 cup	250 ml	mashed banana
⅔ cup	180 ml	buttermilk
2	2	eggs
1 tsp	5 ml	banana or vanilla extract

Fish:

1 ¼ cups	310 ml	fresh or tinned, pitted bing cherries
¼ cup	60 ml	cherry brandy
3 tbsp	45 ml	cherry liquid or apple juice
1 tbsp	15 ml	lemon juice
2 tbsp	30 ml	granulated sugar
6-6 oz	6-170 g	pompano, orange roughy, or salmon fillets, cut into 2" (5 cm) strips
2 tbsp	30 ml	melted butter
¼ cup	60 ml	Shredded coconut

Preparation:

Boat:

Preheat the oven to 350°F (180°C).

Sift the flour, sugar, baking powder and soda together. Cut in the butter. Blend in the banana. Slowly add the buttermilk. Add the eggs, one at a time. Stir in the extract. Pour the batter into a 9" x 5" (22 x 12 cm) greased and floured loaf pan.

Bake for 65 minutes. Cool to room temperature. Remove from pan and cut out the centre, fill the hollow with the fish, use the balance of the loaf to decorate the dish before serving.

Fish:

Heat the cherries in the cherry brandy over low heat until very tender. Press through a sieve into a sauce pan and return the saucepan to the heat.

Add the cherry juice, lemon juice and sugar. Simmer until thick.

Place the fish on a baking sheet and brush with butter. Bake in a preheated 375°F (180°C) oven for 8 minutes.

Place the fish in the banana boat. Smother with sauce. Sprinkle with coconut to garnish. Serve.

Serves 6

Khoshaf with Cream Cheese Pound Cake

Ingredients:

Khoshaf:

1 ½ cups	375 ml	dried prunes
1 ½ cups	375 ml	dried apricots
1 ½ cups	375 ml	dried small figs
1 cup	250 ml	golden seedless raisins
1 cup	250 ml	granulated sugar
3 cups	750 ml	boiling water

Cake:

¾ cup	180 ml	butter
8 oz	225 g	cream cheese
6	6	eggs
3 cups	750 ml	granulated sugar
3 cups	750 ml	flour
2 tsp	10 ml	lemon extract
1 tbsp	15 ml	lemon zest

Preparation:

Khoshaf:

In a mixing bowl add the fruit, sugar and water. Cover and refrigerate for 6-8 hours.

Cake:

Preheat the oven to 325°F (160°C). Butter and flour a loaf pan.

Cream the butter and cream cheese together until very smooth. Add the eggs and sugar, alternating, 2 eggs and 1 cup (250 ml) of sugar. Blending until smooth after each addition. Fold in the flour. Add the lemon extract and zest.

Bake for 1 ½ hours or until a inserted toothpick comes out clean. Remove from oven and cool to room temperature.

Slice the cake and serve with the stewed fruit.

Fun Food Facts

Spice up your cake, omit the lemon extract and zest. Add the following.

1 tsp	5 ml	vanilla extract
½ tsp	3 ml	cinnamon
½ tsp	3 ml	nutmeg
½ tsp	3 ml	allspice

Family Favorites Index

Family Favorites Index

Family Favorites Index

Family Favorites Index

Family Favorites Index

South Pacific

Family Favorites Index

Acknowledgements

We would like to thank the following sponsors for their generous donations.

ELAINE YUKE

TOTO SOEGAND

BRONSON'S CHINA & GIFTS OF TORONTO

BRIAN COOK